Sallie Holley

A LIFE FOR LIBERTY

ANTI-SLAVERY AND OTHER LETTERS
OF
SALLIE HOLLEY

EDITED

WITH INTRODUCTORY CHAPTERS

BY

JOHN WHITE CHADWICK

E.
449
H73
1969

WITH ILLUSTRATIONS

NEGRO UNIVERSITIES PRESS
NEW YORK

Originally published in 1899
by G. P. Putnam's Sons

Reprinted from a copy in the collections
of the Brooklyn Public Library

Reprinted 1969 by
Negro Universities Press
A DIVISION OF GREENWOOD PUBLISHING CORP.
NEW YORK

SBN 8371-2689-4

PRINTED IN UNITED STATES OF AMERICA

PREFACE

I SET out to make this book because my venerable
friend Samuel May of Leicester, Massachusetts,
and his friend Caroline F. Putnam of Lottsburgh,
Virginia, wished to have it done ; but as, in the course
of my work, I have become better acquainted with
Sallie Holley I have counted myself fortunate in being
brought into such intimate relations with her mind
and heart. She was a rarely intelligent and noble
woman, deeply engaged in a great cause, and laying
some of its lowliest burdens on herself in a spirit
of lofty consecration and most patient love. Her
letters admit us to the domestic side of Abolitionism to an exceptional degree : many of them are
"interiors" as vivid as a Teniers could paint ; as
homely, too, sometimes. But my satisfaction in my
work has been a dual one, conditioned hardly less
by Miss Holley's life and character than by her
friend's. Miss Emily Howland, who was well acquainted with Miss Holley and Miss Putnam for
nearly fifty years, and was profoundly interested
in their work, writes to me : " This Memorial will be

iii

a tribute to a friendship that I never saw equalled, of a remarkable woman, quite as much as a record of the worth of her friend." So it appears to me, and will, I trust, to all who read what I have written, and the better part which is constituted by Miss Holley's letters to the friends she prized so much.

I have written introductory chapters to these letters and, for the rest, have tried to give them a setting of anti-slavery history, to this end re-reading, with much else, both new and old, the "Story" of Garrison's life, "told by his children," with a new sense of its invaluable excellence, not merely as a biography, but as an encyclopædia of the anti-slavery conflict. To my introductions to the various chapters I have added a few foot-notes where any explanation or comment seemed desirable.

In editing the letters I have not been at pains to indicate omissions, and some of them may on this account appear more incoherent than they should. I have withheld some things which I did not think Miss Holley would wish to have published, though had I rigidly applied this rule I fear there would have been no book. No omission has ever changed the character of anything printed. In a few instances I have done as I would be done by in substituting other words for those betraying the carelessness of rapid composition, spelling proper names in full where only initials were given, and so on. It is not as if I were editing the Shakespeare folio of 1623 and were bound to preserve every inaccuracy of whatever kind. Whether I have exercised good judgment in deciding how much to print and how much to leave unprinted, the friends of Sallie Holley must decide. It is for them that I have made the book; but not without a hope that it will make new friends for her as it is read here and there by those who did not know her living face and voice.

J. W. C.

Brooklyn, November 5, 1898.

CONTENTS

ILLUSTRATIONS

A LIFE FOR LIBERTY

SALLIE HOLLEY

CHAPTER I

THE ANTI-SLAVERY WOMEN

A YEAR or two before his death I had the pleasure of meeting Stepniak, the Russian Nihilist.
He came to dine with us and one incident of the
dinner impressed us vividly at the time and has often
been recalled. Taking his knife in both hands he
drew the edge of it slowly and deliberately along his
eyes. He was very near-sighted and apparently was
trying to distinguish the edge of the knife from the
back, but so sinister appeared the act in the light of
Stepniak's reputation, so suggestive of the Nihilist's
careful examination of knife-blades with ulterior purposes, that every several spine had its own chill of
nervous recognition. But so much is hardly rele-
vant to my present purpose. An hour or two after
dinner, as he was taking leave, he asked, " May I see

Mrs. Chadwick again before I go?" She came down at once and then I knew that he imagined he would find in her a more sympathetic auditor than he had found in me. He delivered his message with a fervour and passion that were a fuller revelation of the force and spirit of the man. The act epitomised much that I had read as to the part played by Russian women in the Nihilistic conspiracy and propaganda. I could see how much Stepniak had relied upon women for the enthusiasm and devotion necessary to his desperate cause. And not only this. The circumstance was a pregnant comment on the relation of women generally to the world's innovators and reformers.

The sentimentalism of Renan may be offensive, but he does not exaggerate the importance of the women whose devotion to the person and the ministry of Jesus was one of the strongest pillars in the temple of his early influence and fame. The music of the *Stabat Mater* is a music which has found an echo in every great reformer's heart. Like stars that shine through rifted clouds are the names of sainted women that appear here and there amidst the tumult and passion of St. Paul's epistles to the churches that were wearing out the strength of his devoted heart. But for those faithful women could he have endured the burdens and anxieties of his great apostolate? How long Kadijah was Mohammed's sole disciple!—but such an one that all the rest were sure to come in time.

No reform however organised, unorganised, or disorganised has owed a greater debt to women than the reform of which William Lloyd Garrison was the leading spirit. Many were

> "the unknown good who rest
> In God's still memory folded deep";

daughters and wives like Helen Benson Garrison, wife of William Lloyd; sisters like Sarah and Anna Benson of the same vigorous stock, who, doing little in the way of public service, either with voice or pen, sustained the public workers with their perfect sympathy and with their willingness to endure hardness of any kind for the good cause. These made their homes "a garden of refreshment" for the bruised and aching combatants in the hot arena of the time, soiled with its glorious dust; not always conscious of the glory then and there.

We do not think of Wendell Phillips as being much in need of anyone's encouragement, yet it is not to be doubted that if he ever *had* been faint-hearted in the teeth of monstrous opposition, Anne Greene, his wife, would have been ready with some restorative and bracing word. When the women from Massachusetts and Pennsylvania were, as women, denied their seats in the World's Anti-Slavery Convention meeting in London June 12, 1840, it fell to Wendell Phillips to defend their rights upon the floor of the convention. "Now, Wendell," said his wife as they went in, laying her hand upon his shoulder like a knighting sword,—"Now, Wendell, don't shilly-shally, but be brave as a lion"; and he was so, and those who would have shamed their sisters were themselves made grievously ashamed.

All his life long she was the silent partner in the great business he was carrying on for freedom and humanity. And in being this she was not solitary, but a type of many who, in ways even more silent than her own, strengthened the hands and hearts of those whose work was done in the fierce light that beat upon the public representatives of the anti-slavery reform. These willingly accepted penury and social disesteem ; less willingly and yet bravely the alienation of their most cherished relatives and friends; their busy fingers made the dainty things which tempted even the half-hearted and adverse to patronise the annual Anti-Slavery Fair ; they made the negro's bed in heaven when he was on his way to the free soil of Canada; they clothed his naked-ness; they filled his empty stomach and, yet more, his hungry heart.

Turning from these to those who, could they have freely chosen, would have much preferred their in-conspicuous ways, but on whom necessity was laid to speak or write the word that was an inward fire, we find that there were many of them engaged in the good work. And as " when the sons of God came together Satan came also among them," so doubtless with the noble women of the anti-slavery reform there was a mixture of those less admirable women afflicted with that " determination of words to the mouth " which is not an exclusively masculine ailment, and well meaning but extremely foolish persons like that " flea of conventions," Abigail Folsom, so named by Emerson for all time, " but too ready with her in-terminable scroll." If those who managed the con-

ventions did not "suffer fools gladly," they suffered
them with a patience that brought much discredit on
the cause. Free speech was such a sacred right that
it was respected even when the speaker was not quite
" all there."

But the fanatical and insane were few in comparison with the once bright and cheerful and now
ever memorable company of rare and gracious spirits
who had no love of notoriety, no passion to be seen
or heard, but who could not enjoy the advantages of
wealth, or social pleasure, or the fair fruits of literary
fame, so long as black men were denied the fruit of
their labour, and their wives might not regard the
fruit of their bodies as inalienably theirs. There
was Maria Weston Chapman, second to none in her
lieutenancy to Garrison, the captain of the great
reform ; it may be doubted whether any of his male
coadjutors was so necessary to him as this noble
woman, or so able to lift up his heart when it was
sunk deepest in his breast. Of great administrative
energy, she was " the soul of the Boston Female
Anti-Slavery Society " ; in prose and verse the chron-
icler and inspirer of the movement for immediate
emancipation ; of perfect courage, equal to assuming
the responsibility for the publication of the *Anti-
Slavery Standard* at a critical juncture in the struggle, when some, because they dared not counter
Paul's objection to the public speech of women,
broke away from Garrison and set up a new organisation; young, beautiful, full of radiant grace,
lacking no charm of speech or manner or accomplishment fitting her to be a social queen with lavish

homage at her feet, she freely chose to make her-self " of no reputation," to be one of a despised and persecuted band, if haply she might help to break the fetters of the slave.

A reform that cannot sing itself into men's hearts is, by that sign, almost disqualified for victory. The anti-slavery reform could sing itself and never sang itself more sweetly than from the lips of Abby Hutch-inson, one of a family of singers who could hardly find their voices except for some note of the great social anthem of the " good time coming."

And there was Abby Kelley, a woman dowered with a great gift of eloquence, which she never used except with conscious dedication to a cause so great that for the immediate joy of serving it she could endure the heaviest cross and despise the utmost shame men's meanness or their malice could devise. Among her trials perhaps, sometimes, though of domestic virtue all compact, was Stephen Foster, her husband, that erratic genius who measured the success of anti-slavery meetings by the number of windows and benches broken by the mob and by the quality of the eggs thrown at the speakers, and went about to develop these destructive and unsavoury manifestations with an ingenuous and ingenious perversity. Yet was he not devoid of many excel-lent qualities and many winning traits that endeared him most to those who knew him best and made him a public energy for good whatever his defects.

And there was Mary Grew, a cousin of Mrs. Wen-dell Phillips, kin of her soul as well as of her blood, not gifted with Wendell's eloquence, but a persuasive

speaker in her grave and earnest way; in her republican simplicity at home in the most guarded ring; in
her large-brained political insight and sagacity prov-
ing herself entitled to that political equality with men
which to the last, with ebbing physical strength, but
unabated mental vigour, she claimed as earnestly for
women as she had claimed the slave's right to his own
labour, flesh, and vote.   But one can hardly think of
Mary Grew at all without thinking of her friends,
Sarah Pugh and Margaret Burleigh, especially the
latter, devoted to her with that affection *passing the
love of men* which many of the anti-slavery women
manifested towards each other; in the affection of
Caroline Putnam for Sallie Holley finding one of its
loveliest illustrations.

   I attempt no complete enumeration and my
casual mention may neglect some names of more
significance than those which I set down.[1]   But
certainly the brightness of the fame which Lucy
Stone and Susan B. Anthony and Mrs. Stanton
won in their more special field must not blind us
to the work they did on anti-slavery lines.   And
their special work, the enfranchisement of women,
reminds me that the two women who were more

---

[1] The English women who came to Garrison's aid could furnish a
chapter by themselves.   High, if not chief, among them were Elizabeth Pease, afterward Mrs. Nichol of Edinburgh, born in 1807
(whom I set out to see in 1887 and missed my way), a correspondent
to whom in 1837 Garrison wrote one of his most remarkable prophecies ; Elizabeth Heyrick, who was the first herald of immediate
emancipation in Great Britain (1825) ; and Harriet Martineau,
(1802–1876), whose visit to America bore abundant fruit of English sympathy with our abolitionists.

prominent than any others in the anti-slavery period of most bitter animosities, from 1835 to 1840, were Sarah and Angelina Grimké, and that their prominence was due to the fact that they were women doing work which men had arrogated to themselves or left undone. It was not deliberately chosen. They attained it by a process of evolution every step of which led on to the next following by easy and inevitable gradation. They were daughters of Judge John F. Grimké of Charleston, South Carolina, and their brother Thomas had manfully resisted the nullification craze of 1831. Leaving Charleston, they came to Philadelphia when they could no longer endure the poisoned atmosphere of slavery. In Philadelphia they found the Episcopal Church as dumb at Slavery's dictations as it was in Charleston. Whereupon they left it and joined the orthodox Friends.

In 1836, Angelina published an *Appeal to the Women of the South*, which led Elizur Wright, then secretary of the American Anti-Slavery Society, to urge her and her sister to come to New York and explain the nature of slavery to companies of women meeting in private. They came and the companies outgrew the parlours very soon. Then vestries, lecture-rooms, and finally churches were opened for them—women only admitted. But the men wanted to get in. Their wives and sisters brought to them reports of Angelina's moving eloquence. One day in Lynn, Massachusetts, the Rev. Amos Phelps, general agent of the Massachusetts Anti-Slavery Society, stepped just inside the door of the great Methodist church to hear a moment and then go. But he stayed till the last word ; and the door thus opened could not again be shut. The men crowded through it in a steady stream. Mr. Phelps himself, too late remembering the admonition of St. Paul to talking women, put his own shoulder to it violently but in vain. Last came a " Pastoral Letter" from the General Association of Congregational ministers meeting in Brookfield, Massachusetts, pleading for the exclusive right of clergymen to preach the Gospel, or not to preach it, in their parochial limits, and rebuking those who trespassed on these limits, especially women forgetful of their natural modesty (and St. Paul), and those who by their audience encouraged them in such unscriptural and questionable manners. This " Pastoral Letter" drew the fire of Whittier's Quaker gun, and the shot was one that raked it fore and aft. Let those who do not know the verses look them up. They are too good for me to take a part of them ; too many for me to insert them all.

Few and far between the churches that were opened for the Grimké sisters after the pious roaring of the Brookfield bull. It introduced a tendency to separation and disintegration into the anti-slavery movement. Women were admitted to equal membership in the New England convention of 1838 and in the American Anti-Slavery Society in 1839, but in 1840 a strenuous effort was made to reverse that action. It failed because there came a steamboatful of New England Garrisonians who overbore all opposition with their numerical and moral force. But there was a schism in the society and

there was a new organisation and a new organ, and
on either side much bitter feeling, arousing Whittier
to write one of the most noble and pathetic of those
timely songs with which he marked every event or
tendency of real importance in the course of the
anti-slavery conflict. In the meantime Angelina
Grimké passed from the dust of the arena into the
quiet of domestic life as the wife of Theodore D.
Weld, Dr. Lyman Beecher's most intractable student at Cincinnati and the author of a compilation,
Slavery as It Is, which appearing a dozen years
before Mrs. Stowe's *Key to Uncle Tom's Cabin*,
made that superfluous. I saw the wife and husband
just before her death in 1879[1] in a Boston railway
station. The noble pair irradiated all the place with
the combined magnificence and sweetness of their
faces and made its commonness seem sacred and
tender as a cathedral's solemn nave. *Vidi tantum,*
and I was glad, though the "so much" was so
little, because the experience completed my acquaintance with three women of whom I had many
times heard Samuel J. May speak in terms of profound admiration. Of which farther on.

There was another three whose influence in the
anti-slavery conflict was supreme, and whose fame is
bound up inextricably with its great deeds and generous aspirations: Lucretia Mott, Harriet Beecher
Stowe, and Lydia Maria Child. It was my privilege
to know them all, and my rare good fortune to know
Lucretia and Mrs. Child, especially the former, in a

[1] Sarah died in 1873, Garrison, Weld, and Lucy Stone speaking
at her funeral.

very intimate and friendly way. They had different
gifts, but the same spirit. Mrs. Mott was the least
literary of the three; Mrs. Stowe the most. Mrs.
Mott was an impressive speaker upon the public
platform as well as in the meetings of her sect. Mrs.
Stowe and Mrs. Child had no corresponding gift.
Unquestionably it was Mrs. Child who made the
greatest sacrifice upon freedom's altar. Her anti-
slavery writing brought about the ruin of her literary
hopes and plans, while Mrs. Stowe's assured at once
her elevation to a position so exalted that she could
easily afford the hatred and abuse of those who ceased
flinging mud at Garrison that they might have the
more to fling at her. But God fulfils himself in many
ways, and each of the several ways in which these
noble women worked was necessary to the end in
view,—the proclaiming of liberty to those in physical
and moral slavery, the enslaved and the enslavers.

The story of Mrs. Stowe's life is too well known
for any repetition of it to be needed here. She was
born a little late (1812) to be one of the early abolitionists and she was never in full sympathy with
Garrison's principles and aims. She was long in coming to her anti-slavery self-consciousness, retarded
possibly by some filial tenderness for her father's re-
creancy in a time that tried his soul. In studying
her life we are surprised to find how little preparation, intellectual or emotional, there was for the writing of *Uncle Tom's Cabin*. Even such experience as
she had, she had not realised, and the book was written not from inward impulse, but from outward in-
stigation. Nevertheless it was a great creation and a

potent one in anti-slavery affairs.   It did much to
make Republicans who could not rest contented
with the half-way party platforms of 1856 and 1860;
could not be eloquent for the inviolability of slavery
in the Southern States ; could not be satisfied until
Lincoln had forged his war-power into a thunder-
bolt to shatter slavery in the length and breadth of
its inhuman sway.

Lucretia Mott was not obliged to wait for the
trumpet tones of Garrison's *Liberator* to waken her
to a sense of her duty to those who were in bonds.
The voice of Benjamin Lundy had found its way
into her Quaker stillness with persuasive invitation.
She and her husband were readers of his *Genius of
Universal Emancipation* almost from its start in 1821.
When Garrison was released from jail in Baltimore
(August, 1829) and came North with three lectures
he had written there, Lucretia and her husband were
on hand to hear his faithful testimony and to make
him welcome to their home.   Their radical theology
was shocking to his Calvinistic sensibility, but he
lived to thank them for their aid, above all other, in
freeing him from the bondage of sectarian trammels
and theological dogmas.   In 1833, when the American Anti-Slavery Society was formed, she was moved
to speak several times in the convention, of which
she was not a member, encouraged by the president,
Beriah Green, whose closing speech, wrote Samuel
J. May, alone exceeded Mrs. Mott's speaking in its
impressiveness.   Her anti-slavery convictions made
her " a subject of uneasiness " to those who had authority and standing among Friends.   They ex-

horted her to " keep in the quiet," to "avoid all
contention," and to " avoid going out into the mixture." But while careful not to give technical offence,
she " enlarged her testimony " in all possible ways.
Once on a seventy days' journey of 2400 miles, in a
stage-coach for the most part, she addressed seventy-
one different meetings of Friends and never failed
to emphasise the matter nearest to her heart.

For forty years Lucretia Mott's voice and influence and purse and home were dedicated to the
service of the slave. Her roomy house was the
principal station on the underground railroad between Hannah Cox's in Kennett Square and Isaac
T. Hopper's in New York. When John Brown's
wife was on her way to that last sad meeting with
him in Virginia, she tarried with the Motts for several days, enshielded from all idle curiosity, until
her summons came.

Of that mother-wit an ounce of which is worth a
pound of clergy, she had a goodly share. Her native shrewdness served her well, and she was even
capable of a modest ruse if it involved no least concession to an immoral principle. For example:
Once on her return passage from Europe she wished
to call a meeting of the Irish passengers in the steer-
age and anticipate those " friends of the people "
who would await them on their landing on our
shores. Objections being raised, she called them
together to see if they would have a meeting, ex-
plained to them what kind of meeting she wanted,
and even told them what she wished to say in case
a meeting should be called. " Well, I don't see but

we 've *had* the preachment from the woman-priest,"
said one of the company who was not devoid of per-
spicacity. She was, however, no " woman-priest "
but a woman-prophet; and her " preachment," her
prophecy, was always good for all to hear whose ears
had been attuned to such a message of political and
intellectual freedom as she bore. She was so simple
and sincere, so kind and good, that it was no wonder, when she died, that thousands gathered to her
burial in the great city of which she had been for all
the years of her maturity a citizen second to none
since Benjamin Franklin's death in 1790, two years
before her birth. Their common ancestor was Peter
Folger of Nantucket, who bought his wife for £30
of the celebrated Hugh Peters, so that we may trace
back two of the noblest lives America has yet produced to an emancipated slave.[1]

Take away Lydia Maria Child's reformatory energy and she would still be one of the most gifted
pioneers of our American literature. As it was, she
did a large amount of purely literary work. She
would have done much more if there had been no
slaves to liberate, no intemperance to abate, no war
to hate and shame, no bigotry and superstition to
be " withstood because they ought to be blamed."
We may regret that her literary capacity did not
have full swing, but we cannot regret that when
obliged to choose between literary fame and exact-
ing philanthropic cares, she chose the latter without

[1] Theodore Parker: *Historic Americans*. But Franklin's biographer, Parton, and Mrs. Mott's tacitly ignore the incident and so
make it appear doubtful.

hesitation and cast no longing looks behind. She was always striking out into some untried path. Her *Progress of Religious Ideas* was one of our earliest studies in comparative religion, one of the first contributions to that "sympathy of religions" which Colonel Higginson has so aptly named. But her most signal trial of "fresh woods and pastures new" was her *Appeal for that Class of Americans Called Africans*, in 1833. Like Whittier's *Justice and Expediency*, published almost simultaneously, it was a splendid seconding of the motion made in Garrison's *Thoughts on Colonisation*, published the year before. She wrote in the preface: "Should it be the means of advancing even one single step the inevitable progress of truth and justice, I would not exchange the consciousness for all of Rothschild's wealth or Sir Walter's fame." A strong resemblance was remarked in the face of her brother, Dr. Convers Francis, to Martin Luther's. *She* had the features of the great reformer's mind. The *Appeal* stirred Dr. Channing's heart as it had not been stirred before. John Albion Andrew, a boy of fifteen summers, bought it, read it, and gave it to his sisters with an inscription that prefigured the temper of his maturest thought.

Mrs. Child's correspondence with John Brown, whom she would fain have gone to in his prison, reached, when published, a circulation of three hundred thousand copies. Does anyone sitting in "the seat of the scorner" wonder what kind of a nurse she would have made for the old hero? A good one certainly. For all her immersion in great public interests, she had ample time to tend her home affairs with careful diligence and her garden-plot with loving pains. The " ever-womanly " was as characteristic of her most public as of her most private life. Hundreds of society women might have learned of her a more exquisite womanliness of demeanour than they had attained to in their " doll's house " of trivial anxieties. She was as domestic as Lucretia Mott,[1] whom a morning's mending insured the top of her condition. There never was a kinder or more comfortable soul. The years went by, leaving in deeper lines upon her face the impress of those kindly sentiments which were continually welling from her heart. They brought no dimness to her sparkling eyes. At the last she was a little anxious to be gone : she " had so many things," she said, " to tell David " ; not the " man after God's own heart," but the man after hers,—her husband, who had gone on before her to the undiscovered country which never had for her a single doubt or fear.

It is of one who took an honourable rank in this company of anti-slavery women that I am to write, but listening to her own voice as much as possible, in the remaining pages of this little book. She was not one of the greatest of them, nor one of the least. She had her own place and work, and filled the one and did the other with a brave and earnest heart.

---

[1] Of whose economy I have a cherished proof in a set of notes on her most precious book, the *Life of Blanco White*, which she gave me a few years before her death. The notes are written on the backs of old Nantucket letters, as the postmarks and wafers testify.

Some time before I met her and heard her speak in my own pulpit, her name was pleasantly familiar to my ears. Samuel J. May had made it so. Pleading for the fitness of women for the ministry, he would say, " If you could hear, as I have heard, Lucretia Mott, or Sallie Holley, or Angelina Grimké, you would not, could not, doubt the fitness of women for this work." I heard this protestation several times from that dear saint, and across the tract of years I can even now hear the impressive tones, the accent of his speech. I wish that I could draw upon the riches of his memory for the story I have set out to tell,—the story of Sallie Holley's useful and devoted life.

2

CHAPTER II

SALLIE HOLLEY—so she preferred to write her name—was born in Canandaigua, New York, February 17, 1818. The family name is believed to be a variant of the English " Halley," most honoured by Edmund Halley the astronomer (1656–1742), from whom Sallie Holley claimed direct descent. The comet named for Halley may have presaged something erratic in the character of his descendants. Certain it is that members of the family, notably Alexander Lyman Holley, a distinguished engineer and inventor, have shown such mathematical ability as would naturally appear in descendants of the great astronomer. But when we are told that the great-grandfather of Sallie's grandfather came from England and settled in Stratford, Connecticut, the astronomic derivation becomes infected with dubiety. Her ancestry was, however, sufficiently honourable, even if her claim on Edmund Halley should be disallowed. Her mother, Sally House of Canandaigua, New York, whom her father, Myron Holley, married there in 1804, was a daughter of Captain John House,

18

an early settler of the place. He was killed at the
battle of New Orleans, and it was certainly a very
great distinction to be one of the seven killed on the
American side, while two thousand of the British fell.
Sally House was a village beauty, so attractive to
the young men of the region that Myron Holley's
capture of her was hardly a less famous victory than
that of Jackson at New Orleans. With her beauty
she had substantial qualities which made her a good
wife and mother. Intellectual or cultivated she was
not, but no incompatibility with her husband arose on
this account. He was her lover till the last. When
they had been married twenty years he celebrated
her virtues in one of the few poems in which he
indulged his fancy.

Six sons and as many daughters were the fruit of
this marriage. The wife did not share the husband's
liberal opinions in religion, but joining the Methodist
Church with mature conviction, she remained in it
contentedly for the remainder of her life, and had,
in 1838, the satisfaction of seeing three of her
daughters joining her beloved church at once.

Sallie Holley's paternal grandfather, Luther Holley, whose home was in Salisbury, Connecticut, was
an ancestor of whom anyone might well be proud.
When a mere boy the care of a sick father with his
mother and sisters came upon him. He had often to
ride for the doctor after a hard day's work, when he
was so tired that he sometimes slept for miles upon
the horse's back. He never had but five days' school-
ing, but, when suffering from an injury to his knee
that jeopardised his farming prospects, he qualified

himself to teach school and was successful in this
line.   Although his wife, a Baptist preacher's daughter, was exceedingly devout, we find the germs of the
liberal beliefs of her son Myron and his daughter
Sallie in her persuasion that " her own child would
never suffer endless torments on account of a point
of faith."

Luther Holley was evidently not "in all things
very religious" after the manner of the New England Calvinists.   Nevertheless, he was a great admirer of *Paradise Lost* and is said to have known it
by heart.   From this admiration Milton Holley got
his name.   He sent three of his sons to college :
Myron to Williams, Horace to Yale, and Orville to
Harvard.   One of his letters to the Harvard man
has been preserved.   It is an eloquent plea for the
dignity of manual labour, to which, apparently, he
hoped his college-bred son would soon return.   If
the son's college breeding enabled him to write as
good a letter as his father's, it did more for him than
Harvard does for many of its " young barbarians, all
at play," after a century of growth and change.

Myron Holley, son of Luther, and Sallie's father,
was born in Salisbury, April 29, 1779, and he died
March 4, 1841, while the bells of Rochester and all
the country round were ringing in a new president
at Washington, who in one short month would lay
down the office which he ought never to have taken
up.   Myron Holley's life was one of much interest
and importance.   He was intimately and impress-
ively associated with some of the most serious events
and movements of his generation, and the dignity

and sweetness of his nature and his character won
the admiration of those who had no sympathy with
his religious or political opinions. We know little of
his boyhood, but there are signs that he was much
liked by his companions for his open, generous disposition. He was graduated at Williams College in
1799. The next year we find him studying law
in the office of Judge Kent, at Cooperstown, New
York, and, later, pursuing the same study in Salisbury, where the beauty of the situation must have
been a kind of liberal education to one who was
never dull to any pleasing aspect of the natural
world. In 1803, Myron Holley settled in Canandaigua, then an insignificant village, its first log hut
having been built only ten years before. But then,
as now, it was " beautiful for situation," and until
1821 Myron Holley found there a pleasant home,
and ten of his twelve children were born to him. An
unconfirmed tradition represents him as giving up
the practice of the law because he could not conscien-
tiously maintain a cause he knew to be unjust. He
was a man of books and liked to share their contents
with his friends in conversation, reading his favourite authors aloud in a delightful manner. He was
well acquainted, no doubt, with Bacon's saying,
" God Almighty first planted a garden, and indeed
it is the purest of human pleasures," and of the second of these declarations he was well convinced.
Gardening, when not his vocation, was the most
engaging avocation of his life.

" Flowers laugh before thee on their beds,
And fragrance in thy footing treads."

But fruits even more than flowers were his peculiar joy.

For four years (1810–1814) he was town clerk of Canandaigua, and in 1816, at the age of thirty-seven, he was sent to the General Assembly of the State to further a project of great importance to the people of his neighbourhood,—the making of the Erie Canal. The satisfaction taken in the completion of this enterprise did not exaggerate its actual importance. Now we sometimes think of it as " that Serbonian bog where armies whole [of political reputations] have sunk" and millions of the people's money. Then it was a wonderful and beneficent achievement, and no one, not even De Witt Clinton, who has had the lion's share of praise, did so much to consummate the happy end as Myron Holley. He was the most active of the commissioners who carried on the work. Paradoxical as it may seem, his estimate of the cost, about $5,000,000, was very little exceeded. His, too, was the happy thought to make a part of the canal as a kind of object-lesson, one which would raise the demand for its completion to a fever heat. What he expected came to pass, and in 1825 there was a " wedding of the waters " of the Hudson and Lake Erie, and there was a sound of jubilation all the length of " the raging canawl " as Governor Clinton and his party were slowly dragged on their triumphal way.

But for Myron Holley there was a painful shadow on that brilliant consummation of his eight years of hard administrative work. Somehow, his accounts as treasurer of the canal were not straight. There

was a discrepancy of $30,000 between his vouchers
and his disbursements. He asked to be allowed a
commission of one per cent. on the moneys received
and disbursed, but his request was not granted. Not
until 1828 was slack and tardy justice done to him.
In the meantime he was technically a defaulter, and
that damning title was affixed to him with such
malignity as only partisan malice can invent. Even
after he had been formally exonerated, the blistering
epithet was kept as a rod in pickle, to be produced
at any time when it would serve the ends of a political opponent. And it must be confessed that his
business administration was not wise. It was never
so. He managed his own affairs as dubiously as those
of the canal and ended his career a poorer man than
he had been twenty years before. But at all times
his honesty was entire and absolute, and no man
ever did so much for the community with so little
personal advantage.

The next important enterprise in which he was
engaged afforded ample confirmation of his unselfish
disposition and at the same time proved his invinci-
ble courage. This new enterprise was Anti-Masonry.
At this remove the cause is not an impressive one,
but it aroused some excitement in 1826, when William Morgan, having betrayed Masonic secrets, mys-
teriously disappeared, and the body of a drowned or
murdered man having been almost simultaneously
discovered, it was identified as Morgan's by his
friends; with more of passion than of judgment is
not only possible but probable. Anyway, the dead
man, battered past all certain recognition, was " a

good enough Morgan till after election," as some of the baser politicians or their satirists declared. He was " a good enough Morgan " to convince Myron Holley, who, always meaning to be just, may in this instance have mixed some prejudice or passion with his thought. The Anti-Masonic movement culminated in a national convention which met at Philadelphia in 1830. Myron Holley wrote the " Address to the People of the United States " put forth by the convention. He wrote it with no 'prentice hand. He had done much writing of the same sort for New York State and other conventions. It was admirable writing, calm and clear and forcible, fervid without passion, not bitter and yet terribly severe. For a dozen years the Anti-Masonic movement had much local and national importance. In 1838 its gubernatorial vote in New York was 192,-882. It was a bias upon national politics that affected more than one presidential election in a serious manner. And from first to last Myron Holley was a leading spirit in the agitation that stripped the Masonic order of all its prestige and in a few years reduced the number of lodges in the State of New York from three hundred to seventy-five. He edited the *Lyons Countryman ;* he was a candidate for the Assembly ; he left no stone unturned that might be built into his argument. The wonder is that he did not share the supposed fate of William Morgan, and that he did not is one good reason for a serious doubt whether Morgan's death was actually compassed by emissaries of the Masonic order. He invited it by a course of speech and action that was not more distinguished by its fearlessness than by its freedom from all irritating personalities. It was to a system that he opposed himself, and to its apologists only so far as this was unavoidable.

But the supreme distinction of Myron Holley's life was yet to be attained—that of being the principal originator of the Liberty party, the first party to make anti-slavery a matter of partisan politics, a party which developed in 1848 into the Free Soil party, losing at the same time much of its moral purity, and in 1856 into the Republican party, the instrument by which slavery was abolished. Mr. Holley's anti-slavery sentiments were a tardy growth. Anti-Masonry for a dozen years had too exclusive possession of his mind to tolerate a brother near the throne. Not until 1837 do we find him taking a practical interest in the anti-slavery conflict. A nomination to Congress was offered him if he would let slavery alone, but no promise to this effect could be extorted. He became a lecturer of the Anti-Slavery Society, and one not exceeded in efficiency by many of his companions in the field. But he was born too late into the anti-slavery movement.

Garrison's conception of abolitionism as a purely moral enterprise, disdaining, as such, all direct political action, was never thoroughly ingrained with him, and when a good many abolitionists became restless under the sway of the non-voting principle, Mr. Holley quickly fell in with these and by a process of natural selection soon found himself the leader of their company. It was not at all strange that many matter-of-fact people, as earnest and sincere as Garrison himself, could not appreciate his principle, or were impatient of the lingering agony of suspense which it seemed likely to entail. Garrison could not do justice to the motives of those who fell away from him, and he was strengthened in his ill opinion of them by the obvious sordidness of some of these and of others who came flocking to their camp. Especially could he not understand how anyone who had been one of his disciples could decline upon such a wretched notion as the sectionalism of slavery and the freedom of the Constitution from all complicity with it. If abolitionism had taught anything consistently it was that the Constitution was responsible for the existence of slavery in the States. The pleasing fiction adopted by the Liberty party, which later became the Republican party cry *par excellence*, "Freedom national, slavery sectional," did such good service that its success was generally accepted as a proof of its validity. But that it was a pleasing fiction, and no more, is pretty sure to be the dispassionate verdict of the political historian. Moreover, all of Garrison's prophecies as to the effect of political action on abolitionist principles were fulfilled in course of time. From demanding the abolition of slavery, the political abolitionists fell so far off that in 1856 and 1860 the Republican party accepted the Fugitive Slave Law and slavery in the District of Columbia. We have the word of James G. Blaine that in 1861 the general position of the Republicans was that of Daniel Webster in his compromise speech of March 7, 1850. Many were prepared, like Seward, to make even more base concessions, and it was only

Myron Holley

because Lincoln refused to, that war's dread arbitrament became inevitable.

But in 1839 Myron Holley was full of a fine enthusiasm for the organisation of abolitionism as a political party with presidential candidates of its own. He urged this course upon a State anti-slavery convention meeting at Cleveland, Ohio, October 23, 1839. It is an interesting comment on his daughter's ultimate career that one of the glories of this convention, as described by Henry B. Stanton, husband of Elizabeth Cady, was that "no miserable woman question" marred the occasion. A distrust of women's public action was almost inseparable from political anti-slavery in its initial stage. The Cleveland convention very properly, and quite unanimously, refused to endorse Mr. Holley's motion for a presidential nomination, because the delegates had been chosen without any reference to such action.

But already a local convention in Monroe County, New York, had adopted a series of Holley's resolutions, looking to a national ticket, and this action was followed up at a State convention meeting at Warsaw, New York, November 13th, of which Holley was the leading spirit. James G. Birney was nominated for President and F. J. Lemoyne for Vice-President. Both declined the nomination on the ground that abolitionists were insufficiently agreed as to the advisability of forming a new party. The demand for such a party was strongest in New York, where Holley had for his coadjutors, if not for his inspirers, such distinguished abolitionists as Alvan

Stewart, Gerrit Smith, William Goodell, and Beriah Green.

In New England the non-voters were in the ascendant, while in the West the new party movement was decried as too radical, because it would not permit any voting except for abolitionist candidates. It is easy at this remove to see that good and true men could adopt any of these three positions with perfect good faith. When, after the nomination of General Harrison, such a well-grounded abolitionist as Dr. Bailey, editor of the *Philanthropist* (afterward of the *National Era*, in which he gave *Uncle Tom's Cabin* to the world), thought "a tolerably fair case might be made out for the General," the new party men had a good sharp circumstance to "spur the sides of their intent."

April 1, 1840, obedient to the call of Myron Holley's county convention, a national convention met at Albany and nominated James G. Birney and Thomas Earle [1] for President and Vice-President. Delegates from but six States were present and none from the North-west. The new party took no name, and though we now speak of the Liberty party of 1840 it is only by reflecting back a name which was adopted in 1844. The nominations were accepted, though the same reasons existed for declining them as six months before. Garrison's adherents thought nothing could be more significant than the fact that

---

[1] A brother of Pliny Earle, the celebrated alienist, born in Leicester, Massachusetts ; a nephew of Arnold Buffum, " an Old Hickory Quaker abolitionist," one of Garrison's " great allies " and cousin to Elizabeth Buffum Chace, another, who still lives (1898).

they were made on All Fools' Day. But they were supported by a forlorn hope with as much enthusiasm as if they expected victory to perch upon their banner, and by no one with more serious conviction or more moving eloquence than by Myron Holley. He received forty dollars a month from the party treasury for speaking up and down the State. Not for that meagre stipend, but for the joy of battle in what he conceived to be the best of all good causes, he kept up the unequal fight. All the waves and billows of "hard cider" might go over him, but he bated not a jot of heart or hope—not of immediate but of ultimate success ; a hope justified, many say, by the election of Abraham Lincoln in 1860 ; but Abraham Lincoln was not an abolitionist. In the course of twenty years political anti-slavery underwent the change which Garrison had prophesied in 1839. It became "subdued to what it worked in like the dyer's hand " to a remarkable degree. But the Republican opposition, not to slavery but to *the extension of slavery*, was sufficient to drive the South into rebellion, and to bring about something very close akin to Garrison's "immediate and unconditional emancipation." Thus once again it was made manifest that

"God fulfils himself in many ways."

The votes for Birney and Earle were 7069, and it was as if every one cost Myron Holley a drop of his heart's blood. It was not entirely because of his arduous labours and severe exposure "on the stump." He complained of a pain in his chest. Certain it is, he had an aching heart. Elizur Wright, who wrote his Life in 1882, reckons that there were at least 70,000 abolitionists qualified to vote. That only one tenth of these acted as Myron Holley would have had them act must have been a dreadful damper to his hopes. But they shot up like fire out of the ashes. He believed that he had made the right beginning. Meantime he had wrecked not only his health but his fortune, which was but a modest one at any time. From Canandaigua he had moved (1821) to Lyons, where he had a spacious house, and made a lovely home. When the Erie Canal was completed, making the State rich and him a poor man, he moved into a smaller house, set in a five-acre lot of quince and mulberry trees. Whether the mulberry trees looked to a silkworm project as elsewhere in those times we are not told.

The orchard did not prove a profitable one, and about 1835 Myron Holley betook him to a lovely spot on the Genesee, just below Rochester, which he named " Rose Ridge." He made it beautiful with flowers and was not above peddling in Rochester *in propria personâ* the fruits and vegetables he raised upon his land. " Gurowski cannot be degraded," said the Polish Count of that name when someone expressed fear that he was degrading himself by working on a railway excavation. Myron Holley had the same indomitable self-respect, and he *appeared* the gentleman he was, no matter what his occupation. " Why, Doctor," said the rector's wife, " I 've just seen the only *gentleman* I have yet met in Rochester, and he was selling vegetables ! "

And the high-bred rector smiled and said, " It must be Myron Holley." And it was.

For Cincinnatus to return to his farm was no such great hardship. If he had had to give up his farm it would have been a different matter. Our Cincinnatus had to give up his. To run the *Rochester Freeman* during the campaign he had incurred responsibilities jointly with others which the others were not prepared to meet in the cool morning after the losing game. But Myron Holley, selling " Rose Ridge," paid *his* debts to the last cent, and with a residue of $400 went to live in Rochester in a hired house. This was in December, 1840, when but four months remained to him of a life of much vicissitude, too early spent. As the shadow of death enfolded him he was full of tender thoughts and said, communing with himself, or to those who were about him, " I have never deceived anybody in my life."

Myron Holley was a man who did his own thinking in religious as well as in political matters. He was one of a smaller and more despised minority in the former particular than in the latter. He was an exceedingly religious man, but "after the way that some call heresy." At this point I am very happy to avail myself of an account of his religious character and conduct written by his daughter Sallie, than which nothing could be more instructive or more satisfactory :

" Nothing impressed me more, as I grew into young-womanhood, than my father's earnest religious convictions, ever ardent, alive, and all-controlling. I never knew any soul who had such an unfaltering faith in

immortality—more like sight than faith, a habitual anticipation of heaven, that transfigured all human life to him
and dignified every act. He utterly repudiated the
popular theology. He thought it unscriptural, irrational,
and demoralising, and that it deplorably hindered the
coming of the kingdom of heaven upon earth. So he,
as I knew him, could not sanction going to the fashion-
able churches. I never in all my life saw him in a
church. Instead he used to hold a simple service in
our home parlour in Lyons, in which the family and
the poorer neighbours joined. After his removal to
Rochester he convened Sunday morning meetings at the
Court-House, where he preached regularly. There was
no Unitarian or liberal preaching otherwise in the city.
While he occupied the fine fruit and vegetable farm a
few miles north of Rochester, at Carthage, his custom
was to hold Sunday meetings in the poor old district
schoolhouse there. What a curious, odd audience used
to gather to listen and look at him! Every rank in
society was represented. There sat the elegant and
courtly Judge E. B. Strong, with occasionally the ladies
of his household. And the Episcopalian Hoopers, on
Sundays too rainy to get to their St. Paul's in the city,
came to this extraordinary kind of worship, where they
met the poorest and most humble day-labourers, and even
drunkards and outcasts did not feel themselves excluded
from the all-embracing humanity of those ministrations.

"It was not an uncommon thing for families, too
degraded by intemperance and vice to venture to ask
a clergyman, to send for my father to officiate at their
funerals. They saw in their daily intercourse with him,
that his divine tenderness took them all in."

The portrait in Elizur Wright's biography of **My-**

ron Holley is that of a man with a very beautiful face, and all the traditions confirm this testimony. At sixty he was already a venerable figure on the streets of Rochester, strangers pausing to look at him and friends greeting him with a respect that was nigh to reverence. His habits were temperate and clean: he used neither intoxicating drinks nor tobacco. He had great physical strength, once taking a tramp bodily in his arms and carrying him from his daughter's house, where he had intruded, and planting him in the middle of the street. I infer that he was somewhat bald, from the fact that a little granddaughter, whose confidence in his horticultural genius was immense, asked him " why he did not sow hair seed on the top of his head." One of the grandchildren in his arms was not enough. Two or three were better. His delight in them, as in his own children, was unbounded, and in every family relation he was perfectly affectionate and loyal. For his brothers and one sister living in Salisbury, Connecticut, his heart continually yearned, and to visit them was to renew a thousand memories of his early life. Governor Holley of Connecticut was his nephew and the father of Alexander L. Holley, the practical inventor, who was the chief promoter of the manufacture of Bessemer steel in this country. And blood with him was always stronger than water. For any Holley to demean himself would have been felt as a stain on his own honour; for any to do well heightened the beating of his heart.

Nothing could exceed his interest in his children's real welfare, their education, their characters. And

3

they "knew the gift of God"; they appreciated their good fortune in having such a father. Sallie always regarded him as the inspirer of her anti-slavery work. From the Liberty party to the abolitionists was a direction seldom taken in the times of Polk and Taylor. But for Sallie Holley it meant no reflection on the high purpose and integrity of her father and his companions in the new party organisation. She knew him too well to question his devotion to the cause to which she consecrated her whole life. The significant thing for her was that he would not vote for anyone who was not an abolitionist. He was for her as much an abolitionist as Garrison, but wearing the doctrine with a difference which never at any time, apparently, concerned her very much.

CHAPTER III

CHILDHOOD AND YOUTH

SALLIE HOLLEY was the fifth child of her parents and her name was one doubly sacred to her father's heart, because it was at once that of his high-souled mother and his beautiful wife. Sallie's birth was the first anniversary celebration of a day forever memorable in her father's life, February 17, 1817, the day on which he presented his first report as Canal Commissioner. When the work was completed in 1825 she had a lively sense that it was preëminently her father's work, and the booming of the cannon which signalised "the wedding of the waters" lingered pleasantly in her memory ever afterwards. As time went on her perfect sympathy with her father made it necessary for her to do something to carry on his work to larger issues. "No child," says a beloved friend, "was ever more strongly imbued with filial reverence." To do the things that pleased her father was her greatest happiness while he lived, to do the things that would have pleased him was her inspiration after his death. With his blue eyes, she had not the other features of his face, but she had the features of his mind,—his liking for good books, for liberal religion, his passionate humanity, his courage in speaking out his convictions, his love of flowers and gardening. She liked to be with him and to imagine that she helped him when he was at work out-of-doors. She liked to hear his reading and his talk. His battles royal with the Methodist minister were her delight, and while yet a child she preferred his preaching in the court-house to that of the ordained clergymen in the steeple-houses of the town. One of the earliest possessions of her facile memory was a description of the fishermen of Galilee in F. W. P. Greenwood's *Lives of the Twelve Apostles*. She learned the passage to please her father and recited it often to please others. She recited it to Miss Putnam on their first ride together in Oberlin to Vermilion River, and on their last in Virginia to the old Yeocomico church.

There came a day when Dr. Channing, on his way to Niagara Falls, stayed a few hours in Lyons, and preached to Myron Holley's congregation. To be led by his gentle hand from the house to the place of meeting was for Sallie a great distinction and one not to be forgotten. It gave her, possibly, an extravagant idea of Dr. Channing's influence, for when she went to Boston in 1851, she credited the general good manners of policemen, hackmen, and the like to his preaching. Whereupon Garrison, whose idea of Channing's influence was certainly not extravagant, smiled his demur. At an early age Sallie became familiar with the thoughts of Channing and Emerson, and, following her father's lead, with

the great classics, Milton and Dante [1] and Shakespeare.   Her father's interest in her education was
shown in many ways.   In 1830 she received her first
letter, when he was visiting his birthplace in Connecticut, and with, perhaps, superfluous care, he ad-
vises her to get a dictionary and look up any words
she does not understand.   In 1831 she attended, as
a day scholar, a boarding-school in Lyons.   Two or
three local revivalists were let loose upon the school.
This business aroused her father's deepest indignation, and he wrote the teacher an elaborate letter
which is still fresh and pertinent after the lapse of
nearly seventy years.   In 1834 he wrote Sallie from
Hartford: " Before I came here you told me I should
see Mrs. Sigourney.   You were a true prophet."
The whole letter is a pretty picture of the intellectual and æsthetic aspirations of that far-off time.   In
1835 he writes from Rochester to a married daughter in Lyons: " I love Sally with an affection which
nothing shall or even can obliterate, and hope to aid
her advancement in life more hereafter than I have
been able to do for some years past."   But his
affairs were destined to decline for the remainder of
his life rather than to improve.

One of the delights of Sallie's childhood was to go
a-fishing in the canal which flowed hard by the Lyons house.   Her brother Sam was her companion,
but he seems to have been a less capable one than
George Eliot's of the " Brother and Sister " poem.
Once she slipped in, and when rescued by Tom

[1] Probably at first in Cary's translation, and possibly at a period
subsequent to her father's death.

Rooker's father, like Garfield—so a pathetic eulogist described his similar mishap—she was "all wet," but not otherwise damaged. Tom Rooker was a favourite companion, dragging her upon his sled and doing other gallant things with boyish zeal. In 1841 he assisted Horace Greeley in bringing out the first number of the *Tribune,* and his connection with the *Tribune* lasted fifty-six years. How, after long divergence, his lines and Sallie Holley's met again, is "another story," which I will tell in its due place.   One of her girlish attachments was for Harriet Coles, a daughter of Judge Coles of Lyons, and this meant every joy that orchards, barns, and fields can yield a young girl's heart.   Sallie's visits to the Judge's were not more sweet to her than they were prized by Harriet Coles and all her housemates.

After years of separation Harriet and Sallie met again, when the latter came to Lyons in the 'fifties to give an anti-slavery lecture. The Methodist church opened its door to receive her and she was listened to with a respect smacking of kindly memories more than of the general distrust of women in politics. Here was a day to "mark with a white stone," but a rare lily served as well. It was plucked—the Nelumbo—on the shore of Sodus Bay, an arm of Lake Ontario, and it was a great triumph to send so rare a specimen to a botanical friend in Boston,— James Jackson, son of Francis. The love of flowers was always an enthusiasm with Miss Holley and bound the several periods of her life together as with a fragrant wreath. Twenty years later, Harriet Coles came to Lottsburgh to see the Holley School. And

there on the wall of the schoolhouse, which Thomas
Rooker had generously helped build, was a picture of
the man who had been a playmate with both Sallie
Holley and Miss Coles some forty years before.
Verily, "the whirligig of time" brings other things
than "its revenges" into our complex life!

Naturally vivacious and attractive, as she passed
from girlhood to young-womanhood, Sallie Holley
profited by and enjoyed the best provincial society of
Lyons and Buffalo and Rochester under the protection of her sisters, Mrs. Chapin, Mrs. Beaumont, and
Mrs. Kingman. Her temperance principles were of
early date, and when others drank at table she
"turned down an empty glass." For much of the
time during five successive years she was the companion of Mrs. Timothy Childs,—an invalid lady
who had held slaves in North Carolina and brought
one of them to Rochester, a pious old personal at-
tendant. Miss Holley was equally at home with
mistress and maid. "She and Aunt Louisa," said
Dr. Timothy Ledyard, "used to talk slavery and anti-
slavery over their chess, with tears in their eyes, so
earnest was each." At the same time Mrs. Childs
was happy to divide the honours of her drawing-room
with her bright young companion. Bishop De
Lancey [1] also played chess with Mrs. Childs. When,
years afterward, he confirmed " Black Sarah " at
Olean, New York, with a number of white candidates
awaiting the Bishop's blessing, Miss Holley could
not but remember how his delicate, white hands used
to move the chessmen as they were laid more gently

[1] Episcopalian Bishop of Western New York.

on the woolly head than on the fairer ones while he said with special emphasis, " Defend *this* thy servant, O Lord ! "

With General Childs, U. S. A., Miss Holley talked of the morality of the Seminole War in which he had been engaged. He confessed its injustice but pleaded that as a soldier he must obey the commands of his superiors. Miss Holley did not see why. She did not believe in war, yet had no more compunction than Garrison in 1861 as to wishing that Freedom's armies might prevail.

Her first opportunity to worship with a Unitarian society was in Buffalo and she embraced it cordially. Rev. G. W. Hosmer, the minister of the society, baptised her in April, 1841. It is Roman Catholic doctrine that the personality of the priest does not affect the sacrament for better or for worse. But to be baptised by Dr. Hosmer was, it seems to me, a piece of rare good fortune, such a good man was he. It was in Buffalo that Miss Holley enjoyed—I use the word advisedly—another experience of first-rate importance. The story was told by Frederick Douglass, on the day of her burial in Rochester, at a Memorial Meeting of a Woman's Suffrage Convention meeting in Washington. Invited to speak by the president, Susan B. Anthony, Mr. Douglass said :

" An Anti-Slavery Convention was appointed to be held in Buffalo, New York, where Miss Holley then resided. [Was visiting her sister.] It was in the year 1843. The abolition question was then so unpopular that no church or public hall could be obtained in which to hold the meetings ; so we went into an old deserted warehouse, without door or windows, and began with an audience of six or seven men who stood about the open front of the building.

"I continued for six days to speak in this place to an audience (which at last crowded the house) of the common people, who came in their common clothes.

"On the third day of our motley meeting, made up entirely of men, I observed with some amazement, as well as pleasure, a stately young lady, elegantly dressed, come into the room, leading a beautiful little girl. The crowd was one that would naturally repel a refined and elegant young lady, but there was no shrinking on her part. The crowd did the shrinking. It drew in its sides and opened the way, as if fearful of soiling the elegant dress with the dirt of toil. This lady came daily to my meetings in that old deserted building, morning and afternoon, till they ended. The dark and rough background rendered her appearance like a messenger from heaven sent to cheer me in what then seemed to most men a case of utter despair. The lady was Miss Sallie Holley, and this story illustrates her noble, independent, and humane character. She was never ashamed of her cause nor her company."

Here was a good proof of the openness of Sallie Holley's mind. Because her father had broken with the abolitionists, and because they had abused him roundly,[1] she was not pledged to follow the new party blindly and to close her ears and mind against the thorough-going abolitionists. There

[1] Yet Garrison said of him : " As a writer he had few superiors in any country ; and he always conducted his controversies with dignity and candour."

were some of these who followed the banner of the Liberty party for a time and then went back to their first love, as they found the Liberty party getting more political and less moral from year to year. But it was more exceptional for those born into the Liberty party, as Sallie Holley was, to go over into the abolitionist camp. She came in time to be a stout political partisan, but that was after the war, when the Republican party was redeemed and sanctified for her by its providential part in the emancipation of four million slaves.

The death of Myron Holley made the conduct of her own life a more serious question than it had been before. What should she do with herself; with her gifts, such as they were? The way to marriage was not clear. Suitors she had; if not as many as Penelope, several that were considered worthy of her even by those who loved her best. One of them was a Harvard classmate of Wendell Phillips; and of Dr. Rufus Ellis, who urged with some indignation, "Has the young lady no friends to advise her to make this brilliant and eligible match? What prospect has she of doing better?" Miss Holley objected that "he had black eyes and voted for Henry Clay." At another time it was to herself that she objected: she "was not good enough and did not know enough—would be sure to disappoint the hope and affection laid at her feet." What then?

The first gleam of light was the possibility of teaching school in Rochester. But it was a fading gleam. The school-board was ready to do anything for her that she might ask : she chose the humblest and most arduous position in their gift,—a primary school consisting of some sixty little Irish girls. But she felt that her preparation for such work was miserably inadequate. At that time the question, "Should women learn the alphabet?" was much more pertinent than it is now. Miss Holley declared that few young ladies of her acquaintance knew the multiplication table. Meantime her brother and sister-in-law begged her to make her home with them, but such dependence was not to her mind. To "go as a nurse-girl to Cincinnati" seemed a preferable alternative. "No," said Frederick W. Holland, minister of the Rochester Unitarian Church; "go to Oberlin." An uncle of Mrs. Holland had just returned from England, where he had been soliciting help for the Ohio college, and, thanks to its liberality in admitting women and negroes, he had enlisted the sympathy of Harriet Martineau and other anti-slavery people.

Mr. Holland backed up his advice with a gift of forty dollars, and there was a scholarship, established by her friend Mr. S. D. Porter, one of the Oberlin trustees, of which she could avail herself. And so she went out very much like Abraham: not knowing exactly whither, but confident that she must *be* something better before she could *do* anything serious and important. Perhaps I should have said Moses rather than Abraham, for the reason that there were flesh-pots in Rochester, the savour of which seemed pleasanter than ever as she set out for Oberlin leaving them all behind. There were pleasant people there whose society it was hard to forego, and good times that could not be given up without a pang. But she had put her hand to the plough and even if she had foreseen how long and hard the ploughing was to be it is not likely that she would have turned back. For here was one who by nature and experience was fit for the kingdom of God.

CHAPTER IV

AT OBERLIN

SALLIE HOLLEY set out for Oberlin from her brother's house in Monroe, Michigan, in the depth of winter, 1847, taking the stage-sleigh for Cleveland. Those were the days of green barege veils, and hers hid a tear-stained face much of the way as she went doubtfully and yet resolvedly on a journey that was then a tedious one. Her brother had begged her not to expose herself to the insult sure to follow her going to the "nigger school." That was the distinction of Oberlin in 1847 and had been since 1835, when the institution made its good beginning. A romantic story attaches to the origin of almost every college in the United States, but in few cases is the story so romantic as in that of Oberlin. No other educational enterprise was so directly the offspring of the anti-slavery spirit.

In 1833 a new settlement was started in Lorain County, Ohio, by Rev. John J. Shipherd and Philo P. Stewart. The site was determined by a gift of five hundred acres of land from New Haven people, who owned much more in the vicinity. Lake Erie was ten miles away, and Cleveland thirty-three. The settlement had a distinctly economic and religious character. A covenant was subscribed which lamented the degeneracy of the Church, and pledged the signers to hold no more property than they could as God's faithful stewards and while appropriating as much as possible for religious uses. The basis, however, was not communistic.

The start was made with a company of pioneers of high moral character. Oberlin Collegiate Institute, which became Oberlin College in 1850, was chartered in February, 1834. Coeducation was one of the initial purposes, the first circular announcing that the purpose of the college was to be "the elevation of female character, by bringing within the reach of the misjudged and neglected sex all the instructive privileges which have hitherto unreasonably distinguished the leading sex from theirs." It was this aspect of Oberlin that attracted Sallie Holley to its shades—those in 1834 of an impenetrable forest surrounding a rude clearing in the woods. The plan of instruction contemplated a graded course from "the infant school up through the collegiate and theological courses." The lower grades were soon filled to repletion, but the first college class numbered only four young men. With Western Reserve College only forty miles away and already well established, the chances of the new college seemed very poor indeed. But a series of happy accidents, regarded at the time as special providences, gave Oberlin a strong impulsion towards a happy goal.

The action of the trustees of Dr. Lyman Beecher's Lane Theological Seminary, at Walnut Hills,
near Cincinnati, had driven out some thirty of the
anti-slavery students who were not willing to be
gagged. The only trustee refusing to subscribe to
this action was the Rev. Asa Mahan. In December, 1834, Mr. Shipherd, the Oberlin founder, set
out for New England to find a president for his new
college. On the way he heard of the break-up at
Lane, and jumped at the opportunity suggested of
securing Mahan for his presidency. He immediately set out for Cincinnati and made the journey
of 150 miles on a two-wheeled ox-cart, jolting and
plunging over a road that was almost inconceivably
bad. Mahan fell in quickly with the idea, and introduced Shipherd to the protesting students. They
all agreed to go to Oberlin if Mahan was made its
president. Here was, as Dr. Johnson said of Mrs.
Thrales's pots and kettles, "the potentiality of
growing rich beyond the dreams of avarice." So
much for happy accident or special providence
number one.

Number two was not less significant. Putting
their heads together, Mahan and Shipherd agreed to
invite Theodore D. Weld, the most capable and
brilliant of the protesting students, to take the
theological chair at Oberlin. Weld at the time was
on an anti-slavery circuit. But he was followed up
in a team belonging to John Rankin, an immediate
abolitionist before Garrison, and found at Hillsbor-
ough. He was confident that he was not the man
for the position, and that Charles G. Finney was.

Weld, by the way, was one of the many converts made by Finney's flaming zeal. Taking Weld's advice, Shipherd and Mahan went to New York. There they found Finney, but also a letter from the Oberlin trustees saying that they did not feel prepared to admit coloured students. But such admission was a *sine quâ non* with Finney and Mahan and the Lane contingent. It was with Mr. Shipherd also, who wrote that "if the injured brother of colour and consequently brothers Finney, Mahan, and Morgan, with eight professorships and $10,000, must be rejected," he must join himself to those outside the walls. Here was a tremendous "cinch," but the colonisation trustees held out stubbornly. When the final vote was taken it was a tie, and the chairman's ballot was necessary for a decision. Fortunately, the chairman was all right, but worse reasons for doing a good action were never given than in the resolution passed.

Still, the good cause was won and Oberlin was "named and known by that hour's feat," not only as a coëducative but as an abolitionist college, while Finney gave it an intensely evangelical character. He was not engrossed in anti-slavery principles. His biographer, Dr. Wright, to whom I am much indebted for the facts above recited, says: "We look in vain in his sermons for any formal discussion of the subject of slavery. His references to it were frequent and forcible, indeed, but they were casual." The fact that Arthur Tappan was the principal benefactor pledged Finney, and the college generally, to the new organisation when the break came in 1839,[1] though it was too deeply involved in the principle of coëducation to extricate itself from that. If the founding of Oberlin had been delayed until after the birth of the new organisation with its taboo of womankind, it is not probable that it would have welcomed women to its halls. But the irrevocable step was taken in 1834.

To appreciate the courage of those who persisted in opening Oberlin to coloured students, we must remember that the year 1835 was preëminently the year of pro-slavery mobs all over the country. It was the good fortune of Oberlin to be far from the madding crowd of city streets. Its rude buildings, battened with slabs that kept their bark unspoiled, would have made a splendid bonfire if the local population had not been in general sympathy with the movement that brought so many men and so much money to their aid.

It was, apparently, the fact that Oberlin opened its doors to women that attracted Sallie Holley, and not its anti-slavery character, though this was much in harmony with her Liberty party antecedents. The record of her life at Oberlin does not give us such details of her impressions of Finney as we should like to have. If she heard his sermon, "A Seared Conscience," which contained ninety-five subdivisions, and the supplementary one with eighty-four additional specifications, no echo of her thought about them has come down to us. But the moral intensity of the man must have made a profound impression on her mind and heart. It speaks vol-

[1] See the Garrison *Story* for that year.

4

umes for the essential soundness of her judgment
that with a temper so emotional she was not carried off her feet by the flood of his impassioned
eloquence.

She was the only Unitarian in the college. She
was assured that, however her faith might do to live
by, it would not answer when she came to die. She
answered : " Beyond all comparison it is the one to
die by. I never saw any faith so beautiful and sustaining as in my father's death. I have seen Trini-
tarians die, and none approached his peace." She
was asked if she could ask God's blessing on dancing, of which she was fond, as her father had been
before her. She answered: " Certainly ; as readily as
you do in Miss Adams's calisthenics, opened with
prayer. Those exercises are really dancing, and
Miss Adams says I am a great help to her in her
class." Her nature was exceedingly devout, and
she said, " I never had prayer enough till I came to
Oberlin," where every recitation was opened with a
prayer or hymn. Asked if she would partake of the
communion, and seeing that a negative answer was
expected and desired, she felt herself called upon to
testify to the worthiness of Unitarians, as such, to
join in every sacred exercise, and said, " Nothing is
so sacred as prayer, and if you allow me to pray with
you I shall certainly take the communion, and nothing but Mr. Finney's coming down from the pulpit and seizing the bread and wine shall prevent me."

So exemplary was her walk and conversation that
her companions and teachers could not deny that
she was a Christian, while yet more convincing was

her dropping her rings into the contribution box for the Mendi Africans. Her friend, Caroline Putnam, upon whose reminiscences I draw for these particulars, recalls the charming simplicity of her dress, her cottage-bonnet tied with a plain band of ribbon, and her independence here as elsewhere : on the day of her graduation she declined to go with the multitude who kept holiday in white muslin and blue ribbons, yellow being the colour she preferred.

"But she was radiantly lovely," says her friend, "as she stepped forth on that great stage of the Oberlin Tabernacle, animated by the preluding music, her deep blue eyes looking off from her manuscript now and then to more earnestly impress her heretical 'Ideal of Womanhood.' Her ideas put bees in the bonnets of the sages, humming as they did with women's right to vote, to preach, and with the brightest humour, poetry, and satire, ranging for illustration from Hans Andersen's 'Ugly Duck' to Wordsworth's 'perfect woman nobly planned.' Nobody forgot that scene and lesson, or lost its pith and point. The brave soul was there consecrating itself with lofty enthusiasm to the holy war against slavery. The Divine Voice had called, and with instant, reverent obedience she answered, 'Here am I.'"

Miss Putnam, but for whose gentle violence of persistency this sketch would never have been written, was drawn to Sallie Holley at Oberlin, she tells me, by anti-slavery kinship. At an anti-slavery meeting "in York State" a fugitive slave pleaded for his people in Canada, though free, still much in need, and Myron Holley made his last public address.

The recollection of that meeting[1] and of Myron Holley's speaking was Caroline Putnam's assurance of Sallie Holley's friendship when some years later they met at Oberlin and found themselves " the only ultra radicals there "—which means, I suppose, the only Garrisonian abolitionists, not an original distinction, but one to which they ultimately arrived. The friendship thus begun ripened into one of the most beautiful of the many women friendships that were developed by the anti-slavery fellowship. It was like Cleopatra's beauty : age could not wither it, nor custom stale its infinite variety. And since Miss Holley's death her friend has enjoyed a spiritual communion with her which she cannot think has been conscious only on this hither side.

At Oberlin Miss Holley's course was varied much according to her conscious need. She studied mental arithmetic with the preparatory class and read compositions with the seniors that excelled their best. One had a history. It was an autobiographical story, " My First Lie." A friend sent it to T. S. Arthur, and it was printed in his magazine. Later it was pirated and Sallie became Michael. Thus or otherwise transformed, this vagrant turned up one day in Virginia, when Sallie Holley and her friend were rummaging a barrel of Northern contributions to the Holley School. It was a sad story, no doubt ; much like one that harrowed my own feelings, when I was

---

[1] Caroline Putnam went to an anti-slavery meeting with her mother —the girl's first evening meeting—and was sent forward to put a Spanish quarter in the black man's hand, her first contribution to a cause to which she has since given her whole life.

a boy, in the first book I ever owned, and I wonder that I ever read another. Sallie, it seems, was entrusted with a cent to buy a fig. She bought the fig and ate it bit by bit and then told her sister a wicked lie—that she had lost the cent. Then it came her turn to be eaten—with remorse—and to confess her crime to her dear father and to suffer the punishment of his disappointed trust—the moral of the piteous tale.[1]

"At Oberlin," says Miss Putnam, "when her money was gone, she fell into the spirit of self-support in the leisurely way of the students; doing anything from washing dishes to making bread (too good for economy at Mrs. Parmelee's, where she boarded); tending baby and story-telling in Prof. Fairchild's nursery; making the best buttonholes that Prof. Allen ever had in his shirts; dressing dolls for Mrs. Kinney; teaching preparatory classes in composition, or giving private lessons in arithmetic to young coloured men who were trying to keep up with their class; getting for such work from three to twelve cents an hour, and paying a dollar a week for board and twelve and a half cents a week for lodging."

What manner of opposition she had to encounter in her endeavour to achieve a free and independent womanhood may be inferred from the following story, related by her faithful annalist:

"Side by side with the sober-faced and sober-minded young men, searched through and through by President Finney's eagle eye and questions, Antoinette Brown was

[1] Since writing this I have received the identical copy that came to Lottsburg. It does not call for any change in the free paraphrase that I have given of Miss Putnam's rendering.

in the theological course to fit herself for becoming that anomaly of those days, a woman preacher. Her heart was beating at the approach of her turn in President Finney's theological class, to open the recitation with prayer. But Mr. Finney passed right by her and took the next (male) student. Antoinette cried about it, which was duly reported to him, and the next time he saw her, away ahead of him on the street, he called out, loud enough to be heard across the street, 'Antoinette, you may pray ! You *shall* pray ! I did not know as you *wanted* to pray.' So after that she took her part with the others, and we, always alert for the last ray of progress, went to hear her (the only time we were ever in that low-roomed, out-of-the-way closet of the Institution)."

There came a time, many years later, when Antoinette Brown was invited to uplift in prayer the hearts of a great International Women's Parliament in Washington, and when it seemed as natural a thing for her to do so as for the stars to shine or for the grass to grow. *E pur si muove !*

Sallie's was a genuine, natural religion that puzzled the orthodox people at Oberlin, teachers and students, not a little. They could not understand how anyone so earnestly religious could be so without their experience of enmity against God and rejection of his Son. " Oh, no ! " she said, " I have no such sublime rebellion to relate. My sins are that I have n't learned more ; that I do not study my lessons better. This is the solemn religious duty that weighs on my conscience ; not that I have n't prayed enough." It was exactly in the spirit of her father's life and thought that she made "the supremacy of ethics" her controlling principle ; and this, too, with the clearest eye for the most homely duties within reach.   At her boarding-house, to which young men were attracted that they might hear her talk, the mistress was extremely pious, going to five-o'clock morning prayer-meetings, and to others in the afternoon after a midday nap.   She thought Miss Holley should go and do likewise, but her boarder thought it poor religion for her to do these things and neglect her family and boarders, leaving for them skimmed milk and scanty food while she was drinking in "the sincere milk of the Word," and battening on the bread of life.   Miss Holley imparted her views on this subject to the mistress of the house, and also others touching the habits of her children, who were much given to borrowing what their mother should have provided.   This counter-blast had the desired effect : the stream of evangelical expostulation was cut off.

Miss Putnam writes :

"After listening to any sermon from Prof. Finney [made president in 1851], President Mahan, or Prof. Fairchild, at Oberlin, whose theology seemed monstrous, even blasphemous, to her broader views of the Divine character, she would boldly follow to the home and discuss her dissent.   In one instance, when Prof. Fairchild had assumed a literal devil in the story of the Temptation, he, in his beautiful, humble spirit, acknowledged his obligation for her fine, spiritual rendering, then new to him.

"She took notes of the startling prayers that led the

excited devotions in the great Oberlin church.   Also of
what were thought such searching sermons of Prof.
Finney, whose revivalistic methods to awaken concern
in the students, for their own salvation, were to her
highly dramatic.   ' It was so like a theatre,' going to
that immense meeting with its tiers of seats rising in a
circular gallery,—the pulpit at the front of the vast
orchestra stage.

"On one occasion, after Mr. Finney's high-voiced,
sharp, ringing, penetrating arraignment had for a moment
subsided, he abruptly said :

"' Brother Clark, will you pray ? '

"The brother quickly fell on his knees and broke
out :

"' Oh, Lord Jesus ! we would throw our wicked, hateful, and devilish miserable selves right into thy bosom,'
etc.

"Mr. Finney himself prayed :

"' O Lord, if thou shouldst this instant poise thy
thunderbolts and hurl them at the head of each one of
us to thrust us down to lowest hell to perish to all eternity, we should cry, " Just and merciful art thou in all
thy ways, O Lord God Almighty ! " '

"But with all the eccentricities at Oberlin, Miss Holley honoured its earnest people, resolute to bless the
world by spreading its best light and truth, and especially did she honour it for admitting women and coloured
students, alone of all the institutions in our broad land.

"To be sure, its evangelical missions and ministers
were getting teachers, wives, and matrons in these educated women ; but, as the magic mill could n't stop
grinding salt when there was enough in the ocean, so
out of Oberlin's mill came lecturers, doctors, and free-
thinkers and doers.

" Said Miss Holley, ' Antoinette, all this false theology will fall right off of you in time.' And it did, when she had read Emerson."

There were good times at Oberlin, as when our friend Sallie went with others to attend the Commencement of Western Reserve College. The horse was very slow, the waggon neither comfortable nor elegant, and yet the forty miles were not too long, and when Judge Baldwin, their rheumatic host, denounced the oration of the day as " a right Abby Kelley affair," the cup of satisfaction overflowed. There was another outing, when Miss Holley, with two other " ultras," aspired to the best horse and buggy at Oberlin for three days, at fifty cents a day, a charge which was certainly not exorbitant. They went to Akron to a Woman's Rights convention meeting there, and heard Aunt Fanny Gage, Sojourner Truth, Caroline M. Severance, and other champions of the faith, and were vastly entertained, especially by Sojourner's discomfiture and rout of a young preacher who had the temerity to come up against her. But when they were ready to start for home a team of the least possible pretentiousness was brought round. Fortunately, there was a strawberry-mark by which Miss Putnam could identify their own,—a lost rivet in the harness,—and they set out for home, made happier by their relief from an appalling fear : what Mr. Munson would say when they told him of the change his property had undergone !

Oberlin did much for Sallie Holley in many ways,

but she had special courses, not published in the catalogue, that were of more importance than any of her regular studies. All the time she was breathing the air of anti-slavery reform, and as time went on she found herself upon a wave that carried her into the thick of the battle, her place with those of the advance-guard, which, under the leadership of Garrison, the anti-slavery people of Oberlin had very generally come to distrust as rash in its denunciation of the Constitution as "a covenant with death and an agreement with hell."

CHAPTER V

FINDING HER PLACE

" BUT the momentous, the decisive convention of our lives, was the next summer [after the drive to Akron], at Litchfield, Ohio, twenty miles from Oberlin, a fanatical, heretical, infidel assembly gathered through the inspiration and welcome of Josephine Griffing, a wonderful woman both in the Woman Suffrage movement and in the Freedman's Bureau, of which Garrison hailed her the true founder.

"Among the speakers at this meeting was Abby Kelley Foster,[1] who made an eloquent appeal to her hearers in behalf of the slave-woman and asked :

" 'Who in this great assembly is willing to plead her cause ? '

" At the close of her address, and in the recess of the meeting, Miss Holley advanced to say, ' I will plead the cause of the slave-woman.' Mrs Foster welcomed

[1] Born January 15, 1811 ; died January 14, 1887. Wife of the erratic Stephen S. Foster, who was born November 7, 1809, and died September 8, 1881. She was one of the brightest and best of the goodly company of anti-slavery women. She did not " run well in harness," but did her work with much individual freedom, Garrison and other leading spirits being always confident that she would "use her liberty " in a more effective manner than their wisdom could devise.

with warmth and gratitude the proffer and begged Miss
Holley to join her instantly in that Ohio campaign ; to
which Miss Holley replied, that she had another year to
study in Oberlin to complete her course, but as soon as
she should graduate she would join her. Mrs. Foster
said afterwards, 'I looked upon you as a bundle of
enthusiasms.' But the pledge was faithfully made and
faithfully kept. From that day all her plans were made
with reference to its fulfilment. 'Putty, I 've decided
to be an anti-slavery lecturer !' she wrote me,—my first
intimation of the event."

Here was the natural climax of a disposition which
for some time had been maturing in Miss Holley's
mind. It was not reached without much inward
questioning, nor did her purpose pass over into
action without much outward opposition. Her pastor, as she always regarded him, Dr. Hosmer, be-
sought her sister to remonstrate with Sallie to save
her from ruining her reputation by joining those
hated abolitionists. Her sister answered : " Sallie
thinks her salvation depends on not being ashamed of
those hated abolition infidels, Parker Pillsbury, Abby
Foster, and Mr. Garrison." Whenever she went to
Buffalo it was a very tender experience for her to hear
Dr. Hosmer preach, but after Millard Fillmore had
signed the Fugitive Slave Law and returned to his
accustomed seat in Dr. Hosmer's church without
rebuke, she could never partake of the communion
there again.

During her last summer in Oberlin, Miss Holley
received an invitation to address a meeting called to
celebrate the West India Emancipation, August 1st,

A. K. Foster

by the coloured people of Sandusky, Ohio. She asked leave in the customary manner of the Faculty and the Ladies' Board. It was granted, but Mrs. Mahan, the president's wife, said, " We have one condition : You will, Miss Holley, please not accept any invitation to stay in a coloured man's house in Sandusky." Miss Holley replied, " As a matter of truth it had never occurred to me that I should be so invited, but, Mrs. Mahan, now you mention it, I should certainly feel it my duty to accept any such invitation as a testimony to my principles, and, really, to those professed by this Institution." Another troublesome occasion was the election of Lucy Stanton, a bright, able coloured student, as president of the Ladies' Literary Society. Some weeks in advance of Commencement, Miss Holley nominated Miss Stanton as the best presiding officer available and as commended to her companions by her dignity, ability, and faithful service. There was a great outcry. What would everybody say? Oberlin would be more notorious and hated than ever. But Miss Holley did not yield and managed her canvass so skilfully that Miss Stanton was elected and, in the event, presided handsomely, winning deserved applause. A tempest in a teapot, but a teapot in which was brewed a little of the Soma that was to sustain Sallie Holley's fainting heart in other critical adventures. It was perhaps on the night of this victory that she saw in a dream all the angels in heaven riding on white horses and saying to her as they passed by, " We take great interest in you, Sallie."

As her last year in Oberlin drew to its close, Frederick Douglass wrote asking her to engage in behalf of his paper, the *North Star*. She declined because of her promise to Abby Kelley, who, equally faithful to the Anti-Slavery Society, remembered the hope of the young recruit she had enlisted—for a service of ten years, as proved by the event. The first duty assigned her was to join in the Ohio campaign, holding conventions with Parker Pillsbury,[1] Charles C. Burleigh, and Sojourner Truth, together with the Ohio abolitionists, the Griffings, Marius Robinson, editor of the *Anti-Slavery Bugle*, and others. Miss Putnam's account of the work and workers of those days is too good to be curtailed:

" It was in the days of outlawry for anti-slavery, and rarely could the meetings, as we travelled from place to place, find any church, hall, or schoolhouse open to them. But some grove would serve, and in one instance a little shoemaker's shop, which was quite at our service, the man taking off his apron, shoving back his

---

[1] Born September 22, 1809; died July 7, 1898. He represented the extreme of anti-slavery antagonism to the pro-slavery churches. He was so swarthy in his complexion that—so goes the tale—Phillips, agreeing with an innkeeper to share his room " with a nigger," went up to it and found Pillsbury in possession. His *Anti-Slavery Apostles* tells his story well and cannot safely be neglected by any careful student of the anti-slavery times. Charles C. Burleigh was one of a set of brothers devoted to the anti-slavery cause. He was a man of oratorical and religious genius, self-limited by his deliberate peculiarities. Actually and consciously he had the typical Christ face, and cultivated that appearance by allowing his hair to hang in curls about his neck. He was born November 3, 1810, and died June 13, 1878.

bench, and asking us in. Soon the people on the street, passing his door, stopped, to listen to the voice of the young lady pleading so earnestly for the slave-woman ; her beautiful face full of the warm human sympathy of her plea.

" Thus prepared for strong meat, Parker Pillsbury, with dramatic power, unfolded the sublime apocalypse of divine retribution if this country, and especially the Church, failed of its duty to preach the doctrine of ' setting the captive free,' and the State to make good its Declaration of Independence. He said the philanthropic Lafayette, whose love and honour for America were so great that he had a hogshead of American soil carried to France that he might be buried in it, would turn in his grave to protest against this treachery to humanity in keeping in iron bondage three millions of slaves.

" Such sharp arrows of conviction, tipped with harsh truth and severe justice, and winged with the love of man, in the humble guise of a negro slave, kept down in ignorance and chains to the level of brute beasts, denied marriage, the knowledge to learn the Bible, wages for labour, and every right and privilege of citizenship and of humanity, did he send from his anti-slavery quiver, that we were thrilled with admiration,—while others exclaimed,

" ' That Parker Pillsbury is a very bitter devil.'

" We have since heard him in Boston and other places, but never did he exceed the power and lofty strain of eloquence of this small meeting in the Ohio shoemaker's shop, in an obscure village street.

" Following Mr. Pillsbury, would rise, towering, the striking form and features of Sojourner Truth, in her turban, and with wit and pathos she would wring our hearts, and wreathe our faces with smiles, and even con-

vulse us with laughter, at her story of her old slave life
in New York, before the act of emancipation in the
Empire State in 1828.

"At last we reached Oberlin, where Prof. Monroe, a
former agent of the Anti-Slavery Society in New England, came up to our carriage and said, speaking to Parker
Pillsbury, 'I must shake hands with this infidel.' But
there was no cordial welcome to his anti-slavery gospel ;
only anxiety lest the progress of a revival of Mr. Finney's
religion might be checked by it.

"Mr. Garrison on a later occasion remarked on his
cold reception, that if there was any spot on earth where
he would have looked to be welcomed for the sake
of the slave, it would be Oberlin. He referred significantly to the College's great obligation to his friends, the
English abolitionists, for funds.

"I believe this was the only visit Mr. Garrison ever
paid to Oberlin. Only a beggarly handful turned out
to meet him, instead of the throngs of students and others
accustomed to fill the immense audience-room for a
popular lecturer. Miss Holley, quoting Whittier with a
difference, used to say : 'Oh, "the one sacred thing beneath the cope of heaven," there, was n't "Man" but
theology.'

"November's surly blasts were advancing, and we came
from the West into Western New York. There, on the
hills of Cattaraugus, she awaited the orders of the agency
of the Anti-Slavery Society. She had never dreamed of a
salary and compensation,—having literally preached and
taught the gospel 'hoping for nothing again.' Afterwards she saw how unfair it was that, while in Ohio she
was the attraction of the meetings that contributed
money to the collections and subscribed for the *Liberator* and the *Standard*, in response to her appeals,—

the other agents took all, both collections and commissions on papers.   But it was a surprise when Mrs. Foster wrote,

"'You are to be paid ten dollars a week and your expenses by the Anti-Slavery Society, and I will meet you in Syracuse, to begin our winter meetings.'

"That meeting in Samuel J. May's church, Sunday evening, is never to be forgotten by me.   We had heard Mr. May in the morning.   In a burst of eloquence he alluded to the rescue of Jerry, the fugitive slave, the first of October previous [1851].   On that morning no one was so obscure and unknown as Jerry.   But when his rights as a man were assailed, before night of the same day there was no one in Syracuse of so much importance as Jerry.

"The evening brought a packed house, and the sympathetic tears did not run down Mr. May's face alone, as Miss Holley told with powerful pathos, the slave's wrongs, and by every motive of humanity and religion urged his cause on the audience.   In Mr. May's family pew in front, I sat with Mrs. Foster.   She often took her handkerchief from her muff, but not till we entered her room at the hotel,—having walked home with her,—did I dream of the fountains of the great deeps of her soul, that had been so stirred.   With an eloquent passion of reverence and apostolic fervour, she laid her hands on Miss Holley's shoulders and exclaimed,

"'Oh, I have been prostrate before the Throne, all this evening, thanking God that, when I am so worn and weary and feeble, he has raised up one who can and will speak so nobly and winningly in this holy but hated and persecuted cause.'

"Such it was.   Even Mrs. May could not come into sympathy with the pulpit service for a woman.   When
5

we were leaving her house for the meeting and Miss Holley remarked how she dreaded to go, Mrs. May said, 'Ah, I am glad to hear it. That shows your true nature, as the cat in the fairy tale, who had been turned into a fine lady, sprang under the Queen's chair for a mouse.'

"So, pushing through all sorts of opposition, and overcoming all the objections raised to deter her, this heroine of the new departure for women,—like the girl in Turner's *Golden Bough*,—kept her eye, and her heart, and her feet true to the upward path, though every stone along the ascent called with discouraging voice for her to give over the too painful quest. Such, at any rate, was the interpretation which Sallie Holley's personal experience gave to Turner's lovely dream."

For the remainder of the way I shall do little more than stand aside and let Sallie Holley's letters speak for her. A few of them antedate her connection with the Anti-Slavery Society, and these will illustrate the spirit in which she entered on a work that was to end only with her life.

TO MISS PUTNAM

" OBERLIN, Nov. 25, 1849.

"   .   .   .   I have read the *Life of the Martyr Torrey,* a very affecting tale of sorrow and suffering in a Baltimore penitentiary. Even when his physicians pronounced that poor Torrey could live but a few weeks, the Governor refused the petition of the afflicted wife that he 'might die among his native hills' of Massachusetts.

"To the last Torrey nobly sustained his Christian char-

acter and died full of peace and hope. He never would
admit that he did wrong either against the laws of God
or man. His enemies swore falsely. More than a thousand dollars were immediately raised to meet the expenses
of his trial, and, again, when he was about to die, money
sufficient to satisfy the demands of the slaveholder, who
arrested him for running off his slaves, was raised by
his true-hearted friends, and the Governor was petitioned
to pardon him; but he utterly refused unless Torrey
would acknowledge he regretted what he had done,—
own he did wrong. This Torrey could not say, and—to
his everlasting glory be it recorded—he did not betray
the cause of his Maker!

"It seemed to me last night, as I read, almost like
reading the trial and crucifixion scene of our blessed
Master!"

ROCHESTER, January, 1850.

Mr. B. desired me to present you with his best regards. Apropos to Mr. B., Samuel J. May told me that
Mr. B. was once going to strike him! I laughed heartily
as Mr. May told me the following:

"I saw Mr. B. was injuring himself by his excessive
use of tobacco; I endeavoured to remonstrate with him,
saying it was a wretched habit for a young man,—he was
ruining his health and constitution, etc.,—whereupon
Mr. B. drew himself up, saying:

"'It is well, Mr. May, you have years to protect
you!'"

"Oh," said Mr. May, "I am not so *very old* that I
need hide behind my years. Do what you would if I
were younger!"

I have had a charming visit with Mr. May. He is a
truly lovely person. Abby Kelley Foster has been here;

she urges me very hard to go right into the anti-slavery
lecture field.

"ROCHESTER, Feb. 10, 1850.

"I have lately enjoyed the rare pleasure of hearing
two lectures from Ralph Waldo Emerson on 'England
and the English.' The hall was crowded with the beauty
and chivalry of Rochester. How queerly fashion regul-
ates some things in this world! Here was a man of the
most ultra radical views, a Garrisonian abolitionist, a
Unitarian minister of the worst heretical stamp, a dis-
unionist, a transcendentalist, etc., etc. Yet the very
sanctity, piety, patriotism, and boasted conservatism were
all present, dressed in their most good-humoured smiles!
Fashion says that everybody must attend the Athenæum
Lectures."

"OBERLIN. [Undated.]

"We have had no rain for some weeks. The drought
is oppressive. To-morrow is appointed Fast Day, to
pray for rain. All recitations are to be suspended.

"P. S. Saturday morning after Fast Day we had a
very mild, gentle rain. Mr. Smith (the artist) was walking
up-town and met some of the church-members, who said,
'You see, Mr. Smith, the rain has come in answer to
prayer yesterday.' 'Yes,' replied he, 'Prof. Morgan
can bring a little shower, but it is nothing to what Prof.
Finney could do if he were here.'

". . . I am to give an anti-slavery address in the
Chapel, some time in August. I am collecting thoughts
for it as I can. My subject is to be something like this:
The duty of anti-slavery women to keep informed as to
the progress and mode of the anti-slavery reform in our
nation, to be ready to counteract the pernicious influence
of such speeches as Clay's and Webster's on the plastic
minds of all our young men and women."

" TECUMSEH, MICH., Sep. 16, '50.

" I have wished you with me while I have been with Henry C. Wright at the anti-slavery meetings and during the intermissions. He seems to me a deeply earnest, pure-minded, loving spirit. By the orthodox world he is cast out as 'infidel.' I feel there may be in human life a heavenly beauty. I strive and yearn to be established immovably in the very spirit and principles of the Divine Master. My life falls far short of my ideal, yet I think I can apprehend something of the beauty and glory of a truly Christian life. Whenever these visions come up before me, then do I yearn most to be in immediate communion with some of my dear Unitarian friends. It seems to me they have a hold, an insight into the spiritual life, that I do not find in others. Yet, nevertheless, I think I cannot consent that my name shall stand on the books of a church which will countenance voting for any pro-slavery presidential candidate.[1] Think of a woman-whipper and a baby-stealer being countenanced as a Christian ! My anti-slavery sympathies burn stronger and stronger."

TO THE PORTERS

" OBERLIN, June 16, 1851.

" . . . I am surprised and grieved at Professor Kendrick's loss. We all know what it is to be bereaved of dear friends. What could possibly fill up in our hearts the space they occupied and still occupy, and which would emphatically become empty, if we could admit the thought of annihilation ? or of their being in existence and capable of thought and feeling, but eternally separated from us ?

[1] The reference here is probably to Millard Fillmore's connection with Dr. Hosmer's church.

" My feelings revolt with horror from the idea of an endless separation from them ; valuing the doctrine of immortality as the brightest that ever dawned upon the human mind, next to that of the existence of a God and his superintending providence, I think it derives its chief value from the doctrine, naturally and irresistibly growing out of it, that we carry with us forever all the knowledge and sympathies awakened in this life.

" It is this cherished belief that plucks the sting of affliction from my heart, more effectually than anything else could, upon the loss of friends ; for though to the mere eye of sense they are lost when they die, yet, looking with the eye of the spirit, through the truth into the future, we may still behold them, with all the generous attributes of their natures, sharing the ineffable blessing and protection of him whose tender mercies are over all his works, and ready, with their minds expanded by the teachings of eternity and hearts warmed by the immediate presence of infinite and unfailing Love, to welcome us to all the joys of their communion and to participate with us in the highest duties, services, and rewards of which they are made capable under the gracious guidance of the Universal Father.

" I am indebted to my blessed father for the brightness of my visions of immortality. He taught me how to live, and, blessed be God, he taught me how to die. I wish I were a better child and more like my father.

" You ask me to tell just what I am doing. Miss Putnam has just written a letter to her mother, which discloses something we have done, and if you will overlook the egotism and vanity of my copying an extract from her letter, I will do it.

" ' Last Saturday afternoon, Mr. Munson appeared at the door with the same noble and generous horse and buggy of Akron memory, all at the expense of some good anti-slavery people down in Litchfield, whither we were to ride. Our ride was as pleasant as could be, and as Miss H. has an extravagant fondness for swift riding, with our jewel of a horse we found ourselves in Litchfield almost before we were aware. Mr. and Mrs. Griffing gave us a most cordial welcome, and as it was a cool evening, Mrs. G. lighted a fire in the dining-room and Mr. G. read us Andrew J. Davis's Declaration of Independence, to which we listened with much interest, often interrupted by remarks. After a refreshing sleep we woke the next morning, descended to breakfast, and read and talked until meeting time. Then with Mrs. Griffing and her daughter we walked to the Presbyterian church, where, in the absence of the pastor, the deacon read a sermon.

" ' At the close of the usual exercises, the deacon read a notice to the effect that Miss Holley of Oberlin would speak on anti-slavery in the afternoon. So at the allotted hour we found ourselves at the church again. As the beautiful hymn containing " When men of virtue fail " was read, a waggish friend whispered in Miss Holley's ear, most significantly—" Then we call upon women." The deacon offered an appropriate anti-slavery prayer, another hymn was sung, and then Miss Holley gave us an earnest, powerful, and deeply interesting address. Everybody gave the best possible attention, and as she related several thrilling and affecting facts, the big tears coursed down many a cheek. It was a time of stirring sympathy and awakening interest in the cause of the oppressed and crushed slave. At the close she offered a very touching and simple prayer. Then they sung a hymn and the meeting was dismissed.

" ' Afterwards one of the deacons expressed himself as

having been highly gratified, and said that others who had some scruples about allowing the church to be used on *Sunday* by a *woman*, were very much pleased indeed with the lecture and were glad the house had been given up for that purpose. Miss Holley's countenance wears a very benign expression while speaking, and I think would remind you very forcibly of her father.

"'The anti-slavery people regarded the affair as a great triumph. The church had never before been allowed to *anyone* for an anti-slavery discourse on Sunday.'

"So you see I have not been idle. I thought you would be glad to know that I succeeded so well."

CHAPTER VI

THE ANTI-SLAVERY IDYLL

ONE of the most delightful evenings of my life was spent at the house of John and Hannah Cox at Longwood, Pennsylvania. It was for these excellent people that Whittier wrote his "Golden Wedding at Longwood." They were anti-slavery saints, and their house was the first station on the underground railroad across the Maryland border. I was attending a meeting of Progressive Friends, and in the evening many of them gathered in the living-room at the Coxes'. What a great, big room it was, and what a remarkable company! Garrison was there and Oliver Johnson, Robert Purvis and Lucretia Mott, Mary Grew and Margaret Burleigh and Sarah Pugh, and with these many others. The war was over, slavery was abolished, and there was much talk about the anti-slavery crusade. Garrison read to us Wordsworth's "Happy Warrior," and the event is bracketed in my memory with Emerson's reading[1] of Wordsworth's "Intimations of Immortality from Recollections of Early Childhood," and I

[1] Somewhat later, at a friend's house in Brooklyn.

could not say which was the more impressive. But it was the more genial side of the reformer that impressed me most. No one could have a keener sense than his of the humours of the anti-slavery conflict. His account of Stephen Foster was as good as Lowell's famous characterisation, and he told how Charles C. Burleigh, who wore his hair in long curls about his shoulders, once arrived at his house, with his pack of anti-slavery literature on his back. He was covered with the dust of his pedestrian journey and his curls were flying in the wind, and the children fled before his face as if the wicked one were after them. "A clear case," said Mr. Garrison, "of hair 'em scare 'em." There never was a happier company, and I am well assured that it gave a very just impression of the average gathering of anti-slavery leaders and followers when they were in the thick of the fight. They were no solemn, sour-faced Puritans, but folk of kindly disposition, serenely confident that they were engaged in a good work and that the good time was " coming right along."

If I had ever doubted this I should have been convinced by Sallie Holley's letters. Their value for me consists, to a very great extent, in the picture which they give of the anti-slavery idyll, the enjoyment of the workers in each other and their work. The idyll had its seamy side and the enjoyment was augmented or abridged according to the domestic habits of the people who received the wayworn travellers. I recall no other letters and journals of the period that furnish us with so vivid a conception of the work done by the agents of the Anti-Slavery

Society. As we read, it is as if we, too, were going
to and fro in the land, and up and down in it, enduring many hardships, enjoying much delightful
hospitality, alternately elated and depressed, pathet-
ically pleased with very modest contributions, sitting
in heavenly places with some of the best people in
the world, and in others less celestial with some of
the most peculiar and fanatical. There were even
those who seemed to think with Tolstoi that cleanli-
ness is inimical to social equality and that the dirtier
they were the better.

When in the fall of 1851 Miss Holley became an
agent of the American Anti-Slavery Society, it had
left far behind the brilliant period which, before the
divisions generated in its ranks by the theological
spirit and the passion for immediate results, had
multiplied the local societies far and wide and promised to enlist before long the sympathy of a majority of the people of the Northern States. Garrison
had made the logic of his position more and more
intelligible and severe, if with considerable loss of
numerical support, with a more than compensating
gain of coherency and passionate sincerity. From
its abandonment of the Garrisonian doctrine that the
Constitution gave what Daniel Webster called " solemn guarantees " to slavery, the Liberty party had
so far retreated as to admit that it did give such guarantees to slavery *in the slave States*. The next step
was to the doctrine of the Free Soil and Republican
parties, that slavery in the slave States was to be
patiently endured, while the extension of slavery into
new territory was to be strenuously opposed. The

Liberty party vote in 1840 was 7069, and in 1844 it
was 62,300. But the increase in 1848 to 291,263
meant gain of votes at the expense of principle, and
it also meant that Van Buren's friends were knifing
the Democratic candidates in revenge for the substitution of Polk for Van Buren in 1844. How unreal
was the Free Soil vote of 1848 is shown by the fact
that in 1852 it fell off to 155,825 ; but this loss of
nearly one half was, however, owing partly to the
fact that many ill-knit anti-slavery people had after
the Compromises of 1850 settled back on them as
on a bed of roses and gone to sleep; Horace Greeley,
for example, voting for General Scott, and William
Cullen Bryant's paper supporting Franklin Pierce.
Clearly it was a time demanding from the abolitionists an unequivocal assertion of their characteristic opposition to slavery as such wherever it existed
in the United States, and it was with the clearest
consciousness of the nature of the situation and the
principles involved that Sallie Holley chose her path
and entered on it with a courageous and yet trembling heart.

For hers was a temperament that shrank from the
publicity of the platform and felt keenly the stigma
which was imprinted on her by the conventional
spirit of the time. When ladies who had been proud
of her acquaintance crossed the street to avoid
speaking with her, she was not indifferent to the
stab. The fact that she was a woman presuming
upon public speech and action made her even more
intolerable than her abolitionism. When, a little
later, Mrs. Stowe was in the flush of her fame from

Uncle Tom's Cabin, her brother, the great Brooklyn preacher, declared that he would not like to have her appear on a public platform ; and, if such was his feeling, that of the general crowd can be easily imagined. Those were the days of phrenology, and the examiner, asked if Miss Holley could be a public speaker, answered, " With such an organisation it would be impossible." It was nonsense, but with a kernel in it.

Samuel May [1] of Leicester writes me :

" You know that she became one of the agents of the American Anti-Slavery Society. As such she came to my knowledge. I had a considerable part in laying out her work for her, and introducing her. Once introduced she did all the rest. I am told that her New Testament readings and comments were of wonderful force and

[1] A cousin of Samuel J. May ; born April 11, 1810, about a month before his Harvard classmate Wm. Henry Channing, and a week after his classmate James Freeman Clarke. Their class was Dr. Holmes's, that of 1829. Mr. May became General Secretary of the Massachusetts Anti-Slavery Society in 1847. The Garrison children dedicated to him their " Story " of their father's life, as one " who freed from toil and care the declining years of William Lloyd Garrison " ; which means that mainly by his efforts a gift of more than $30,000 was amassed for Garrison among his friends. Mr. May is still living, and doing and enjoying much, though, in his eighty-ninth year, his health is not robust. Miss Holley had no better friend, nor had Miss Putnam. Miss Holley wrote to him in 1866 : " I cannot repress a keen regret that the dear revered Massachusetts Anti-Slavery Society should so fall out with each other along the route of their extraordinary career of noble fellowship and glorious work. How good and pleasant, dear Mr. May, have been all my years of labour with the society, with you for general agent ! Not a jar or discord in all my relations with you. No miserable misunderstanding or doubt."

beauty, and that her lectures invariably moved to tears.
I never heard her speak !   So sensitive was she that even
when she lectured in Leicester, she made a point that I
should not go, though my wife was going.   She little
knew how much good she might have done me.   But
she said that she could not *be herself* in the presence of
any of those whom she recognised as leaders in the work.
For this reason she *never* spoke in the large conventions,
etc., when any such were present.   Caroline Putnam is
the one to tell you of this."

Her testimony is:

"Miss Holley's reverence for the Boston abolitionists,
especially for Wendell Phillips, made her refuse all so-
licitations to speak in Boston.

"In Abington she enjoyed a lyceum lecture by Edmund
Quincy, and at the close thanked him for the pleasure.
'Bless me !' replied he, 'are you here ?   Why, if I had
known it I should n't have been able to speak, for I am as
much afraid, I assure you, of speaking before you as you
can possibly be of speaking before me, and' (making an
elegant bow) 'with quite as much reason.'

"In Mr. Quincy's delightfully interesting report as
secretary of the New England Anti-Slavery Society, he
congratulated the society on having a *lady* for its new
agent ; and in arranging for the meetings, Mr. May,—
general agent, — had the happiness of sending Miss
Holley into private homes of culture, where her social
qualities made entrance for the hitherto unwelcome
doctrines and pleas of the abolitionists.

"Her enthusiastic praise of the leaders,—Garrison
and Phillips,—and of the *Liberator* and *Standard*,
won admission to many new hearts and planted the ultra

banner of ' No union with slaveholders ' in many pulpits that allowed her lips to expound with acceptance their teachings.

" How winning she was ! One of her converts, who remained her grateful, attached friend for forty years, was Mrs. Anna Shaw Greene [an aunt of Colonel Robert G. Shaw], whose first contribution, made through her, to the anti-slavery cause, was continued by hundreds of dollars to the last. She worked [*i. e.*, Miss Holley] so patiently, so faithfully, so truthfully, so heroically !

" Like the first Christian apostles, we went *two*, and in humble homes as well as in grand ones, were glad to receive hospitalities. Sometimes in a lonely farmhouse, with a table spread with a tin pan of sweet milk and a corn-meal ' johnny-cake,' as all the house afforded ; sleeping in a log house with one room,—but with such good, innocent people ! Presto !—the scene would be changed, and we be welcomed to the brightest home in every respect,—parlour, library, drawing-room, dining-room, music, elegance, superior intelligence and manners.

" At Colonel William B. Greene's she wrote me, ' I am in the most luxuriously furnished room I ever occupied.' It was only a few weeks afterward that we shared the plain but scrupulously neat farmer's milk-pan, set on the coarse but clean linen table-cloth. We got up as soon as it was day to see the Oreads dance on the high hillside of the Cattaraugus woodlands.

" She had versatile talent, humour, and vivacity. Who ever forgot her ringing, joyous laugh ? What happiness she gave the children, the grandmother, every member of the household ! Even the dog gave his tail an extra wag of joy. Eagerly expected for any repeated visit, she filled the whole house with life and gladness."

TO THE PORTERS [1]

"Huntington, Sep. 30, 51.

"You are aware that I have already entered upon my work of anti-slavery lecturer. My love and interest in the great cause increases and swells and brightens every hour.

" It does seem to me that I have at last found out my 'sphere.' Miss Putnam, Mr. and Mrs. Griffing, Parker Pillsbury, and myself compose our travelling party, in one carriage. Every few days Sojourner Truth joins us and aids in our meetings. She travels in a buggy by herself. An anti-slavery friend loaned her a pony and buggy for the entire summer. She is quite a strong character and shows what a great intellect slavery has crushed. She talks like one who has not only *heard* of American slavery, but has *seen* and *felt* it. As she eloquently exclaimed last evening, ' All the gold of California, all the wealth

---

[1] The head of the Porter family, living in Rochester, New York, was Miss Maria Porter, who lived to be ninety-two years old, dying in 1896. With her lived her aged father and his wife and three unmarried sisters, the Jane, Libby, and Almira of the letters. Besides the regular family and boarders, generally college men, the house was always open to all vagrant abolitionists. High and low, from Beecher and Curtis to old black Harriet Tubman, piloting her gangs of runaway negroes to Canada, came and went unceasingly. From first to last the house received almost everybody prominent in the anti-slavery cause. It was equally hospitable to Unitarian ministers. The family had come to Rochester from Philadelphia, where Dr. Furness had been their minister and made them " lively stones " for Myron Holley to build, with himself, into the Rochester Unitarian foundations. Samuel Porter enlisted early in the abolitionist ranks, and his house was a recognised station on the underground railroad, the last this side of Canada and liberty. There Sallie Holley went habitually to recuperate when tired out with her lecturing and canvassing. The Porter name is now extinct in Rochester, but there are from forty to fifty people who are glad to own the blood.

of this nation, could not restore to me that which the white people have wrested from me.'

"I am very much pleased with Parker Pillsbury's mind and character as revealed in our few weeks' acquaintance. So sublimely Christian ! So full of mighty faith !

"When I see you I shall take great pleasure in detailing to you all my adventures and excitements in this my first anti-slavery trip.

"Oh, my dear Mrs. Porter, you cannot know how richly rewarded I feel, how full my enjoyment is, in going about with these anti-slavery friends.

"Yesterday we rode over from Clarksfield to this place : Mr. Pillsbury gave us some very interesting and thrilling passages in his experiences with Stephen S. Foster, N. P. Rogers, Garrison, and others: How many times Mr. Foster had his coat torn to pieces, was pitched head first downstairs, dragged out of meeting-houses, and shut up in jails. It all reminds me of the days of Jesus and the Apostles more forcibly than anything I have known in my life.

"Gerrit Smith's noble and beautiful letter in Frederick Douglass's paper in which he bears testimony to W. L. Garrison's Christianity is worthy of Mr. Smith."

"AT GERRIT SMITH'S, May 27, 1852.

"Yes, I am in this great and good man's home. His affability, his sociability, his gentleness, his grace, and his noble spirit are all very beautiful.

"He received me so cordially, so kindly, with open arms and beaming eyes. Such an atmosphere of love and goodness as breathes around him must be a foretaste of heaven.

"When I left Rochester I did not think of visiting Mr.

Smith so soon as now ; but, while I was lecturing in
Cazenovia, ten miles distant, Mr. Smith sent his son-in-
law, Charles Miller, for me. I could not leave that day,
but came over the next, and here I am enjoying his hospitality, his attractive conversation, his benevolent manners, his generous spirit, and surely it must be a miserably
stupid being who could see all this, without having the
better emotions, the better and holier aspirations of his
soul awakened, quickened, and strengthened into higher
intensity for a like spirit, a similar character.   One thing
you will particularly admire in him, and that is his inviting all his domestics every Sunday to dine with him, and
they seem to look upon him with all the reverential admiration of a Catholic for a patron saint.   They do not
seem uncomfortably oppressed in his presence.   No ; he
is too truly great for that.   Among the family portraits
was one of a nurse who has lived in the family thirty
years.   Her picture hangs by those of his father and
mother.

"He told me that if he had all his money to give over
again he would give it all to *women*. They, he said, were
more trustworthy, economical, and would use it to better
purpose.   He had not yet heard of a single instance of a
woman misusing the money he had given her.

"Mr. Smith's home is in much humbler style than I
had anticipated.

"A lovely daughter of James G. Birney is here, also a
Miss Fitzhugh from Maryland ; and an enthusiastic
Catholic young lady is visiting here.

"The first day I was here, Mr. Smith's daughter and
her husband, with other friends, dined here. The daughter was in Bloomer costume. Mr. Smith is an earnest
advocate of the dress ; he said, laughingly, he considered his daughter the best-dressed lady in America.

" Mr. Smith is constantly receiving letters from a great variety of people. He tells me he has received in a single month requests for money more than covering the whole amount of his property. And to give you an idea of the vast multitude of such requests, he says he does not comply with one in a hundred. He said that people seem to think he has 'a sort of pecuniary plethora that requires constant bleeding to assure health and vigour.' He hopes both of his children will be farmers.

" Mr. Smith said to me : ' I am glad you are lecturing with the American Anti-Slavery Society. I think you will do good ; you will bring about a more friendly and harmonious understanding between some of the members of the Liberty party and the Garrisonians. I love William Lloyd Garrison, I believe him to be a Christian. His is a beautiful spirit.' "

"CANASTOTA, N. Y., June 6, 1852.

". . . On Thursday afternoon, Elizabeth Fitzhugh, a fine, independent girl, took Gerrit Smith's uncovered buggy and drove me over here. There were four ladies in our party, who returned to Peterboro by moonlight, after my lecture here.

" Gerrit Smith has a remarkably close and tender sympathy with poverty. He is all interest and sympathy when told any case of sorrow. The very home of his soul is Love, a divine charity. I expect Jane and Almira will say, ' Sallie has gone off into one of her enthusiasms. When we first knew her it was Frederick Douglass. The next winter, Abby Foster and Parker Pillsbury ; and now everybody fades away before Gerrit Smith.' They may laugh as much as they please. I shall go on loving and admiring everybody I can, and express all the enthusiasm which I feel.

"The friends in Madison County, especially Mr. Smith, did everything to favour my meetings there, and urged me to remain."

"MRS. FOSTER'S, June 16, 1852.

"I have had a week of balmy quiet and needful repose here. And here I have seen Abby Kelley Foster at home, 'in woman's proper sphere.' She is a very neat housekeeper. Her little daughter is the very incarnation of sweetness and simplicity; though she is a child of decided character. She is five years old. She cannot read books at all, but knows the names of all the garden and field plants, the habits and food of chickens, and a great deal about cats, dogs, and horses. All this came out unconsciously as I talked and walked with her, and asked her questions. She evidently has picked up this kind of knowledge from her own observation. I never saw a child of extraordinary parents that answered my anticipations before. She is just what you would naturally expect from her father and mother.

"Next Saturday evening I am to make a speech in Worcester. On Sunday Mr. Garrison and Mr. Phillips are expected.

"Worcester is adorned with fine old trees, even the business streets. I saw the house where an aristocratic lady once asked Frederick Douglass at how much his master valued him. The reply was, 'One thousand dollars.'

"'Then,' responded this woman, 'you have robbed your master of one thousand dollars you ought to return.'

"I have received a very kind letter from Miller McKim of Philadelphia, inviting me to lecture there Sept. 1st. The heat which prevails in that climate prevents all lectures during the three summer months."

TO MISS PUTNAM

"SCITUATE, Aug. 9, 1852.

" Lewis Ford brought me to this place on Saturday. Yesterday we held a meeting in the Town Hall.

" I have passed three weeks delightfully at the Water-Cure establishment in Worcester, and derived great benefit from the use of water. Dr. Rogers is a very true man on the reforms. I was very sorry when the time to leave came. I am now to lecture in Plymouth County three weeks. Lewis Ford takes good care that his County does not lack for anti-slavery lecturing.

" I have good meetings wherever I go. The other day at Concord I saw the ground where the British were first forcibly resisted. The monument is plain and simple.

" I rode by the ' old manse ' where Hawthorne wrote *Mosses from an Old Manse*, and saw where Mr. Emerson and Mr. Hawthorne live. Very common looking houses.

" Mrs. Emerson was an auditor of mine. She is a delicate, shrinking woman. We had a delightful August celebration. The most charming grove I ever saw. Mr. Garrison appeared almost divine. Edmund Quincy is a very aristocratic looking personage.[1] Theodore Parker appears something like Samuel J. May, though not so fine looking.

" Lucy Stone wears the Bloomer costume. She is a little, independent piece. I wish I had her self-possession. She is quite a favourite speaker and speaks well. She is to be in Syracuse at the Woman's Rights Convention in September. W. H. Channing [2] will probably be

[1] Colonel Higginson writes of him as carrying this appearance farther than Wendell Phillips.

[2] See biography by O. B. Frothingham.

there. He has accepted a call to be pastor of the Uni-
tarian church in Rochester. I am invited to lecture in
Warren in a few weeks and shall call on your aunt Sally
Putnam.

"Mr. Pillsbury has gone to Ohio, and now we shall
have his letters in the *Liberator*."

"SOUTH BRIDGEWATER, August 19, 1852.

"My adventures and experiences as a lecturer are not
very dissimilar to ours of last winter. Sometimes, the
people where I go are extremely warm and cordial ; evidently feel it a pleasure and privilege to entertain the anti-
slavery lecturers. Again I stay with those who seem to
think of us as Topsy did of niggers, ' They ain't nothin'
nor nobody.'

"It is very grateful when we go to a family where the
woman is cut off from her neighbours' symathy on account
of her anti-slavery position, and to see and talk with us
is a rare and rich treat. Oh, the lighting up of the face,
the kindling warmth of the whole expression which I
have seen on such an occasion is a whole year's refreshment."

"PLYMOUTH, Aug. 22, 1852.

"To-morrow I am to visit Pilgrim Hall and sit in old
Governor Carver's chair. I asked a curious old gentleman what he thought of the so-called spiritual manifestations. ' It is Satanic influence,' was his reply,
and then, with deepest gravity, ' Now is the seventh vial
being poured out.'

"Monday.—Had a large, crowded house last evening.
Bourne Spooner says ' The *saints* shall judge the world,'
and adds, ' None but saints *can* judge the world.' You
would like this Bourne Spooner. (He is the "pious

SALLIE HOLLEY
(About 1852)

deacon " of Edmund Quincy's *Standard* letters).   He is
full of good anecdotes and quotes scripture very happily."

" ABINGTON, Aug. 26, 1852.

"You see how I flit from place to place.   An anti-
slavery lecturer's life has something apostolic in it, if
it only be in going from town to town to preach the
everlasting gospel.   To-day I was entertaining myself
making out a memorandum of all the places and times
I had lectured.   I made out one hundred and fifty-six
times.

"September 2d.—Day before yesterday Lewis Ford
took us in his carriage from this place to Duxbury.   The
weather was delightful.   We rode twenty miles through
beautiful woods.   We alighted at a large, old fashioned
mansion, a little before six o'clock and were cordially
welcomed by two maiden sisters who ushered us into a
plain, old fashioned parlour.   The chairs, sofa, and table
looking so quaint, as if belonging to a bygone generation.
Then the mother made her appearance, a lady eighty years
old, but, in spirit and conversation and manners more
like eighteen than eighty.   Indeed she proved to be a
most charming old lady.   I was quite captivated with
her, so fresh, so youthful, so beautiful.   She seems to
have read almost everything.   Was delighted with
David Copperfield, and *Dombey and Son*, and spoke
of Theodore Parker with glowing enthusiasm.   (He
makes their house his home when he goes to Duxbury).   She admires Andrew Jackson Davis's writings,
particularly his views of death.   She loves Mr. Garrison
and Stephen and Abby Foster ; knows Lydia Maria
Child.   Mrs Child used to spend a great deal of time
next door.   Laughed when she told me Mrs. Child wrote
a cook-book when she had been housekeeper and cook

only a month or so. I told her it reminded me of Mrs. Swisshelm, who has been married a great many years, but never had a baby until last winter, and when the child was three weeks old began a series of 'Letters to Mothers.'

"Here I met with a sister-in-law of Mrs. Child—Mrs. Francis, wife of Professor Convers Francis of Harvard Divinity School. I told her of my great desire to see Mrs. Child. Mrs. Francis said she thought Mrs. Child would be glad to see me, though she sees very few people now-a-days ; lives in a retired, quiet way ; does her own work. Mrs. Francis politely said she would offer to accompany me but she thought I should be more successful alone. We both agreed that Lydia Maria Child belonged to the public and that she ought not to shut herself up so. Mrs. Child is preparing a memoir of Isaac T. Hopper.

"Yesterday morning[1] early, we all rode to the beach and then to Daniel Webster's beautiful domain. It is called 'Green Harbour,' and is close to the sea. It is a charming and particularly beautiful place in the summer time. The beach is something marvellous to me, being of great breadth and of splendid, hard, floor-like sand : and when this is covered by the rolling Atlantic, the waves come almost up to the green grassy fields. Very high waves cover them.

"A fine wide walk and carriage road lead up to the house and garden. On both sides is a handsome hawthorn hedge. The house is an old one, built before the Revolution by an old Tory. During the war a hundred British soldiers were quartered in it. Mr. Webster has enlarged and improved it very much. It is an exceedingly comforta-

---

[1] This was September 1st, and Webster had gone to Washington a few weeks before. He returned September 8th, and died October 24th, a tragically sad and disappointed man.

ble looking house ; the windows opening to the ground and a piazza all round it.

" It must be deliciously cool, protected from the sun as it is, by the overshadowing masses of foliage of a most magnificent elm. This colossal tree stands just before the house, and is preëminently beautiful. It seems to unite in its one gigantic person the exquisite and exceeding grace of the weeping willow, with the strength and grandeur of the towering elm. Underneath and in its shade are some rustic, but very picturesque looking chairs. We walked through the lovely garden and through a winding and romantic path up to a bower house, Oh, so bewitching, all covered with creeping vines.

" Mr. Webster's farm here consists of fifteen hundred acres. He has one hundred head of cattle. We saw his beautiful geese, both wild and domestic, and three beautiful Llamas, with very fine eyes, some friend had sent him. They appeared as gentle as lambs.

" September 5th.—Yesterday at Bridgewater I saw the *National Era* [Dr Bailey's paper in which *Uncle Tom's Cabin* had appeared] and read Grace Greenwood's delightful letters from England. They began last June.

" Last evening I was enchanted to hear my favourite among birds, the whippoorwill. I had not heard it before for years. I must tell you the barberry grows wild here in great luxuriance ; also in June the laurel was everywhere in lovely bloom. It looked beautiful along the roadside.

" The other day after the storm, we saw on the beach, immense quantities of 'kelp,' as they call it,—a seaweed that grows curiously on submarine rocks.[1] Farm-

[1] Apparently it seeks the light, for sometimes its beautiful stems are six hundred feet long.

ers use it for manure. Last year Daniel Webster had a thousand cartloads put on his farm at Marshfield.

"September 10th.—Yesterday I was in Boston. Francis Jackson took me to see a beautiful portrait of my uncle Dr. Holley, who was one of the " one hundred orators of Boston." [A predecessor of John Pierpont and Starr King in the Hollis St. Church]. Then we drove to Bunker Hill monument ! Ascended the nearly three hundred stairs ! From the top you have a fine view of Boston Harbour ; ships of war, islands, Independence Fort, Chelsea, Mystic River, etc. Eighteen thousand visitors were here last year and the number gains this year.

" It seems to me the anti-slavery reformers have the best right to visit here, as the monument was erected to commemorate the *abolitionists* of that day.

"We visited Mr. Carew's who made the beautiful medallion of my father at Mt. Hope Cemetery, and saw busts of Daniel Webster, General Cass, John Pierpont, and others.

"On Wednesady evening we went to the Museum and what should be the play but our old favourite, Goldsmith's *She Stoops to Conquer !* William Warren acted the part of 'Tony Lumpkin' to admiration. I could not but think how you would enjoy it, and wished you were sitting by my side."

CHAPTER VII

IN JOURNEYINGS OFTEN

THE publication of *Uncle Tom's Cabin*, March 20, 1852, was the great anti-slavery event of that year. Twenty thousand copies were sold in three weeks and eighty thousand in eleven weeks. Before the year was out, eighteen English editions were on the market. But little of the honey of this swarm went into the abolitionist hive. Wendell Phillips wrote Elizabeth Pease, one of the staunchest English friends, that, while it brought the anti-slavery fair more goods from England, it brought the fair but few more purchasers. Some of the faithful made up a purse at the fair and bought a beautiful French bronze statuette of a negro and gave it to Mrs. Stowe. Her evangelical piety stood in the way of her full sympathy with Garrison who, if he had not, as her brother Henry wrote, "the deep piety of Wilberforce," had a deeper piety of his own. Strangely enough *Uncle Tom*, appearing in a presidential year, did little to increase the vote for Hale and Julian, the Free Soil candidates. It was, as we have seen, very much smaller than in 1848. But that it increased the hatred of many for the Fugitive Slave Law is certain, though there were not enough of these in 1856 to express their hatred for it in the Republican platform on which Frémont stood. The best effect of *Uncle Tom* was in its wider diffusion of that anti-slavery sentiment which, when the Civil War was raging, forced the hand of Lincoln to write the emancipation proclamations of September, 1862, and January, 1863.

The meagre vote for Hale and Julian meant, for one thing, that some of those who had been united with the Liberty and Free Soil parties had concluded that, after all, Garrison's was the better way. Frederick Douglass was in the nominating convention, contending that the Constitution was an antislavery document and demanding the extermination of slavery in the States, but Gerrit Smith was also there declaring slavery " incapable of legislation," while Hale, the presidential candidate, was ready to do " everything that might be required for the support and sustenance of American slavery, to the extent of the Constitutional obligation, to the last letter of the bond." Whatever Sallie Holley's opinion of such Liberty party doctrine as that of her father in 1840,—vote for abolitionists only,— when it had come at last to this Hale complexion, she had plainly no use for it whatever, though she had cherished friends in the political movement whom she clung to with the warmest personal fidelity.

Another question that was uppermost in antislavery discussion in 1852 was the right attitude towards Kossuth, whose complacency with slavery in America but ill-agreed with his devotion to Hungarian freedom. Miss Holley was unequal to that strict and rigid logical application of a principle which was so easy and so inevitable for Garrison and probably her view of Kossuth was more nearly that of her beloved Dr. Furness than that of Garrison and the stricter sort. But her admiration for Garrison was at all times high enthroned above the reach of any minor differences and even of those which later estranged Garrison and Phillips from each other. It was at an anti-slavery convention in Adrian, Michigan, that Miss Putnam met Garrison for the first time,—October 9, 1853. She writes:

"What a revelation it was—his broad, humane principles and their application to American slavery. Never was the Bible more glowingly quoted than in his rendering of 55th Isaiah, ' Break every yoke and let the oppressed go free.' We stood with him beside the grave of Elizabeth Margaret Chandler [1] whose tender verse Miss Holley used to quote so lovingly when pleading for the slave mother :—
      " ' While woman's heart is bleeding
        Shall woman's voice be hushed ? ' "

Garrison wrote an account of this meeting to his wife : " I was agreeably surprised while speaking in the afternoon to see Sallie Holley come into the meeting with her travelling companion, Miss Put-

[1] " The first American woman who devoted her time and talent to the cause of the slave," says the Garrison *Story*. She began to write for Lundy's *Genius* in 1826, when in her nineteenth year. She died November 2, 1834.

nam. She has been labouring with great success in Detroit and other places, and will probably be induced to remain in the State a short time longer." He writes that he spent an hour at the grave of Elizabeth Chandler and wrote with his pencil a sonnet on her memory on the railing of the plot. It was on an elevation in a large wheatfield without any monument or stone. Again he writes (Detroit, October 17th), "Sallie Holley has recently lectured here, to very general acceptance, as she does everywhere,—her addresses being of a religious character, without dealing with persons, churches, and parties in a way to probe them to the quick, yet doing good work for the cause." It was his uniform commendation that no other agent got so many subscribers for the *Liberator ;* "and no other," adds Miss Putnam "worked so hard and faithfully to get them."

September 14, 1852, Anne W. Weston, a sister of Maria Weston Chapman, writes her from Weymouth that just then there is no church for her to speak in as the Universalist is closed for repairs and the orthodox is out of the question. The same letter contains an invitation to a private visit, which in its consummation added several days to those already " marked with a white stone." September 30th, she writes to Miss Putnam from Nantucket :

TO MISS PUTNAM.

" ISLAND OF NANTUCKET, Sept. 30, 1852.

"'Our life is all checkered,' etc. In New Bedford I found a very kind and gentle friend in Daniel Ricketson. He lives in a beautiful place about a mile from the city. A man of taste, refinement, and wealth.

" He gave one hundred dollars towards purchasing a home for W. L. Garrison. He is a correspondent and ardent admirer of William and Mary Howitt. They have just sent him Mary's picture engraved and William's daguerreotype, both accounted very good likenesses. He is full of love for all the old English poets : writes himself for Edmund Quincy's *Liberty Bell.*

" Mr. Ricketson's place is very fine. He has the simplicity of a child. He took me all through his yards and gardens, barn, and carriage-house : showed me his horse, and said he liked the man who remarked that he wanted to treat his horse so that he would not be ashamed to meet him in the next world. Then his two fine cows were brought up and caressed. I can't give you a just idea of Mr. R.'s gentle, delicate, refined taste and humanity. Everything about his place wore the look of culture, refinement, and kindness.

" I assure you it was a great pleasure to me to find such a gentleman-abolitionist, with so much order, neatness, and good care in his home. Some of the houses I stop at are so intolerable. I think I have encountered more filth in the last year than in all the other years of my life. We are now at a dreadfully dirty place. The woman and her two little boys (one of whom I just heard her call her little saint) do not look as though soap and water had ever come nigh them. Oh, *so* untidy !

" ' Our life is all checkered,' truly ; but some of the checks are dreadfully soiled.

" Mr. Ricketson read me some interesting letters he had received from the Howitts. He has all their writings and loves them devotedly. I had a good time with Stephen Foster at the convention. I like him more and more. He appears a truly noble man.

" Yesterday I visited the Athenæum and was introduced to Miss Maria Mitchell, a lady who has discovered a comet and the King of Prussia sent her a gold medal. The comet takes her name. To-morrow I go to Siasconset village to visit a Quaker family, Nathaniel Barney's. He is quite a cultivated person. The woman with whom I am staying keeps a small variety store and such smells as proceed out of it when our room door opens are really distressing. If I had your wit I could write a funny letter."

" PHILADELPHIA, Oct. 24, '52.

"Mrs. Garrison and I have just returned from an ineffectual attempt to attend a Quaker meeting. We went to the gate but it was shut. It seems they are in the habit of locking up their gates after a certain minute, and after that there is no possible ingress. I never felt so like one of the foolish virgins spoken of in Scripture. We knocked but it opened not unto us. They don't recognize any eleventh hour sinners there. I was *so* desirous of being there this morning, as I hear the Quakers are tightening the ecclesiastical screws upon Lucretia Mott more than ever. She will continue to be a faithful witness to all their shortcomings, to their excessive annoyance. The latest charge they have brought against her is, the *report* that at the recent Syracuse Woman's Rights Convention she requested someone to offer prayer. This is entirely untrue. She is particularly careful to avoid violating any of the rules that are laid on Quaker ministers.[1]

"You can't think what delightful times I am having here as guest in Lucretia's Mott's spacious mansion. Oh, the Quaker conveniences ! comforts ! There is nothing

---

[1] Yet she gave me permission to advertise her speaking in my pulpit,—saying, " The Spirit always gives me about twenty-four hours intimation." But this was farther on.

Wm. Lloyd Garrison

like them. So beautifully neat, too. The whole air of
the house and its lovely mistress constantly suggest to
me the purity and fragrance of a sweet, fresh-blown rose.
James Mott is a very tall, dignified, and spiritual-faced
man, in the dress of a Quaker. Our party staying here
includes W. L. Garrison, Mrs. Garrison, and a daughter
of Frances D. Gage, about sixteen.

  "Mrs. Mott told me last evening that Mrs. Gage wrote
to Oberlin, making enquiries of one of the Professors
about the Institution with a view of sending her daughter
there. She received an answer saying they would 'be
very happy to receive her daughter and particularly at
this time, as a very interesting revival was in progress
and the daughter might be hopefully converted.' That
decided Mrs. Gage against sending her daughter there.
Lucy Stone is also here. Oliver Johnson dined here
yesterday.

  "Mrs. Garrison is a free and easy person with the least
possible pretensions, and has a very natural, artless sort
of way. She told me how 'awful 'fraid' she was of me
when she first saw me, and when I told her that was just
my embarrassment on seeing her, we both had a hearty
laugh. We are both writing now at the same table. She
asked me as we sat down if I carried a pocket dictionary
with me. I nearly laughed myself into fits. 'Oh, you
need n't laugh so;' said she, 'usually I'm not at all particular, but put down just what comes uppermost and in
any way I can, but I'm going to write to Ann Phillips,
and Wendell is *so* particular.'

  "You would like Mrs. Garrison's talk and simple ways ;
no starched-up stiffness to scare a body out of their wits.
Mr. Garrison talks most and best ; though there is nothing to choose (in this particular) between him and
Lucretia Mott.   Lucy Stone too, is a great talker."

7

"WILMINGTON, Oct. 31, '52.

"I saw some young ladies from Oberlin last evening. Dear old Oberlin ! It has many fond recollections for me.

"Sunday afternoon.—I have just returned from New Castle. There I saw a whipping-post. Is it not barbarous ? What an indignity to humanity !

"The Brandywine River, on which Wilmington is situated, is a romantic stream. It takes its name from the loss of a vessel laden with brandy and wine. The fact that I am in a slave state constantly presses upon my mind. It is such a new experience for me. It seems very strange and awful. I am told the pillory is in use in this city. Persons who steal are publicly whipped, both men and women.

"I am in the house of Thomas Garrett. He tells me that he has assisted upwards of eighteen hundred fugitives to a land of freedom. You know when we heard his story last Winter it was fourteen hundred [ultimately 2700]. He is rather a stout built man, with light hair and dark eyes, with immense firmness and decision ; would n't be afraid to face—you know *whom*. He says he was never intimidated in his life, though three times he has had a loaded pistol presented to his breast by slavery folks and several times been threatened with bowie knives. He is a smart, energetic, business man ; firmly-knit frame ; looks as if he were destined to a long life. Very large benevolence and plenty of good humour and fun.

"I gave my first lecture in Wilmington Saturday, October 30th. A crowded town hall listened with great respect; some slaveholders present ; collection $7.06 ! Quite a surprise to the anti-slavery folks here. Thomas Garrett drove me about the city. The streets are dreadfully dirty. Oh, the quantities of dirt I have to encounter in my meanderings, both in houses and places !

" Lucy Stone says Antoinette Brown is electioneering for Gerrit Smith and Gerrit is really afraid he will be elected. Whigs, Democrats. and Rummies come to him and say, ' I shall vote for Scott & Graham, but I shall vote for you to go to Congress ' : or, ' I shall vote for Pierce & King, but I shall vote for you to go to Congress.' If he is elected it will show a grand anti-slavery feeling unknown before in that region." [1]

[" From PENNSYLVANIA.   No date.]

" Shall I tell you what anti-slavery hospitality is in Pennsylvania? It is to be ushered into a small, close, stove-heated room, where seven or eight grown up persons and children have already breathed over the air two or three times ; introduced to a tall, unshaven, uncombed unwashed man with terribly dirty clothes and boots thick with mud and manure ; your things taken off, you are presently invited out into a dirty, dingy kitchen to sit down to highly-spiced sausages, or a dish here denominated ' scrapple,' and hot, thick, heavy pancakes, picking out two or three flies from your drink whatever it may be.

" And though you have been lecturing an hour and a half that day, besides riding through rain and mud several miles, you are expected to entertain the friends with how delighted you are with anti-slavery in Pennsylvania ; how you enjoy travelling about and seeing their beautiful State ; how much you enjoy their warm-hearted hospitality ; how liberal friends are in this region, etc., etc. An hour passes and you are asked to ascend to a cold, uncomfortable, half furnished apartment. There you

[1] Here is one sign of many that Miss Holley's anti-slavery sympathies were not narrowed to her particular school. But as her father's loyal friend, Gerrit Smith was always sainted in her eyes.

lie until morning, when again you go through the charming experience of the evening before.

"Then you ride eight or ten miles to the next appointment. All along the road you are told that Lancaster County is the greatest wheat-growing county in the world ; that Chester County contains more woman's rights women than any other in the world ; that my style of lecturing being so 'moral and religious,' so mild, not exciting anger or resentment, is *remarkably adapted* to this region.' "

" PHŒNIXVILLE, Nov. 22, '52.

"The last four days I 've been passing in an uncommonly amiable and interesting family, consisting of a father, mother, and seven children. Such an atmosphere of mutual love and confidence as their house exhaled was truly refreshing. The father and mother are no scholars in the technical sense of that word, but have what is higher—a real thirst for knowledge and appreciation of education. Such sweet unaffected simplicity of character was really beautiful. The father said to me,

" ' When I was a young man I was educated as well as my neighbours, but since I have become acquainted with these abolitionists I find myself quite behind the times and feel the need of a better education.'

"I replied that all true souls had something of the same experience ; it had been the great grief of my life that I knew no more.

" 'Oh !' said he, "in you those are what I should call unjustifiable yearnings.'

"The family belong to the religious society called ' German Baptists ' ; they wash each other's feet, baptise by immersion, and, beside the regular communion service of the churches, have a supper once a year, in imitation, as they believe, of the first apostles.

" And now I am staying with a brother of that man. I saw him in meeting yesterday and was impressed by his beautiful prayer. He thanked God 'that all hearts are not obdurate. We can still perceive the workings of Thy spirit in hearts consecrated to truth and righteousness.' I feel refreshed in heart and strengthened in hope by contact with that family, and am much affected by the gentle and genuine cordiality and kindness these brothers have shown me.

" November 23d.—Yesterday afternoon we rode to Valley Forge, saw the house where Washington was quartered during that dreadful winter of 1777-8. 'Friend Jones,' an old Quaker lady, now occupies the house. As I sat down she remarked, 'Thou art now in Washington's parlour.' The house is an old stone building. The windows of thick glass. The woodwork looks ancient and worn. I visited the hill where the army encamped and saw the remains of the intrenchment they threw up. I also saw the house where Quaker Potts lived, who thought Washington was a Christian because he caught him praying behind a rock. Two hills near are called Mount Joy and Mount Sorrow, because in early times, William Penn got lost in the vicinity and was for some time bewildered. When he ascended the hill where he could see the surrounding country and by that means ascertained his whereabouts his gladness was so great he named the hill Mount Joy. The other hill, behind which he was lost, he called Mount Sorrow.

" BYBERRY, PA., November 26, 1852.

" I am now staying at the elegant country home of Robert Purvis. It may be called 'Saints' Rest,' for here all the abolitionists find that 'the wicked cease from troubling and the weary are at rest.' The house and extensive grounds are in tasteful English style.

" Mr. Purvis is a coloured man, but so light that no stranger would suspect it. His wife is very lady-like in manners and conversation ; something of the ease and blandness of a southern lady. The style of living here is quite uncommonly rich and elegant. Upon my arrival I was ushered into a beautiful room where there was a fine large wood fire blazing most delightfully in an open fireplace. It was so charming to me after my twenty miles' ride through the mud and cold.

" What a pity that homely, gloomy stoves should be allowed to take the place of open fires ! Why, in a few generations more the words *hearth* and *fireside* will have no meaning. People will have no idea what they signify. The golden age of open fires is indeed departing.[1] I am writing in a very cheerful ' upper chamber,' and feel remarkably amiable, staying in such a beautiful home. As Mr. Skimpole said of his lying on the soft grass and looking up through the trees to the blue sky, it ' must be what I was made for, it suits me so exactly.'

" Mr. Purvis took the highest premium on poultry at the late fair in Philadelphia. While speaking of it he told me this anecdote. During the poultry exhibition or ' Hen Convention,' as it is called on the spot, a gentleman came near Mr. Purvis's exhibit, and as he was admiring them and remarking on their rare beauty he said to Mr. Purvis (not knowing him), 'And these belong to that black nigger down in Byberry.' Mr. P. replied, 'Why, friend you put it in rather strong language, but you can judge for yourself—I am the man.' The other man turned and went away.

[1] But it has since come back as a very common luxury both in country and city houses.

" Mr. Purvis is an elegant man in his manners, conversation, and bearing.   He was educated at Edinburgh." [1]

" NEWTOWN, November 28, 1852.

" I am now in Bucks County.   J. G. Whittier said, years ago, that in Massachusetts a Bucks County farmer would starve."

" WRIGHTSTOWN, November 30th.

" I am stopping at the place where Parker Pillsbury quietly remarked, when he first drove up to it, ' This looks like making great sacrifices for the slaves.'   It is a large and productive farm.   The Chapman family reside here.   Two sisters and two brothers, all about fifty to sixty years old.   They are firm abolitionists and like Mr. Pillsbury exceedingly.

" I have always felt myself drawn toward Quakers by their extreme simplicity of life and great sincerity of manner and I have not felt less so since I have seen these lovely Pennsylvania ones, some of whom inspire my warm admiration.   Their quiet homes and retired places bring to mind those beautiful lines of Gray,

" ' Far from the madding crowd's ignoble strife
        Their sober wishes never learned to stray ;
   Along the cool, sequestered vale of life
        They kept the noiseless tenor of their way.'

" I find many elevated spirits engaged in the great work of emancipation ; an angelic phalanx of the good and true.   Heaven prosper the work of their hands and may their hearts convert the world.

" Many slaveholders have their families residing in Philadelphia while they stay on large plantations at the South. It is said they keep their families at the North for safety.

[1] Born in Charleston, South Carolina, August 4, 1810 ; died April 15, 1898.

"John Randolph said, 'Every slaveholder is a sentinel at his own door.'"[1]

TO THE PORTERS.

"Newtown, Bucks Co., Pa., Dec. 2, 1852.

"I am endeavouring to hold up our glorious banner of anti-slavery as well as I am able. I heard a touching story the other day : a poor coloured man, who has lived a few years in this State, joined the church one year ago but has not yet partaken of the sacrament. His minister secretly asked him why he had not.

"'Oh,' said the poor fellow, 'I once had a brother, and he was sold to buy communion plate, and, somehow, I can't partake.' 'Dear kindred blood, how I love you all!' Daniel Webster was not alone in that holy sentiment. Strange that one who could so tenderly love his own 'kindred blood,' should not have had more thought about the slave's 'kindred blood,' when he made that cruel Seventh of March Speech! But ambition can change a man into a fiend.

"You would have laughed as I did to hear the boasting of a Dutchman from the dark hills of Berks County, he had such a large county pride. Said he, 'Berks County is the grandest in the State. It has the best corn, the finest cows, the biggest apples, the handsomest gals, and fewest niggers of any county in the State.' He evidently did not agree with the poet, who says, 'What constitutes a state? Men, high minded men.' I am in a quiet, pleasant (anti-slavery) farmer's family ; and while the good woman in the other part of the house is playing 'Cinderella,' I am in the parlour, not 'counting out money,' but

[1] But the Civil War furnished a remarkable commentary on this saying. The slaves were faithful sentinels at home, while their masters went off to the front to rivet their chains.

reading Henry Giles's eloquent discourse on *Life* and writting letters to friends. The cheerful little rag-carpeted parlour and shining stove look significant to me, and very friendly, after my long ride in the cold and through the mud.

"I have long wanted to know how W. H. Channing and our church agree in Rochester. How happy I should be to receive a long, good letter from *you*. How I should like to drop in among you all again, and take my old seat at table, and in the parlour. How kind you all were to me. Love to all from your weary but happy friend."

"PHILA., PA., Dec. 12, 1852.

"This morning I went with Miller McKim to hear your dear Mr. Furness. He gave us a most encouraging and inspiring sermon. 'Sanctify them by thy truth,' was his text. I felt my own soul quickened and blest by his words. After church, Mr. McKim introduced me to Mr. Furness. He was very kind and said he should love to hear *me* preach. Mrs. Furness, I hear, has no opinion of anti-slavery or woman's rights.

"I return to New England to-morrow."

TO MISS PUTNAM.

"MELLICO HILL, N. J., Dec. 5th, 1852.

"I have just returned from Woodston, a nine miles' ride from this place, where I had an overflowing house, great numbers having to stand. All listened with absorbed interest. I cannot but feel good was accomplished. The collection was $12.24.

"Some of our Quaker friends rather object to taking collections. They fear that the moral influence upon those who receive will be bad. I tell them they have looked too exclusively at the moral influence on the receivers and too little at the moral influence upon the givers. They do not remember that it is more blessed to give than to receive. Giving to the anti-slavery cause opens the blessed sympathies of the soul ; opens a way for anti-slavery truth to enter and impress the heart.

"I have been for the last two or three weeks in those places which witnessed the happiness of Mr. and Mrs. Foster when they were lovers. They used occasionally to steal away from the lecture room and snatch an hour from the throng that they might be alone together. Several times in different places remarks like these were addressed to me : 'This is the room where Stephen and Abby sat when they were lovers.' 'Here is where Stephen met Abby after many weeks' separation.' They have many warm friends in Pennsylvania.

"In my recent readings[1] I found this passage, which I copy for you, it is so true.

"'After all there is much of one's life that is not unfolded, much that remains uncommunicated, and that is uncommunicable. The very medium, language, by which spirit holds converse with spirit is inadequate to transmit the plainest thought as it is in the mind of the speaker. Language is not representative but suggestive, and no merely spiritual idea is exactly the same in any two minds. No word therefore can be to any two minds the sign of an import that absolutely corresponds in both. How much of life passes within us that we make no attempt to impart, that we have no opportunity to impart.'"

[1] One of Miss Holley's loveliest habits was that of sending to Miss Putnam and other friends passages that delighted her. I have seldom reproduced them, though they are bright reflections of the beauty and the wisdom of her spiritual life. This one, if not Horace Bushnell's, is in close agreement with one of his most significant utterances,

WORCESTER, December 19, 1852.

From Philadelphia I went to Belleville, New Jersey, to visit Theodore Weld, Angelina Weld, and Sarah M. Grimké. Theodore Weld is a remarkable man ; he is full of brilliant conversation and has a strong mind. Angelina and Sarah are full of mental vigour. They talk much of the great principles of life—how human life can be made harmonious and beautiful. Angelina is a believer in spirit manifestations and a great admirer of Andrew Jackson Davis. Sarah is deeply interesting in conversation but *shockity* in personal appearance. She reminds one of Charles Lamb's " Mrs. Conrady," where he attempts the refutation of the popular fallacy, " Handsome is that handsome does." Neither can you say of Sarah Grimké " I think I have seen that face before, somewhere, but can't tell where." Seeing her is an event of your life. It is like seeing Stonehenge. Both the ladies wear the " American costume." Such folornities ! But then their talk ! Oh, it is angels' food ! Not coarse, earthly fare, such as most people set before you. How you would expand and grow under such ideas !

Mr. and Mrs. Weld and Sarah have laid aside all the forms of religion. Mrs. Weld said, " We endeavour to teach the children principles." (Mr. Weld has a school of about twenty scholars.) " I used to pray with my oldest boy whenever he had done wrong, but at last I thought it injured the child. He got so that whenever he did anything wrong he would come to me and say, ' Mother, now let us pray over it and I shall feel better.' It was to him a wiping out of the trangression."

Theodore was once stiffly orthodox, but, as he expressed it, " It all fell off naturally as I advanced. I did not have any conflict or doubt or struggle. I found it was all nothing to me. An earnest, true, real life was the only essential."

"When we first came here to reside," said Mr. Weld, "for months no one came nigh us but the doctor and the butcher. The butcher supposed we ate meat. We had no influence in the community for months. People seemed horrified at us. Now the whole community put together has not the influence of us three. People came and begged me to be superintendent of all the schools in this county, and here I have been for five years putting in and putting out what teachers I think best. I am amused when the Methodist or Presbyterian or Baptist minister comes to me and says, 'Why, Mr. Weld, there is not so much difference between us after all.'"

We have had some splendid meetings lately. Mr. Pillsbury related several facts showing that even Whigs, Democrats, and Free-soilers hated the Fugitive Slave Bill. One was :

"A few days ago a member of the vigilance committee took me to see a young woman just escaped from the South; she was as white as any lady in this room, with two children of whom any mother might be proud. She, with these children, one two years and the other five months old, had arrived in Boston by train not knowing where to go. An Irishman took her where she could get warm, and, leaving the youngest child, she wandered about in search of employment. Asking a man in a drug store if he knew where she could get work, he said there was a great call for women's work in the city, that good women could always find employment.

"'Can coloured women ?' said she; 'I am a coloured woman.'

"'Where's your colour?' he inquired. Ascertaining where she came from, he went to a member of the Vigilance Committee who made the case known to anti-slavery friends and she was at once provided for.

"This merchant was one of the most forward and staunchest supporters of General Pierce's election in the city of Boston."

At Framingham I was cordially welcomed by Dr. and Mrs. Stone. Dr. Stone told me a good story which I must repeat to you. Last winter Dr. Stone tea 'd at Theodore Parker's in Boston, where was also Mr. Brace (the man who was confined in a Hungarian prison), and Mr. Parker related this story to them. Years ago Dr. Francis Parkman went over to Lexington, Massachusetts, to hear Ralph Waldo Emerson preach. The day after he met George Ripley on the street in Boston and said to him in a tone of alarm, and almost breathless with astonishment, "Have you heard of the outrage in Lexington? Ralph Waldo Emerson?"

"No," answered Mr. Ripley, "what outrage has been committed upon Ralph Waldo Emerson?"

"Why," returned Dr. Parkman, "if you can credit it, Mr. Emerson preached a sermon without taking any text!"

"Well," said Mr. Ripley, "I know of a very popular sermon that was preached by a very popular preacher which had no text."

"But," interposed Dr. Parkman, "Mr. Emerson did n't have any prayer either before or after the sermon."

"Well," replied Mr. Ripley, "if I remember right this popular sermon had no prayer before or after it was delivered."

"Why, what sermon do you mean?" said the curious Doctor.

"The Sermon on the Mount," was the triumphant

answer ; whereupon the Doctor was completely silenced and left.

At the West India celebration meeting I wish you could have seen Wendell Phillips's countenance when administering rebuke to Frederick Douglass [who had been consorting with the Free-soilers] for the paragraph suggesting that the executive committee of the American Anti-Slavery Society had designedly kept Wright, Pillsbury, and Foster from the Anniversary in New York City as a propitiation to a slaveholding church and a New York City mob.

Mr. Phillips in a burst of noble, beautiful feeling exclaimed, " I am proud to associate with Henry C. Wright, Parker Pillsbury, and Stephen S. Foster. They are men whom my soul honours. When I shall have laid upon the altar of human freedom and human progress the labours, the sacrifices, the glorious faith of these great reformers, I can thank God I have not lived in vain." (I can only give the idea, not the burning and shining words)

Douglass in his answer appeared better than I should have supposed it possible for him to appear. He is certainly a remarkable man, of wonderful self-control, shrewdness, and talent.

Some in the convention said Mr. Phillips's rebuke was untimely and in bad taste, not good for the " cause." I am entirely willing to leave " the cause " to such men as Wendell Phillips and his brave associates, feeling well assured that they who have so long, and through such a wilderness, borne the " ark," will know best and do best for it now. The past proves too absolutely for me to doubt that their love is true. Fire cannot burn it ; many waters cannot quench it ; persecution and famine will not change it.

Wendell Phillips

CHAPTER VIII

WANDERING ON

" Oh well for him that finds a friend,
Or makes a friend, where 'er he come,
And loves the world from end to end,
And wanders on from home to home."

THE year 1853 was a significant one for Sallie
Holley. It was marked by the most important
of the earlier Woman's Rights conventions, which
met in New York early in September and was presided over by Lucretia Mott with the utmost dignity
and impressiveness. The same year, in May, a
"World's Temperance Convention" was held in
New York and the proposition to place a woman on
a business committee was clamorously voted down;
women were refused a hearing and finally excluded
from the convention as not having been invited. A
secession of those otherwise minded, headed by Col.
Higginson, immediately followed, and a " Whole
World's Temperance Convention " was called for
September and was held in New York, Wendell
Phillips doing valiant battle in the rival organisation,
holding its convention a few days later, for Antoinette
Brown, who had been elected a delegate. Another

convention of the same year was the Bible Convention
which met in Hartford, June 2d, and " hell was moved
to meet it "—a mob of students from the Hartford
Theological School. Here was a business of the
greatest interest to Sallie Holley, whose Unitari-
anism, following her father's lead, was very rational
and liberal. If none of these things made much
impression on her correspondence it does not mean
that she was not interested in them, but that she had
her own work to do and on her journeys—frequently
remote from the great cities—the echoes of their
doings came to her with but the faintest intonation.
Moreover, the record of her life made by the letters
herewith printed is, like the geologic record, an imperfect one: there are many missing leaves. It may
be that other letters would reflect more than these of
the more public aspects of the anti-slavery and other
reforms. She very properly assumed that what her
friends were most interested in was her own experiences in the missionary field. For Mr. Garrison a
better acquaintance with Mrs. Stowe was one of the
important incidents of the year and of this there is
some vivid intimation in Miss Holley's letter of May
21st, though for a full account of it one must go
to the *Story of his Life told by his Children*, pp.
395–401, vol. iii.

TO MISS PUTMAN

" BOSTON, Jan. 6th, 1853.

" I am at Francis Jackson's house.[1]

" On Sunday evening last I lectured in Fall River to

[1] Francis Jackson was one of the most faithful of Garrison's friends,
" a very tower of strong will, solid judgement, shrewd forecast, sturdy

1500 people. The largest anti-slavery meeting ever held there. For the first time in Fall River Mr. Garrison's name was cheered.

" On Tuesday evening I heard Mr. Phillips speak at the Anti-Slavery Bazaar. He said, among other things, that, when Sir T. F. Buxton invited Mr. Garrison to breakfast with him in London and had invited Dr. Lushington with others to meet him, when he (Buxton) came forward to meet Garrison he exclaimed, ' Is this Mr. Garrison, the great advocate, of black emancipation in America ? Why, I thought you were a black man ! ' It was, said Phillips, the greatest compliment Mr. Garrison had ever received. Mr. Garrison had so far emancipated himself from American prejudices and influences as to view the matter from the black man's position. Phillips said, ' Americans think merely of the white man's interest when calculating upon this subject. If the slaves could all be made white to-night, they would all be made free to-morrow.'

" I never [referring to one of Alcott's conversations] can talk with these Boston people. My mental faculties seem completely paralysed when I am in their company."

common sense." One of " the Garrison boys " was named for him. He was born March 7, 1789, and died November 16, 1861, glimpsing but not entering the Promised Land. He was president of the Massachusetts Anti-Slavery Society in its most trying years and Garrison always found in him, as did John Pierpont and Theodore Parker, a friend whose loyalty was equal to all possible events. It was at his house, November 18, 1835, that Harriet Martineau did her life's bravest thing, when in a company of 130 anti-slavery women she declared herself in full agreement with the principles of Garrison. This was to strew her pathway in America with burning marl and cinders, when otherwise it would have been '' roses, roses, all the way."

8

"WEYMOUTH, Jan. 9, 1853.

"I am now in the home of the Westons : name so near the heart of the true abolitionist. Maria Chapman was a Miss Weston. Anne W. Weston is a most lady-like and agreeable person. Is about forty, but appears much younger. Is full of intelligence and a great talker. Mr. Garrison says she talks the best, for a person who talks so much, of any woman he ever knew. She is small in stature, with a light, delicate complexion, light hair, and hazel eyes. There are four sisters at home. They seem to be real heroines in the battle of life. Active, energetic, eccentric characters. Have taught school for years.

"Caroline Weston, who has recently returned after passing four years in Europe, told Mrs. Foster that she had earned and spent twenty-five thousand dollars. That gives an idea of her business tact and talent. These ladies are splendid instances of what woman can do with self dependence, or when she devotes herself to a great principle.

"I suppose the Boston Bazaar would be shut up if the Westons were not in the country.[1] Anna does a great deal of foreign correspondence on anti-slavery topics with the women of England, Ireland, and Scotland. She has a great dislike of the Bloomer costume and will not ask Lucy Stone to speak at the Bazaar because of her dress. She even said to me that if she could prevent it, the Anti-slavery Society should employ no agent who indulged in eccentricities of dress or appearance like Charles C. Burleigh, Lucy Stone, and others. She thinks Mrs. Foster showed great good sense in saying she

[1] Lowell called Maria Weston Chapman "The coiled-up main-spring of the Fair."

wanted people to hear what she said, rather than to observe the length of her dress.

"How you would bask in the sunshine of the talk of these ladies !

"You are right in thinking it was a 'rest and satisfaction' to be again with my loved friend Mrs. Holland. She is a very superior woman and has been a great student. She converses in French, Italian, Spanish, and German almost as fluently as in English ; has a most delightfully familiar acquaintance with all our best English literature, and reads nearly everything."

"BOSTON, Jan. 25, 1853.

"At the breakfast table this morning something was said of the complaint about abolitionists being misunderstood. Mr. Pillsbury said, 'The last time I saw John Pierpont it was in this very room ; he introduced me to a gentleman who was with him, thus : " Let me introduce you to Parker Pillsbury, the man who has the misfortune to make himself understood." '

"This evening Theodore Parker is to speak. Everybody asks me to speak, but my little speeches would be absolutely nothing at all in such company. I have a great dread of making a failure. I have not only the cause of the slave at heart, but also the dignity of women to sustain. I do wish I could speak here, but I know nothing good enough to say before such as Garrison and Phillips."

"BOSTON, Jan. 30, 1853.

"Yesterday I had a happy talk with Mr. Alcott. Among other things he asked me, 'If I felt most or thought most ?' I said I felt most. 'Your feelings,' said he, 'need to flower into thoughts.'

" This morning I heard Theodore Parker in Music Hall. An audience of three thousand. Subject, ' Earnestness and Frivolity.' At the Annual Anti-Slavery Meeting I heard Abby Folsom.[1] She is sometimes very bright in her sayings. Once when two men were carrying her upon their shoulders out of the room, she said : ' I 'm honoured more than my Saviour was. He went into Jerusalem riding an ass. I go out of this room riding upon *two*.' "

" WEST BROOKFIELD, Feb. 5, 1853.

" I am now at Deacon Henshaw's, or at least he was deacon before anti-slavery times. But the church could n't tolerate anti-slavery, so he ' came out.'

" I asked his good wife if she also was a ' come-outer ; ' ' No, I am a " thrust-outer," ' she said.

" I was to have given a lecture in North Brookfield this evening, but a kind, good storm blows and whistles and rains so hard that I am prevented. Storms, real driving ones, are often great blessings to the poor, tired, jaded-out anti-slavery lecturers."

" UPTON, MASS., Feb. 28, 1853.

" Yesterday I left Hopedale after passing three very pleasant days there. There are about two hundred belonging to the Community at Hopedale. They have six hundred acres of land, ' redeemed,' as Mr. Draper said to me, ' from war, slavery, and intemperance.' No one can join who is not a non-resistant. Adin Ballou [the founder] seems a beautiful character. He has been

---

[1] Miss Abigail Folsom, whom Emerson called " that flea of conventions " ; a sore trial to the patience and the non-resistance principles of the abolitionists. She died in Rochester, New York, Aug. 8, 1867, aged 75.

head of the Community for ten years. Now Mr. Draper is head. They began poor and have suffered many privations. Their houses are small, but very neat and comfortable."

"WORCESTER, Mar. 22, 1853.

"I admire Mrs. Foster's character[1] very much as I see her in her home, so beautifully just to every member of the household. Her real reverence for humanity is shown by her ways towards the Irish girls who have lived with her during the past summer.

"Wherever I have lectured for the last ten weeks the abolitionists at whose houses I have stayed have been so kind, so attentive to all my wants, so assiduous to provide me with every comfort, that I feel a strong impulse to acknowledge it in a letter to the *Liberator*. How much I wish I could furnish to the *Liberator* such good letters as Mr. Pillsbury writes.

"It interested me much to hear that Mrs. Stowe is anxious to know the distinguished people in her own country before going abroad. I learn that she invited Whittier to visit her and that he declined."

"ABINGTON, March 31, 1853.

"I was very fortunate in being in Abington last evening. Mr. Edmund Quincy lectured upon the domestic life of the early Puritans. It was no vulgar order of character that clung closer to an idea than to a country, and for a principle braved a dreary exile. Such a profusion of allusions to characters and incidents in history and romance and poems made the lecture sparkle all over. He spoke enthusiastically of Ben Franklin, of his birthplace in Boston; of the house, which yet stands, from

[1] Abby Kelley Foster.

which, as a boy, he issued with that world-renowned whistle ; and of that cellar where he asked his father why he did not ask the blessing over the whole barrel of pork at once, rather than in detail. He was full of humour. He told us of the drought that occurred in Boston which the people believed to be a mark of displeasure, not that they had hung too many victims, but that they had not hung more.

"After the lecture, when nearly everyone had left, Lewis Ford lingered to speak with him, so of course I had to stay too. I wish you could have witnessed Mr. Quincy's manner, his elegant bow and face as he approached me with extended hand : ' Why Miss Holley, I am very happy to meet you. I did n't dream you were listening to me. If I had known you were to be here I don't know that I should have lectured. I am as much afraid of lecturing before you as you are before me ; and with quite as much reason.' You would have been vastly amused by his nonsense."

" BOSTON, April 7, 1853.

"For the last week I have felt in better health than for weeks before. I attribute it to passing a week where I could walk every day and lie in the open air as much as I pleased. I have walked many miles and enjoyed it highly.

"The walk from Lewis Ford's house (where I have been staying) to the Post Office is through a pleasant wood, and some of these blossoming spring days I have enjoyed it keenly. As I walked, the little birds seemed to talk to me, and the music of the frogs at close of day instructed me. As you say, ' All joy and success attend their little lives of song and love !' I was vividly reminded of that charming walk that Sylvester Judd's little Margaret had 'to the village,' when the birds spoke and sung to her and the little squirrels had something for her.

"Professor Allen of McGrawville College is in town. He is married to a white lady. They leave for England in a few days to stay four years. What an accursed country this is! I hope she is a woman of sterling character. It will require superior virtue to walk safely and triumphantly along her path.

"James Jackson is quite a botanist and cultivates many beautiful and rare flowers. To-day he has been showing me a beautiful Ixia Virida Flora in bloom, an azalea, etc."

"DOVER, N. H., April 14, 1853.

"Here I am in the house of Mrs. Mary P. Osborne, sister of my old friend Lizzie Gordon. I am to lecture here this evening.

"While in Portsmouth I made particular inquiries after the descendants of Washington's slave, but found the only two children she left had died within a few years. I saw persons who knew her very well and often had her to work for them. She always said she liked her master, but loved liberty better.

"The last slave in New England—Dinah Rollins—is the subject of an article in an old *Liberty Bell*, by Edmund Quincy. It is well told. I have just been reading it. The family with whom she lived died, 'and poor Dinah was left without anybody to take care of her. The reader will perhaps conclude from this, her unhappy predicament, that she immediately took to begging, if not to stealing. No such consequences ensued, although we are credibly assured that such must be the inevitable effects of emancipation. She migrated no farther than Portsmouth, where she obtained an honest livelihood by serving as hostler in a livery stable.

"'I am apprehensive lest my Dinah should seem to some masters in our Israel to have been "impatient of her proper sphere," and to have stepped forth to assume the duties of the man in her choice of a field of labour; and that she may even come within the fulminations of the Pastoral Letter of the Massachusetts General Association of Congregational Ministers and be exposed to be likened unto "a vine whose strength and beauty is to lean upon the trelliswork and half conceal its clusters,"—but however great may have been her deviation, in this particular, from the gentle elegancies and graceful proprieties of perfect womanhood, it was not owing to anything unfeminine in her education. I can assure the fastidious reader that she is perfectly innocent of a knowledge of the classics, of metaphysics, of the higher mathematics, and, in general, of all the masculine branches of learning.'"

"MANCHESTER, N. H., May 1, 1853.

"I left Portland yesterday morning after a very pleasant ten days' stay. The day previous Dr. Farrar accompanied me to see the Reform School. The building is large and handsome, almost offering a temptation to commit crime, so attractive does it appear. It is pleasant to anticipate a time when a glorified humanity will be far beyond the reach of low temptations.

"And now I am in Manchester where a brother of Margaret Fuller's preaches, and where her little boy lies buried.

"May 6th.—Yesterday morning I visited the grave of Angelo Eugene Philip Ossoli. It is a lovely spot, all surrounded by beautiful trees, running waters, and lovely

green grass. A marble slab marks the hallowed spot.
On the marble is carved the cross with a water-lily on
it ; very touching and beautiful."

"Milford, N. H., May 10, 1853.

"Before leaving Manchester I had the happiness of
twenty minutes' conversation with the mother of Margaret
Fuller. She appeared as Margaret used to speak of her,
'dear, gentle, angelic mother.' She talked beautifully of
her child, said Margaret's faith was more like *sight* than
any person's she ever knew. Spoke of the heavenly
serenity Margaret manifested on the approach of death,
as Mrs. Hasty had told her. Mrs. Fuller said to me, 'I
thought as I listened to your lecture of the deep interest
Margaret would have taken in your mission.'

"At Manchester I took the cars for Nashua, and when
at noon I found myself in the depot, the cheering (?) intelligence was conveyed to my delighted (?) ear that I
must wait only (!) six hours before I could proceed to
Milford. The day was heavenly, the 'Ladies' room'
agreeable, and having the *Commonwealth*, I yielded
myself up to the pleasure of reading a full account of
the Hale festival.¹ Mr. Garrison was cheered to the
echo,—longest, loudest, and gladdest of all; and he made
a most felicitous reply.

"May we not congratulate ourselves on the future
betokened by the blush of morn now reddening the
horizon?

"As I was waiting in the depot an elderly lady in
black came in, and laying aside her bonnet and two

¹ In honour of John P. Hale, whose term as Senator had recently
expired. Charles G. Atherton, who succeeded him, was the infamous
author of " Atherton's Gag," the subject of one of John Pierpont's
most characteristic poems.

shawls and seating herself in the coolest place she could find, remarked, 'How perfectly simple to have a hot fire such a day as this ! I am almost suffocated. I don't think I shall get over it in a week.' I responded as consolingly as I could. 'And then to have to wait here three hours.'

"I was eating some hickory nuts I had bought, having borrowed a hammer and used the register for a stone ; so I said, 'I have some nuts to entertain myself with' ; to which she brightly remarked, ' Nuts are very engrossing.' So we fell into a pleasant chat. I found she got out of the cars at Milford, so when I came to this house where I am stopping I mentioned her. One of the young ladies said she knew her ; that she was the fourth wife of her husband whom she buried last fall. When she had a marble slab placed at the grave she wished to have put on it, ' My Husband,' but somebody told her that would look as though she wished to monopolise him ; then she suggested 'Our Husband' ; that looked a little ridiculous, and she finally decided upon ' Oh, Husband ! ' And so it is. "

" BOSTON, May 21, 1853.

"Last evening I came from Mrs. Foster's after passing a day and a half with her. Little Alla was six years old on the nineteenth, which was Thursday. She is a very interesting child. The other day when Mrs. Foster went to New York she took Alla with her as far as Connecticut to visit her little cousins there. They frequently said (as is the fashion with most children) to Alla, 'Will your mother let you do this?' 'Will your mother let you do that ? ' At last Alla looked at them in deep surprise, replying, ' My mother lets me do just as I please. If she wishes me to do a thing I generally do it.' This was said in perfect simplicity. The cousins could not seem to understand how a child could be 'let' do just as she pleased. Alla, who had never heard of any other way, was equally unable to understand why all children should not be so 'let.' You know Mrs. Foster is very conscientious not to use the least worldly authority over her child, and she is richly repaid by the unbounded confidence and affection which the child so beautifully reposes in her mother.

"Mr. Garrison told me of a conversation Mrs. H. B. Stowe had with him last winter while she was writing the *Key to Uncle Tom's Cabin*. She said to Mr. Garrison, 'Are you a Christian?' 'You could not possibly ask a more indefinite question,' said Mr. Garrison. Mrs. Stowe: 'Well, are you such a Christian as *I am*? Mr. G. : 'That is, if possible, more indefinite than the other.' (When I related this last question to Mr. S. S. Foster, he said, 'I should have answered, " I hope not." ') Mrs. S. : 'Well, Mr. Garrison, do you believe in the atonement?' Mr. G. : 'Ah, now, Mrs. Stowe, your question is a definite one'; and he answered, 'I do not. Jesus could not, in the very nature of things, be good for me, nor good for you. He could be good only for himself. I regard the doctrine of the atonement, as it is called, as monstrous, unnatural, and unlike God.' Mrs. S. : 'What do you do with such passages as this,—" Jesus Christ formed within us the hope of glory," etc. ?' Mr. G. : ' Jesus, as the representative of the Love Spirit, must be in us the hope of glory. Only a love spirit like his can redeem us, can ever redeem the world from selfishness and sin. Our spirit, our character must be like his or we die in our sins.'

"I only give you a meagre sketch of the conversation. Mrs. Stowe received it very quietly and kindly and afterwards wrote a beautiful letter to Mr. Garrison expressing affection for him and confidence in his goodness, saying something like this : ' I used to think you were a wolf in sheep's clothing, but now (pardon the simile) I think you a sheep in wolf's clothing.' [1]

"May 22d.—This morning I heard a fine sermon from Theodore Parker.   His prayers are beautiful.

"When I see other people so bright, so full of intellectual life, I feel deeply my own poverty. I ought to know more, be more faithful to my mind's wants. Now in this season of resurrection and growth, in this springtime, why can't I rise and grow too, mentally and morally ?   I can apprehend the exceeding beauty of knowledge and holiness, but, alas ! I cannot attain unto them.

"May 23d.—Henry C. Wright called with little Fanny Garrison to take me to Mount Auburn. We stopped at Hannah Adams's monument. She was the first tenant of Mt. Auburn. The martyr Torrey lies here. His likeness on one side of the monument, a slave-woman chained on the other.

"May 24th.—The Abolitionists and Free-Soilers are rejoicing this afternoon over the defeat of a proposition from the Whigs in the Legislature to appropriate $10,000 by the State to erect a statue of Daniel Webster, to be placed beside that of Washington in the State-House. It was lost by four majority.   As the Democrats and Free-Soilers together are a larger number than the Whigs in this State, such a thing would have been very much against the wishes of a majority of the people (legal vot-

[1] No such infelicity occurs in Mrs. Stowe's letters to Garrison as printed in the Garrison *Story*, and I am tempted to say, as a kind-hearted and simple-minded woman said of the crucifixion of Jesus, " Let us hope it never happened."

ers), who loathe and detest the memory of Daniel Webster. A good deal of excitement has prevailed in the city concerning it. Mr. Jackson thinks that even if this Legislature had succeeded in getting the statue, the next would have trundled it out of the State-House[1]; or perhaps it would have been served as the figure of Gen. Jackson was."

[During Jackson's administration, Commodore Elliot, with U. S. money, caused the full-length figure of General Jackson to be placed upon a ship of war (as figurehead) lying in the Navy Yard here in Boston. One dreadfully stormy night the head was cut off and no one knew who did it, and this notwithstanding the sentinels were fore and aft.—C. F. P.]

" WEARE CENTRE, June 9, 1853.

" For the first time in my life, during the last year I have encountered *good* people who doubted about a future life and I have listened to them with keenest anguish. I would fly from such a doubt as I would not from famine or plague. Scepticism about a blessed hereafter seems to me to sap the very springs of hope, to wither the life of all happiness here, and lead to deepest and darkest melancholy. It is going into outer darkness, yielding up the sweet breath of heaven."

" CANTERBURY, June 18, 1853.

" Mr. Pillsbury drove Mrs. P., Nellie, and myself over here to Stephen Foster's father and mother this morning. I am to lecture here Sunday.

[1] On the contrary, it was set up in bronze, in the State-House grounds in 1859, not without much vigorous opposition. Wendell Phillips called it " that ill-used iron."

" Yesterday Caroline Foster drove me to her brother David's, the old homestead where Stephen, his father, and grandfather were born. The location is very beautiful. Hills in every direction. Old Mr. Foster is eighty-eight years old and his wife is eighty-one. He was in the ' War of the Resolution,' as old Rainey used to say. He was one of Arnold's life-guards. I asked Stephen's mother if she had ever heard Stephen lecture. ' Yes,' she replied, ' I have heard Stephen lecture when I wanted to lecture him.'

" June 20th.—The Fosters wished to have my lecture Sunday afternoon in the Orthodox meeting-house. The minister thought it his duty to call Saturday evening to inquire of me if I believed in the plenary inspiration of the Bible,—in the Sabbath,—in the institution of the ministry,—in the ordinances of grace, etc.

" You would have been highly diverted by our talk. At the close he said, ' It is not considered polite to discuss theological tenets with a lady, and I have not.' But he had to open the house ' because he feared the people.'

" One aged minister here protested against my going in at one o'clock : it was such an innovation on the ' ancient landmarks.' This same old minister said to Miss Foster, that if he had thought his wife would ever have claimed an equality with him he never would have married her. Miss Foster replied that people generally thought the loss would be quite as great for him as for his wife."

" ROCHESTER, Dec. 6, 1853.

" If I go to Oberlin it will be to go where I am not popular. The fact is I am so pestered with attention that it will be a great relief to get where people don't like me. I think in Oberlin there will be a cessation of attention that will be very agreeable to me. I wish the art of 'letting alone' was better understood in the world.

"At the close of the Convention a lady to whom I was introduced, taking my hand very warmly, said to me, by way of encouragement and consolation for us women lecturers, 'We shall one day be where the wicked cease from troubling and the weary are at rest.' 'Oh,' I returned, 'I 'm there already ; I 've arrived.' She looked as if a new light had dawned upon her mind.

"Ernestine L. Rose is a charming woman and at times playful. After a talk I had with her about a future life, which she does not believe in, I said, 'But I think I shall meet you in a life beyond and above this.' She said,

"'Then you will say to me, "I told you so," and I shall reply, "How very stupid I was !"'

"She does not believe that personal consciousness survives the dissolution of our physical organism. The same elements will continue, for, as nothing was ever created, nothing will ever end.

"She remarked that 'Superstition is religion out of fashion, and religion is superstition in fashion.'

"She seems to me to be a candid, reverent, loving spirit.[1]

"She is the daughter of a Jewish Rabbi, educated in the strictest manner. She has suffered much.

"Sunday eve.,—after ten o'clock.—I have just come from an admirable speech of W. H. Channing's. He closed by saying that the Scandinavians had a fable of a tree that had three roots, and unless these roots were watered by three women, the tree would not be kept

[1] This is a very interesting tribute to one of the worst-abused women of her time. Garrison, *Story*, vol. iii., p. 385, speaks of her "great dignity of carriage and unusual ability."

living, green, and beautiful. 'So,' said he, 'our tree
of immortal life cannot be fresh, green, and living unless its three roots, Home, State, and Church, receive
the influence and power of woman.'

"Mrs. Rose also spoke. She is far before any woman
speaker I ever heard. She is splendidly clear and logical.
She reasons thus :—

"I suppose you all grant that woman is a human
being. If she has a right to life she has a right to earn
a support for that life. If a human being, she has a
right to have her powers and faculties, as a human being,
developed. If developed, she has a right to exercise
them. The women who act in this great reform have
been stigmatised as 'strong-minded women,' and for
herself she accepted the stigma. If a gentleman flatters
a lady you may be sure he does not consider her one of
the 'strong-minded women.'—

"But, oh ! I cannot give any idea of the power and
beauty of her speech. I can only stammer about it a
little."

TO THE PORTERS

"Genoa Hollow, December 9, 1853.

"'Our way has been so delightfully pleasant, that we
almost fear we are not in that of the good old Pil-
grims ; but then, you know, "wisdom's ways are pleasant."' (Quoted from Miss Putnam's letter.)

"For the last three weeks, we (Mrs. Foster and myself) have been holding meetings continually. Giving
two lectures every day, and Sundays we give three, like
the famous 'Old Grimes's hen.'

"Mrs. Foster told me an anecdote of S. J. May that
will cause you to laugh, I know. One day a Methodist
minister walked into Mr. May's study. He wore a lugu-

brious visage, and taking a seat near Mr. May, began: 'Mr. May, I have thought it my duty for some time to call upon you and warn you of your danger. I regard you with a deep and tender love. There is no minister in this city whose *outward* life is so much like that of Christ's as yours is, but, you know, there is all the more danger. You hold dangerous errors, and if you do not renounce them your soul must be eternally lost. I have wept over you in secret places. Be entreated in time.'

" There is no end to the number of neat, quiet, serene Quaker families we have visited. At least I thought so until yesterday, when we left Friend Hutchinson's. He told us he was the last Quaker on this route and now we were to go among Presbyterians. Miss Putnam replied, 'Well, I have enjoyed visiting with my Quaker friends, but am now glad to go once more among my Presbyterian brethren.'

" Miss Putnam went on to say, 'We are received very kindly everywhere, our meetings are well attended, and I cannot but believe we are doing a great and good work. I am so grateful that at last I am doing something in this world.'

"In one of those moods of philosophical pleasantry and erudite whimsicality in which the worthy Archbishop of Dublin sometimes relapsed from weighty affairs, he is reported to have made the following quotation and comment:

" ' Old father long-legs would n't say his prayers,—
Take him by the right leg, take him by the left leg,
Take him fast by both legs, and throw him down·
    stairs.'

" ' There,' said his grace, ' in that nursery rhyme, you

9

may see an epitome of the history of all religious persecutions. Father long-legs, refusing to say the prayers that were dictated and ordered by his little tyrants, is regarded as a heretic and suffers martyrdom.'

" Parker Pillsbury says, ' The reason why the younger religious sects are not as cruel, oppressive, and persecuting as the older ones are, is because their teeth and claws are not yet grown.'

" I believe Maria takes the *Christian Inquirer.* If so I want her to send me the number that contains a letter from S. J. May, giving an account of the anti-slavery lecture I gave in Syracuse. I heard that he had written and I wish to see the letter.[1] I will receive it as a great favour if she will send it to Ithaca, where we shall be in ten days.

" Last evening we lectured in a high pulpit that for tallness will vie with the hills about the village. I assure you when once we reached it we occupied a commanding position.

" My dear Mrs. Porter, I hope you will excuse this silly letter. Bishop Heber said, ' None but the happy can talk nonsense.' If so, you will judge by this letter that I am at the summit of human felicity.

" I have no words to express how happy I am to find that my good opinion and hearty respect for Mrs. Foster does not at all abate, as I come to know her more, and to understand her spirit and character better. She is no ordinary character, but clear, beautiful, upright, with a sacred devotion to duty in the anti-slavery cause, and she is very lovely and agreeable in private life.

" This little village is a pleasant one, surrounded by high hills that seem to reach the sky ; reminding me of

---

[1] I have tried to look it up, but the only file of the *Inquirer* of which I am aware is in too distant private keeping to be made available.

Jack the Giant-Killer's bean-stalk. We are staying in a
nice Presbyterian family. They have never heard anti-
slavery lectures before. The eldest child, a young lady
of sixteen, is very promising, I think. She plays the
piano and sings delightfully. Miss Putnam returns
home in the course of a fortnight. I shall miss her very
much. She joins me in kindest regards to you all."

CHAPTER IX

FROM HOME TO HOME

THE year 1854 offered no temptations to the abolitionists to relax their efforts in behalf of a straightforward, thorough-going policy of anti-slavery reform. The dream which even many anti-slavery people permitted themselves to cherish after the compromises of 1850, was rudely shattered. The pro-slavery party did not rest content with the concessions it had won, but went on to other victories. May 22d saw the passage of the Nebraska Bill, which cancelled the Missouri Compromise and threw open to slavery 400,000 square miles of territory heretofore unpolluted by its noisome trail. To Stephen A. Douglas the nation was preëminently indebted for this action, which did much to make the issue clear, to exhibit the essential spirit of the pro-slavery party, and to make many say, " Something too much of this."

Another cause for ultimate gratitude was the rendition of Anthony Burns, a fugitive slave who was arrested in Boston, May 24th. The shame of that rendition did much to harden the anti-slavery tem-

per of many people in the North, and especially in
New England, to resist the growing insolence of the
slave-power and the increasing complacency of its
Northern apologists and allies.   But to the abolitionists it seemed—and there was much to justify
their opinion—that opposition to slavery-extension
was not only inferior to opposition to slavery, *per se,*
but that the former, adopted as a political principle,
tended to obscure the latter and to weaken it.
And so the abolitionists went on steadily with
their insistence that the Constitution was a pro-
slavery instrument, as the South believed, and as the
Free-Soilers, with their doctrine of the inviolability
of slavery in the slaveholding States, practically admitted.   Miss Holley's work for the year was of the
same general nature as before, and it is reflected in
her letters with those lights and shadows with which
it was diversified through all its course.

TO MISS PUTNAM

"ROCHESTER, Jan. 10, 1854.

"You have, I suppose, read reports of Mr. Phillips's
lecture.   One thing you may not have seen.   He said,
' Water-cure was not a modern discovery.   Charles Lamb
said, " It was neither a new nor a very good thing.   It
existed before the deluge and in Noah's time it killed
more than it cured."   To which a water-cure doctor
replied, " It saved all that were worth saving." '

"I accompanied Mr. Phillips to Mr. Hallowell's,
where we sat until he left for the cars, it being one
o'clock that same night.   In telling us of the Bazaar he
said Lydia Maria Child was there and wanted him to
buy a statuette of Calvin, saying, ' You ought, Mr. Phil-

lips; you are a Calvinist and believe in the Five Points.'
'How much is it?' said Mr. Phillips. 'Three dollars,'
replied Maria. 'Just sixty cents a point,' returned Mr.
Phillips. To which Mrs. Child said, 'And very dear at
that.'

"Mrs. Stowe was there one day and wished an intro-
duction to Mrs. Child, but Mrs. Child had gone home.
The next day when she came back, Mr. Phillips told her
about Mrs. Stowe's wishing to see her. Mrs. Child said,
'I don't want to see a lion.' Mr. Phillips replied, 'But
one lion may look upon another, I suppose.'"

" Lyons, Jan. 12, 1854.

"The people have expressed themselves surprised and
delighted with my lecture of Wednesday evening. An
audience of nearly six hundred. As I usually do, I felt
anxious before the lecture.

"This apprehensive state of mind which almost always
attacks me just before the lecture, is a great plague, a
devil that I long to cast out, but as yet have not the
power. I believe it is one of the kind that 'goeth not
out except by prayer and fasting.' To a person full of
composure and Christian sympathy, the perplexity I suffer about accepting or declining the invitation to Albany
would be astonishing. Last evening I was asked if I
would actually associate with blacks. When I said that
I had done it for years, the astonishment was extreme.
Oh, this anti-slavery movement is revealing the spirit of
Christianity with new power !

"Again I was told of Parker Pillsbury's 'bad temper.'
I said, 'Then why don't you mild-tempered people do
the work ? What do you leave this Christian work to
infidels for ?'

"On Tuesday evening I listened to a very able and

interesting lecture from Theodore Parker. His subject was ' The Progress of Mankind.' Speaking of the advance steps of each generation, he said, ' Franklin taught the lightning good manners ; taught it that when it came down it must not burn up the deacon's barn or the minister's house. We had sent it to school and taught it to read and write.' "

" Lyons, Jan. 18, 1854.

" ' This night I shall be in Paradise,' I involuntarily exclaimed as I arose this morning, in view of my taking this afternoon's train for Rochester. The memories of the past are sweet to me. But oh, how much happier and richer my life has been than I ever expected it would be ! The old story that is usually told to children was told me—that childhood was the happiest time of life ; ' the brightest days are young days,' etc. Lies, all of them. Dr. Channing's definition of a happy life was, ' Great efforts from great motives.' "

" Rochester, Jan. 24th.

" I have an invitation to a party this evening that quite surprises me. For since I have ' chosen to suffer affliction with the people of God, rather than enjoy the pleasures of sin for a season,' some of my old acquaintances don't know me.

" Professor Agassiz is lecturing here. He has been requested not to say anything in his lectures against the Bible. Mr. Channing has recently returned from Washington. He says no one for a long time has made so deep an impression in Washington as Gerrit Smith. Mr. Channing describes a speech of Mr. Smith's which he heard, as ' kingly and commanding.' "

" ' I 'm afloat ! I 'm afloat !
The world is my country
And the " cause " my bride.'—

" Such are my feelings this morning.   As I enter the
cars alone and see no familiar face, I often wonder if
the other women I see there are as cowardly as I am.
Oh, I am only an apology for a woman !   Oh for the
whole armour of Christianity, that panoply divine !

" I am now writing in a front ' upper chamber' of
Judge Cady's great, elegant house.[1]

" The Judge is eighty years of age.   It is beautiful to
look at him : so refined, so gentlemanly, so pure.   He
has a finely moulded head.   He is of the John Quincy
Adams type of man.   He has the appearance of one
who has always been obedient to the laws of temperance
and health.   Mrs. Cady tells me he has always been an
early riser and a great student.   He wished to resign his
office this winter, but his daughters urged him to continue one year longer and then he would have practised
law fifty years.   Mrs. Cady was a Livingstone and is a
sister of Gerrit Smith's mother.

" Sunday.—This morning I attended the Episcopal
church, built in memory of Sir William Johnson, who
lies in a vault under the church.   I was glad to find
that the Episcopalians pray for the ' captives and the
oppressed.' "

" EASTON, Feb. 21, 1854.

" I came to this place Saturday morning.   The
weather intensely cold.   Sunday afternoon I spoke in a

---

[1] Judge Cady was the excellent father of Elizabeth Cady Stanton.
Concerning him and her, see her *Eighty Years and More*, a most
vivacious book, published in 1898.

Gerrit Smith

fifty-year-old Quaker meeting-house to four hundred people. As usual in Quaker neighbourhoods, there is a feeling against taking a collection ; so I gave out word that any donations for the cause would be gratefully received, and the result was seven dollars. One old Quaker who seems to be thoroughly emancipated from sectarianism and its superstition, said to me that Quakers believed it a duty to minister to the necessity of saints, and taking a collection was the same thing."

" UNION VILLAGE, Mar. 1, 1854.

"Without cant or affectation I may exclaim that this evening has been to my soul a time of refreshing from the presence of the Lord. A large audience assembled to hear Frederick Douglass; seven o'clock came and no Douglass. Then seven-thirty, and still no Douglass. I was invited and urged to begin speaking. It seemed a pity to allow that large gathering to disperse without one anti-slavery word, especially those who had come for the first time to hear of the American slave's wrongs and outrages. No one felt a greater disappointment in Mr. Douglass's not coming than myself, yet when I thought of the cause of the slave-woman I could not find it in my heart to refuse my mite ; so I made a little speech, which, when I heard, as I afterwards did, the noble speech of Leonard Gibbs, of this place, seemed like the lispings of a child. My sustaining consideration was the probability that among the audience were those who, in anti-slavery truth and light and love, were only children, and it is said that sometimes children can impart to children an idea with better success than those of larger growth.

"To the first call, Mr. Gibbs, being in delicate health, did not respond, but the call was repeated,—warmly,

cordially repeated.   He rose and poured out such a living tide of breathing thought, and such searching, burning words, that it seemed to me the hearts of the people
fired, glowed, throbbed, and beat as the heart of one man.
One could feel the soul growing and expanding under
the divine influence.   It more than did credit to the
head of Mr. Gibbs ; it was high honour to his heart.
You know it is the glory of our natures to yield to the
incitement of its strong and tenderest sensibilities.

" It was not only that the speech was complete in its
circuit of thought, so grandly apropos to the present
time in this country's affairs ; not merely the lawyer-like
keenness, the subtlety and cunning of genius that took
captive my admiration.   I was exalted, elevated, trans-
lated by the noble humanity, the heavenly benevolence,
the great sympathy with the slave that filled, quickened,
and inspired, and shone from all parts of the speech.

" He repudiated the idea of opposing the Nebraska
Bill *because* it was a violation of the Compromise of 1820.
The Whig party had no love for the slave, neither had
the Democratic party, nor the other party.   The bill
must be objected to on higher grounds.   He dwelt with
power and pathos on the truth that no real, efficient anti-
slavery work will be done, unless based upon a living
sympathy for the suffering slave.   We must be fully
baptised into his wrongs, pierced with his woes ; take
him in our arms, and on the wings of love, hope, faith,
and prayer, bear him up towards happiness and God.

" He said of the Lemmon case that some Virginian,
aided by some Georgian slaveholders, were about to carry
the decision of the New York judge[1] up to the Supreme
Court of the United States.   And that five out of the

[1] Of the New York Court of Appeals.   The decision was that
slaves, as such, could not be brought into the State.

nine are slaveholders. 'And,' continued Mr. Gibbs, with
heightened emotion, 'if *my* freedom, so help me God,
were left to the decision of those five, or the Northern
four, I should take the five slaveholders, for I believe
they are not so corrupt, not so false to conscience, as the
Northerners.' "

TO THE PORTERS

" NORTH EASTON, PA., Mar. 8, 1854.

" Your sweet and friendly letter, my dear Mrs. Porter,
reached me yesterday, and was as grateful and refreshing
to my spirit ' as cold water to a thirsty soul.' But I
must hasten to tell you something of my Albany visit ;
I enjoyed being with my Uncle Orville very much. He
is feeling very happy in having Mr. Simmons in the
church. He says, 'the Orthodox people attempt to dig-
nify the doctrine of the Trinity with the name of Mystery, but there is no mystery about it. It is a plain
contradiction, a flat absurdity.' "

TO MISS PUTNAM

" PITTSTOWN, RENSSELAER Co., March 20, 1854.

" At the close of my meeting yesterday afternoon, held
in Friends' Meeting-house, an old withered crone of a
Quaker woman made her way up to me with the following : ' Is thee a married woman ? How old is thee ? Does
thee live in Massachusetts ? Thee resides with relations ? ' And for the thousandth time I answered those
questions. Don't you think it would save time and
trouble if I were to furnish the *Liberator* a list of questions that are constantly put to me, with all my answers,
and thus forestall future interrogations ?

" You would laugh to hear all the criticisms these
Quakers are guilty of regarding me. One said she

thought I dressed too gay ; another that I laughed too
much ; a third that I did not visit enough. A fourth
wished I would speak oftener, and a fifth said I did not
eat enough, and that I had large self-esteem. Still another said I ought not to receive money ; to her mind it
was just the same as a ' hireling ministry.' "

" MECHANICSVILLE, Mar. 24, '54.

" For the last few days I have understood more forcibly than I ever did what Parker Pillsbury means when
he subscribes his letters ' From a field-hand.' The rough-
and-tumble kind of a life the anti-slavery lecturer experiences is equalled by few, I imagine. Yesterday
morning I had a fine ride perched up on a high-seated
lumber waggon. The recent snow looked pure and
beautiful. In consequence of a break in the road, most
of our way lay through fields and woods, the fences
having been opened for that purpose. The fields were
large, and our solitary waggon going through the wide
waste of snow, at once suggested the idea of ocean, and
when we met a waggon (as we did) it seemed like one
ship at sea meeting another.

" Saturday.—My first lecture in Mechanicsville has been
given. It was in the Methodist meeting-house. After
I had concluded, a man arose and said, ' If what we have
heard is infidelity I am an infidel.' After he took his
seat the Presbyterian minister rose and passed some
compliments on my lecture, but said I did not do justice
to the church and ministry ; that the Northern Methodist Church had separated from the Southern on account
of slavery. Then the first man got up and replied triumphantly, showing that it was the South which separated, and that 27,000 slaves were still held by Northern
Methodists.

" After we came home, my host said of a man in this
village, 'He is an excellent abolitionist ; to be sure
politically he is pro-slavery.' 'And ecclesiastically ?' I
said. 'Why, yes, I believe so,' was his reply. 'Then,'
said I, 'he *must* be an excellent abolitionist.'"

" MILTON, ULSTER CO., N. Y., April 15, 1854.

" Some people's influence in this world upon me is to
congeal me into a solid, stolid, flesh-and-blood statue.
Others are like the mild sun : melting, opening, warming,
ripening, making happy, inspiring joy. This latter influence is that of Sarah Hallock. She grows upon my
admiration and love every hour. I will attempt giving
you some of her sayings, but you will lose the spirit and
sparkle of them :

" ' After hearing Wendell Phillips lecture on the
"Lost Arts" I wanted to write him, telling him most
gratefully that he had relieved my mind of a difficulty that had troubled it from a child. That was how
Cinderella could dance in glass slippers, they must be
so stiff : but Mr. Phillips tells us the ancients had the
art of rendering glass pliable ! Of course that solves the
difficult problem.'

" Yesterday as we were in the parlour, I admired a
little plaster image of a boy and said, 'I am happy to
find them all around, they are so pretty.' 'Yes,' she
responded, 'they are cheap poetry for the people.'

" Talking of the amiable self-admiration of the Philadelphia abolitionists, she said they all seemed to be in a
state of beatification all the time ; some making speeches
and others admiring them.

" Once she said, 'Where do you find words ? If I
knew anything, I have n't words to tell it. I should die of
suppressed knowledge,' "

"N. BUFFALO, May 29, 1854.

"In the lightning express I left Adrian at noon, and at Toledo went on board the delightful steamer *Western Metropolis*. The afternoon was very lovely, and I thought as I sat on deck by myself, looking around, above, below, that I never knew before the exceeding fascination of the ever-varying hues and changing aspects of sky and water. The shore was full of the young summer foliage, the trees bewitching in their fresh, tender green. How eloquent is the resurrection of the outward world of that more beautiful resurrection, that we all cannot help believing in, of the human life out of flesh and blood into the immortal spiritual world!

"On the *Metropolis* I was amused to see posted up in various places that no *gentleman* must go to bed with his boots on, and that, if he does, he shall pay five dollars. It reminded me of the notice [at Clifton Park, Niagara Falls], 'Visitors are particularly requested not to tease and poke the buffalos.' What comments on our civilisation!"

CHAPTER X

KEEPING RIGHT ON

" Still nursing the unconquerable hope,
Still clutching the inviolable shade
With a free onward impulse."
MATTHEW ARNOLD.

FROM May, 1854, until September, 1855, there is a gap in Miss Holley's correspondence, which represents either a temporary rest from her exhausting work, or such steady enjoyment of Miss Putnam's companionship as deprived her of the incitement which that beloved friend, when absent, always afforded her expansive sympathy ; yet hardly more than the Porters. It will, moreover, be noticed that the letters for the years included in this chapter, 1855–58, as in the next succeeding, are disproportionately few compared with those of the earlier years in which she did " the work of an evangelist." Often, possibly, when she had most to tell, her whole head was weary and her whole heart faint with the way she had come and its possible incidents of disappointment with herself or the imperfect sympathy of others. If she had had the skill of some to economise the more doleful elements of her experience,

143

we should have had many a vivid page where now we have a blank. But the pleasant side of her apostolate impressed her much more than the other, to say nothing of her indisposition to be a bearer of ill-tidings. To share her happiness with her friends was much more to her taste than to communicate her petty miseries.

The years 1855–58 were " significant of much " for the anti-slavery conflict. They saw the Republican party taking shape and rolling up a vote of 1,341,264, only 500,000 less than the vote for Buchanan, and 500,000 more than that for Millard Fillmore, Miss Holley's Unitarian coreligionist, with whom she could not take the sacramental bread and wine. (So strict were her total abstinence principles that the wonder is she did not always content herself with " communion in one kind.") The year of the election, 1856, saw " the crime against Kansas " in full tide and Sumner struck down in the Senate-chamber for rebuking that crime in words that hurt like blows. It is easy to see that, however Miss Holley might doubt the logic of the Republican position and deprecate the cowardice which demanded in the party platform neither the repeal of the Fugitive Slave Law nor the abolition of slavery in the District of Columbia, she found herself from year to year in livelier personal sympathy with the most ardent and efficient leaders of the Republican party. It may be surmised that her father's connection with the Liberty party (as yet unnamed in 1840) made her a more genial critic of political anti-slavery than she would otherwise have been, and that she was drawn to Garrison and his party less by the logic of their principles than by the spirit in which they engaged in their propagation and defence. Colonel Higginson, who was averse to Garrison's non-resistance and disunion logic, has told how much more stimulating the meetings of the Garrisonians were than those of the " New Organisation," so that it was necessary for the adherents of the latter to attend the meetings of the former, where they would get a new supply of coals from off the altar for their lips. It was his privilege to feel himself at home in either house and always welcome, even by Stephen Foster, who said at a convention meeting in Worcester, " I love my friend Higginson, but if there is anything I loathe it is his opinions."

TO MRS. PORTER

" ABINGTON, Aug. 2, '55.

" I was very happy to receive your beautiful letter of July Fourth, and if my answer only gives you half the joy I had from yours, it will be more than I dare hope.

" One week ago last Tuesday we left the home of that noble woman, Abby K. Foster, for Boston. Wednesday we visited Mount Auburn where is the Torrey monument, inscribed to the shame of Maryland and the honour of the man whose remains repose beneath it. It bears a faithful and valuable testimony to the thousands of visitors who flock to Mount Auburn.

" Here too lies the beloved Channing, and on a new part of the ground, on a pretty eminence, not far from the Tower, as we were strolling about, we came most unexpectedly in view of a handsome monumental stone with a woman's face in pure white upon it. The ex-
10

quisite chiselling instantly attracted us, and as we came nearer, the name of MARGARET FULLER OSSOLI appeared. The head is a most admirable one, and we wondered as we looked upon its fine and noble development,' and on her face, full of character, generous enthusiasm, and high aspiration, that she should be spoken of as plain-looking. I thought of what the *New York Tribune* said of the bust of Wendell Phillips, ' It will be difficult for posterity to believe that such a head belonged to a bad person.'

"As we had not heard of a stone being erected here to her memory, this burst upon us with most agreeable surprise. As we stood there thinking of her truth, strength, and nobleness, I felt the impulse of a quickened and newer life, as if I would make a fresher struggle after all self-improvement. No other presence or memory in Auburn had this effect upon me so powerfully as did hers. The little Angelo is at last buried here, but the sea still holds his father and mother.

"On Thursday evening, as Mr. and Mrs. Garrison, Miss Putnam, and myself were sitting in their parlour, a little after nine o'clock, there was a very gentle ring at the door-bell. It was a rainy night and Mr. Phillips had come to spend the night in a fraternal sort of way, with his 'frantic friend' Mr. Garrison, his own house being shut up for the season—his family staying in Lynn. He was on his return from giving his lecture on the ' Duty of Scholars '—to identify themselves with the reforms of their age—at Dartmouth College.

---

[1] A phrenological word and one of many in Miss Holley's letters. Phrenology furnished a convenient set of pigeon-holes for those who were assorting mental traits. Henry Ward Beecher availed himself of them in a very liberal manner, and so at one time did the alienist-reformer Pliny Earle.

"Mr. Garrison humorously inquired if there were 'Gods many, Lords many' there, in reference to President Lord.[1] Mr. Phillips replied, 'Yes, there were seven Lords there, sons of the Doctor.' On his way to Dartmouth he met a friend who said to him, 'For once, Mr. Phillips, I hope you will not be *on the Lord's side.*'

"Mr. Phillips was at breakfast with us next morning, and so quiet and gentle and beautiful in his manners and conversation and whole presence, that I said to Miss Putnam, 'It seems as if we had breakfasted with an angel.

"We made a call of several hours on Dr. Harriot K. Hunt. 'My little doctor,' as Miss Bremer called her, is a lively and entertaining person. She gave us a droll account of the 'Presbyterian Sunday' in Oberlin. She was at the house of Prof. Cowles. After the two long sermons, and before the evening lecture, Prof. Cowles announced their usual custom of family religious service, inviting Mrs. Severance, who was with Dr. Hunt, to pray. She excused herself, saying that she was a Quaker in regard to prayer, praying silently. Then he asked Miss Hunt, who replied, 'I am a Swedenborgian, and we never use any other than the Lord's Prayer.' She could say that if he liked. Then they all repeated in turn some verse from the Bible. 'Such doleful selections,' said Dr. Hunt, 'such as " Howl, ye waste places of Jerusalem ! " ' 'When it came my turn,' she said, 'I thought I should be suffocated with the awful solemnity if I did n't do something to turn the tide of lugubrious sentiment ; so I must out with " Bless the Lord, O my soul, and all that is within me bless his holy name ! " If a cannonball had been shot through the room the effect could not have been more startling.'

[1] A notable apologist for slavery.

"At the Athenæum we saw the superb bronze statue of Beethoven, which has recently been added to the gallery of sculpture. At the library we pored with delight over the fascinating volumes of Audubon's birds. There was one dear picture of a Jenny Wren and her family—their nest in an old hat with the top all out. It was the house wren and as natural as life.

"Mr. Garrison took us to the studio of the artist who is executing the bust of Mr. Phillips, in marble. Mr. Garrison expects it will yet grace Faneuil Hall. Shame on the Bostonians that they do not spontaneously delight to honour this truest and most eloquent advocate of Liberty in their midst!

"Yesterday we celebrated West India Emancipation. Mr. Edmund Quincy did his admirable presiding, and also spoke exceedingly to my satisfaction.

"The occasion was so blissful that I could fervently feel,

   "'My willing soul would stay
   In such a frame as this.'"

"FELTONVILLE, Sept. 24, 1855.

"You will be interested to know I saw Miss Sarah Pugh the other day. She was attending the Woman's Rights Convention and visiting Mrs. Follen.

"The convention opened on Wednesday morning under the personal auspices of Mrs. Paulina Wright-Davis, Mrs. C. H. Dall,[1] Mrs. Severance, Dr. Channing (son of Dr. W. E. Channing), Mr. Higginson, Dr. Harriot K. Hunt, to say nothing of Mr. Wendell Phillips on the business

[1] Caroline Healey Dall, a valued friend and correspondent of Theodore Parker, author of many books, and full of serious reminiscences of the Transcendentalists and their contemporaries. Born June 22, 1822.

committee. The morning session, so often dry, was filled
out plump with interesting matter. Dr. Hunt, who is
round and short and merry, took us home to tea. There
we met Miss Sarah Grimké, Elizabeth Peabody, Mrs.
Davis, Mrs. Severance, and others, and had a very
agreeable time.

" Miss Putnam was very grand and happy to take cold
water by the side of Miss Peabody and to be her audience at the tea-table. I had never seen her before. All
that is said of crushed bonnets, disorderly hair, poverty
of dress, every conceivable negligence of arrangement, is
literally true. Yet, the childlike innocence in the face,
the rare and exquisite grace of expression that the thought
comes clothed in from her lips, make a mantle of decen-
cies ample enough to cover crushed bonnet and tumble-
down hair.

" Of all the women who spoke, Mrs. Dall most thrilled
and interested me. Everything she said indicated culture
and genius ; with noble thought and solemn consecration.
She reminded me of Margaret Fuller. [Whom Mrs. Dall
knew very well and whose conversations she has reported.]
Mrs. Davis was graceful and beautiful in a blue satin
dress. Mrs. Severance always looks pleasing and lady-
like. Miss Brown, Mrs. Blackwell,[1] Susan B. Anthony,
Mr. Garrison, Mr. Higginson, all spoke during the course
of the convention ; but Mr. Phillips's speech surpassed
all others in power and in pertinence.

" The last evening Ralph Waldo Emerson addressed
the convention. Mr. Phillips exalted me. Mr. Emerson
entertained me. The convention closed with a poem by
Mrs. E. Oakes Smith. She is a lady of fifty. She was

---

[1] Lucy Stone, who married H. B. Blackwell, but kept her maiden
name. Miss Brown (Antoinette L.) married Mr. Blackwell's brother,
George.

dressed in a very thin white muslin, with four embroidered flounces edged with pink taste ; low neck and bare arms, a very thin white scarf pinned on the shoulders with gold arrows. Two bracelets on each arm, an immense pin on her bosom, and her hands glistening with rings. Her head rigged in the latest fashion. There was a perceptible shock of surprise when she made her appearance. She seemed like a picture out of an old novel.[1] Some of the women-reformers almost wept at this conclusion of the grave and important deliberations and discussions. 'She is a self-intoxicated woman,' said Elizabeth Peabody to me as we left the hall. I laughed myself nearly into fits over it.

"The last day of the convention we dined at Mrs. Garrison's with Mrs. Follen and her son Charles. She is a lovely old lady.

" After Dr. Channing's beautiful speech, Miss Peabody said she felt moved to rise and make a speech. She was very glad a son of Dr. Channing had spoken. This was a cause she had drunk in with her mother's milk.

" Miss Putnam and I left Boston Saturday and came to these kind anti-slavery people, who make us fully at home in their comfortable farmhouse. Here is a peach orchard with thirty varieties. Apples, tomatoes, and grapes, and not a pig on the premises. A woodchuck is being cooked for dinner !—the first meat cooked in the house since we came. They are almost purely vegetarians, which quite suits us. We have been sitting before an open fire, with bright brass andirons, which was very pleasant as well as very comfortable. With kind love for you all."

[1] Later we shall find this mercurial woman, who had, it seems, " a soul above buttons," visiting Miss Holley in Virginia and giving a very interesting and appreciative account of her work.

" To-day is really the twenty-sixth, but I thought it would be a pleasant little fiction to fancy it the twenty-fifth, so I could wish you a 'Merry Xmas.'

"Yesterday was very grum and scowling ; raining, sleeting, and snowing ; evidently 'got up' for the occasion ; while this morning we were not only greeted with the ordinary 'heavenly light of day,' but every shrub and tree and grass-blade glistened gloriously with the frozen sleet. Not even Rachel with her girdle of pearls was arrayed like these.

" I see by the papers that Mr. Thackeray is going West to lecture, and I cannot wish you a greater happiness, I am sure, than that you may hear him. Two weeks ago he gave his charming lecture on George III. in Worcester. Miss Putnam says she shall always esteem it one of the best fortunes of her life that she heard it. Unfortunately I was away lecturing and so missed it. She says it was altogether what he characterised the 'Selwyn Letters,'—'very pleasant.' He spoke of 'the amiable Miss Burney,' and of Cowper as the ' trembling pietist.' The chief grace of Mr. Thackeray's style to Miss Putnam was the absence of all exaggerating epithets ; nothing of the Yankee 'eternal, everlasting, and thundering big.' He treated with great tenderness and pathos the last miserable years of the poor, stupid old king.

" It is no wonder that he was specially invited to repeat this delightful lecture in Tremont Temple, Boston, which would afford so many more people a chance to hear it than were present in the small hall where he first gave it, with others of the series, ' The Four Georges.'

" I think you would be amused at the little snatches of conversation we overhear in the street—how constantly and unvaryingly the theme is dollars and cents, here in

Yankee-land. Even gentlemanly and scholarly Mr. Hoar, who presided, and introduced Mr. Thackeray at the lecture, in a few remarks, when he meant to say 'several thousand volumes,' tripped and said 'dollars,' instead. Miss Putnam said he looked chagrined all the evening, as if he were legitimately spiked for a satirical passage in some future 'Notes on America.'

"Mr. Thackeray's very grey hair is quite remarkable for a man but forty-three years of age. He has a fine, large physique, and only disappoints you by a somewhat insignificant nose,[1] which someone has called 'the index of the will,' 'the rudder of the character'; arguing that if one has a snub, or any sort of a nose beneath the standard one, therein lies the secret of indecision, and other faults pertaining to the character ; so, if this philosophy obtains, we may yet hear little bursts of mortification finding vent in the exclamation, 'Oh, my nose !'

"We lately chanced to make a rarely agreeable acquaintance with Mr. Abram Firth and his pleasant family. He has a cultivated taste in literature, pictures, etc. He read us very choice passages that he loved, from Southey, Mrs. Jameson, Humboldt, Steele, and others. I was much delighted with Browning's 'Pied Piper,' which I did not know before. Mr. Firth is a native of England, and there was an air of English comfort about everything around him. There are in the library little statuettes of Dante, Tasso, Ariosto, and Petrarch. This happened while we were there, and it diverted Mr. Firth

---

[1] Miss Holley was evidently not aware that it had suffered an injury like Michael Angelo's, which suggested Thackeray's pseudonym, Michael Angelo Titmarsh. Staying with George Ticknor and getting sentimental, he suddenly pulled himself up with the exclamation, "How absurd for two such broken-nosed old fellows as we are to be talking sentiment !" From which it would appear that Ticknor, too, had been unfortunate.

considerably : A Quaker countrywoman had rode with
her husband and little boy five miles to my lecture, which
was to be at five o'clock Sunday evening. These people
were seated in the library to warm themselves, when the
woman, looking about, remarked the statuettes and addressed Mr. Firth with the question,

"'Is thee a Catholic ?' innocently adding, 'I see thee
has some saints here.'

"Mr. and Mrs. Firth kindly expressed a strong liking
for my style of lecturing, and I held three good meetings
in their vicinity, they taking me in a snug covered buggy
and returning after the lecture.   They are earnest Unitarians and Mr. Firth has built a pleasant hall where he
invites different ministers to preach and teach.   I met
Rev. E. E. Hale there last summer [1] and heard him
preach.

"These people and their pleasant, attractive home
show how genial and graceful life may be to those who
know how to make it so."

" BEAR SWAMP, TOMPKINS COUNTY, N. Y.,
Dec. 6, 1856.

"We are now staying with a very kind anti-slavery
family, close by the famous ' Bear Swamp,' though I believe only two bears were ever actually trapped there by
the early settlers.

"Did you read an article [by Charles A. Dana] in a
recent *New York Weekly Tribune*, headed 'The Art of
Living '? If so you can sympathise with the itinerant
lecturer's life.   I rejoiced to see such an article in the

---

[1] Then or soon after deeply interested, with Eli Thayer of Worcester,
where Mr. Hale was then preaching, in the New England Emigrant
Aid Society for the free settlement of Kansas, concerning which Mr.
Thayer has written (1889) *The Kansas Crusade*, a sadly egotistic
book, in honour preferring himself above all others.

Tribune, as it may help to cleanse and smooth the pillow, purify the table, and sweeten the air of the sleeping-rooms for some of the victimised fraternity. It is evidently the extorted expression of the experience of some live lecturer during the recent election campaign.

"All this region of our State seems rich with fertile farms and great orchards. We hear a good deal about this being a year of scarcity, but hardly know what it means, as we see tables abounding in delicious sweet baked apples, preserved peaches, pears, plums, raspberries, blackberries, currants, cherries, and white honey, pickled fruits of all kinds in quantities undreamed of in dear, frugal New England.

"All these are often pressed upon us with such large hospitality that sometimes when asked, 'What will you take next?' we are tempted to exclaim with the man in the story, 'If you please, we 'll take breath.'

"Sleighing began last Monday and the exchange from waggons to sleighs is very agreeable. In the last week we have changed houses, people, beds, and tables six times. We have been kindly welcomed to Methodist homes, by excellent Presbyterians, then at a 'Come-outer's' house, in a Universalist family, and to-day with the Baptists.

"Nearly all the Methodists are strongly attached to the former editor of the *Northern Christian Advocate*,—Rev. William Hosmer, who has become the object of Methodist pro-slavery hate and persecution. He was to preach in Dryden, Sunday morning, but was detained at Andover with fever and ague. I spoke there in the afternoon to a crowded house."

"Farmersville, Cattaraugus Co., N. Y., July 13, 1857.

"It is a fortnight since I rejoined Miss Putnam, to whom I gave messages from you. To the last, she responds, that the peacock is in fine feather, constantly on parade, exhibiting that 'pride goeth before a fall.' A few days ago he was caught exercising his valour in an extraordinary manner. Like all cowardly bullies (if the phrase can be applied to so genteel a presence), he takes advantage of unguarded weakness and goes to strangling the young turkeys and tossing them over his conceited head, which had, after all, sense enough in it to feel his own meanness, for, when caught at his trick, he sneaked off quite conscious, and was not seen for a day or two. 'The shafts of contempt can pierce even a tortoise shell,' says the Persian proverb. The young boy is already subsidised to pick up the feathers as his Glory-ship drops them, and what will be his loss, shall be Maria's gain.

"The quiet retirement here is vastly agreeable to me, and I have already accomplished more reading than I usually do in months elsewhere. The fields around here are red with ripe strawberries. I went out and picked several quarts. The absence of all company here gives me something of Charles Lamb's feeling when he declared he had an estate in Time. It is a very pleasant feeling. Yesterday morning Miss Putnam and I took a ride of fourteen miles before the dew was off the grass, to Cuba,[1] where I gave an anti-slavery lecture."

TO MR. PORTER

"FARMERSVILLE, CATTARAUGUS Co., N. Y., Sept. 3, 1857.

"I was very sorry your errand after poor Henry Dixon proved bootless. How shameful is the exultation of the

---

[1] And where the plain hospitality of the widow Bruce (mother of Mrs. Teller, wife of Senator Teller of Colorado) was a variation of the ever-shifting scene, from the clover in which Misses Holley and Putnam were wading deep at Farmersville and Bear Swamp.

pro-slavery press, and how mean and despicable to cite his insane wish to remain in slavery as a proof of the content of the slave! All summer I have faithfully discoursed, to the best of my ability, what anti-slavery I know to the people in this part of the State. Some complain that I lecture as though they were not anti-slavery. Can we call New York a free State so long as she does not exert the disposition and ability to redress the outrage upon her citizens, who are kidnapped and kept in slavery twelve years, as in the case of poor Solomon Northrup, and this more recent case of Henry Dixon with its sad and fearful termination?

"The other Sunday afternoon we happened to arrive at the meeting-house before the Methodist Class Meeting was over. The minister asked me to 'express my feelings.' I said, My feelings were that the Methodist Church could not be a Christian church while holding, as she does, many thousands of God's dear children as property,—keeping them on a level with the brute beast. The whole manner of the minister was as much as to say, If anybody had such unreasonable feelings as these, it would be more convenient for him if she would keep them to herself. He only said, however, that we had not time to discuss the administration of the church. To which I insisted, 'But it is the gospel of Christ.'

"A week or two ago at a common-school celebration in this village, the County Superintendent invited me to address the children. Accordingly I told them of the slave-children of this country, who are not allowed to learn to read or write or spell or commit to memory the multiplication table which they had just repeated so well. Whereupon two Buchanan men rose up and left in high indignation that 'an abolition lecture was poked on them.' I am very sorry to even seem rude and 'fanatical,' but know not how to avoid it and be faithful to the cause of the slave. In fact, nothing else is so important and proper for all occasions, to be talked of, as the slave and his cause.

"It would be most fitting in every sermon, every oration, every prayer, to remember earnestly the astounding fact, that *Christian* America to-day holds four million men, women, and children in slavery!"

TO MRS. PORTER.

"EXETER, N. H., Mar. 18, 1858.

"I need not assure you that your letter of February 25th was a joy and a charm to me. And your good husband's postscript amused and pleased me much. How I wish you could write often to me!

"Last Sunday we were in Haverhill, Massachusetts. It was a beautiful, spring-like day, and an anti-slavery friend called for us, and took us to Groveland, in a chaise, to hear Mr. Wasson [1] preach. Mr. Wasson was educated in the Calvinistic faith, but has emerged with great thanksgiving. The sermon was full of power and interest.

" The subject was the beneficence and love of God, and retribution ; showing how friendly to us all is the discipline of life and how impossible it is for us to escape the suffering which *must* always follow ignorance and vice. That all this suffering was merciful, and worked out the purification of the spirit.

"Mr. Wasson relies upon his consciousness of God and an immortal life, and while he trusts calmly and

[1] David Atwood Wasson, who at a later period took up Theodore Parker's ministry with great power and vision but too little health. He was a man of great philosophic and poetical genius and tragical experience. The story of his life was written by O. B. Frothingham.

gladly, he lives energetically.   I have met with few
persons who discerned spiritual things so clearly, and
regard my meeting with him as a great blessing.   I feel
a stronger purpose that my life shall come more fully
under the control of great and ennobling ideas.

"We are now in Exeter, that has been so long noted
for its Phillips Academy where so many Honourables have
graduated, among them the lamented and lamentable
Daniel Webster.   The Hon. Amos Tuck has his residence here and is among those who welcome me and
my mission.   They seem newly revived to this effort or
crusade against conservatism, and wonderfully chival-
rous about getting a woman to speak in an orthodox
lecture-room of a Sunday in this old, aristocratic, evangelical town.

"Dear Samuel J. May!   I am glad you have had him
to preach in Rochester.   The other day I was amused
when a lady told me that Mr. Alcott said, 'Mr. May
had too much humanity to enter upon the divine life.'"[1]

TO THE PORTERS

"BOSTON, Mar. 26, 1858.

"Last Friday evening the Tremont Temple was nearly
filled to hear the fourteenth lecture of the anti-slavery
course, by Henry Wilson, the new senator of Massachusetts.   Charles Sumner sat on the platform near him.
Mr. Sumner is a very handsome, gentlemanly man.   He
was most enthusiastically cheered by that immense audience on his entrance with Mr. Wilson, and also when
Mr. Wilson spoke of the honour he had of standing side
by side in the Senate with one 'who brought genius,

[1] This dubious oracle may have meant that Mr. May thought " the
divine life" as lived by Mr. Alcott lacking in " humanity," and especially in consideration for the maintenance and comfort of Mrs.
Alcott, a sister of Mr. May.

generous learning, and principle to the altar of anti-slavery.'

"After Mr. Wilson had heightened our expectation by the manly and noble declaration with which he began the lecture, he was suddenly interrupted by a rush of blood to his head, and as his physician thought it imprudent for him to resume, the lecture will be given on a future evening. It is expected he will make a clean breast of it and give his highest and best convictions, all living and warm, in behalf of humanity.

"Last week a Board meeting of the American Anti-Slavery Society was held here in Francis Jackson's parlours. It was called at the wish of Mrs. Stowe, who was present, and, as Mr. Jackson said, 'Two things were transacted here that day. One was, Mrs. Stowe's donating two hundred and sixty-five dollars to the Tract Fund, and the other, Mr. Parker Pillsbury's appointment as agent for Great Britain by the committee.'

"Mrs. Stowe urged that there should be a tract written on the Bible in reference to slavery. 'But,' said Mr. Garrison, 'the Bible is held as confidently by the slaveholders to be on their side, as we abolitionists hold it to be on ours. Still,' he continued, 'we have no objection, and if you will find the person to write it, we will print it.' 'My brother must write it,' said Mrs. Stowe.[1]

"Tell Maria I have ordered my beautiful painting, *Humanity*, to be sent by express to Rochester to her. She must keep it until I come."[2]

---

[1] Her brother Charles wrote it and it was published by the Society.

[2] This painting was one of the most precious of her possessions. It represents a beautiful woman holding a white and a black child with equal tenderness. It may be seen in the illustration representing her school-room arranged in a highly characteristic manner by Miss Putnam for the celebration of some memorable day.

" Day before yesterday we left Boston, dear delightful
Boston, for a month or more, and wended our way
hither through a variety of town, village, and farming
country, glimpsing, as we passed along, many sweet
landscapes, well worthy the artist's pencil.   Among
these, Walden Pond, on whose banks Thoreau *hermited*,
and where on some forenoons he sat in his hut door, in
such a near communion with God and Nature that his
' soul grew like corn in a summer night.'   And immediately after, we halted at old Concord, where, on the nineteenth of April, '75, that shot was fired, ' heard round the
world,' as Emerson sings, and as Bancroft quotes in his
last historical volume.   There too, since Mr. Sumner
was beaten, the church bells do not mockingly ring the
national jubilee of Freedom on the Fourth of July, but
keep stern and reproving silence.   What a sin and shame
it is that Mr. Sumner should be obliged again to seek a
foreign land for health so barbarously prostrated by the
slave-power of the country !   And so, on we came
through pleasant valleys, green woods, with here and
there the finest prospect of upland, stretching away
and up to the distant horizon, till at length, Monadnock,
in his grand and massive strength, appeared to us in a
succession of views for miles of our shifting progress.
At last we cross the river and are in the State of the
Green Mountains, where I am to lecture a month or
more.

" The event of most memorable note while we were in
Boston, was the funeral of Ellis Gray Loring.[1] He was a
gentleman of the highest social position, fortune, culture,

---

[1] Born in Boston, April 14, 1803 ; died May 24, 1858. The con-
text gives his standing.

and of the rarest conscience.   He heartily and nobly espoused the anti-slavery cause in its earliest and most despised day.   Very touching and eloquent were the tributes paid to his memory by Wendell Phillips and Mr. Garrison in the Anti-Slavery Convention in Boston.

"The funeral services were publicly held in James Freeman Clarke's church.   We arrived early.   All who came in seemed moved by a very near and friendly respect and affection for the dead.   Miss Putnam says she 'never saw or imagined such dignified sorrow, such tender friendship, such profound religious faith, such absolute consolation.'   It was indeed a hallowed hour.

"Rev. Mr. Bowen read the Sermon on the Mount.   I never heard it read with more touching and consoling power.   It came home to the heart with a fresher, higher meaning than ever before, and the deepest conviction of its immortal truth.   Here was one for whom those divine beatitudes seemed no exaggeration, whose life had been a perpetual fragrance, whose memory was blessed. Then a few voices in the choir chanted the Twenty-third Psalm, and a sense of those words of calm trust and holy joy seemed to sink into all souls with an uplifting power. Mr. Clarke read a short but feeling portraiture of the character of his friend and closed by asking any others of Mr. Loring's friends present to speak.   Mr. Josiah Quincy, Jr., rose in his seat and spoke so tenderly and truly, with great tears in his eyes, of 'his most intimate friend for thirty-six years.'   He saw him daily and never knew him to do an act, or speak a word, or, so far as he knew, think a thought, that in such an hour as this he could regret.   Then he recited, with beautiful effect, a passage on immortality, from Wordsworth, which he said Mr. Loring repeated to him during their very first interview.

11

" There also sat Mrs. Lydia Maria Child, Mr. Phillips, Mrs. Chapman, Edmund Quincy, Francis Jackson, and many other personal friends. What sacred memories stirred those hearts ; what new vows to duty were made ; what renewal there was of faith in the everlasting realities of Justice, Truth, and Virtue ; what confirmation of hope in God and heaven !   All this I was inexpressibly grateful to feel.

" I quite yearn to hear how you all do this summer. Accept my kind love for you all, and oh, how delightful it would be to get a long letter from you ! "

CHAPTER XI

THE CROWNING QUALITY

" Endurance is the crowning quality,
And patience all the passion of great hearts."
LOWELL.

" THE crest of time now reached by the abolition movement after the lapse of a full generation was the Pisgah outlook over the Promised Land of universal emancipation." So write the Garrison sons, who have told with so much amplitude and exactness the *Story* of their father's life, when they come to the year 1859. But their figure of speech is not in strict accordance with the facts. There were many who in 1859 foresaw disunion, but few imagined that it was less than two years away, and of these a part believed that a separate slavocracy would have many years of morbid growth and lingering decay before the inevitable end. The logic of events was moving steadily on either side to some great consummation. Buchanan's administration was only two days old when (March 6, 1857) the Dred Scott decision of the Supreme Court had affirmed, in Judge Taney's words, that black men,

" either socially or politically, had no rights which
white men were bound to respect," and this succinct
expression of the force of the decision furnished the
Republicans with one of their most effective party
cries during the next three years. In Kansas the
miserable struggle between Slavery and Freedom for
the possession of the State went on with rival incidents of extreme barbarity, those of John Brown's
" Pottawatomie executions "—called by the less humorous, " massacres "—not easily outdone ; while
the National Government lent itself with tolerable
consistency to the pro-slavery side. No wonder that
Lincoln, in June, 1858, found the nation to be " a
house divided against itself," and declared it could
not stand, that " it must be all slave or all free " ;
and that Seward on the following October 25th had
announced an " irrepressible conflict between opposing forces." A tremendous impetus was given to the
practical energy of these sentiments by the John
Brown affair of Harper's Ferry, October 16 and 17,
1859. The Old Testament hero's assurance that " it
would pay " in any event was fully justified. It was
the most important factor operating in the political
complications of the next presidential year. It made
so tense the bond of Democratic party-union that it
broke and made Lincoln's election possible by a
popular *minority* of about one million votes.

The abolitionists had little difficulty in adjusting
themselves to the situation. Non-resistants they
might be and generally were, following the lead of
Garrison ; but, when a fight was on, they had as
little hesitation in choosing the better part as if they

were habitually men of war. At a public meeting
on the evening of John Brown's death, Garrison
said : " I am prepared to say, Success to every slave-
insurrection at the South and in every slave country.
And I do not see how I compromise or stain my
peace-profession in making that declaration. Whenever there is a contest between the oppressed and
the oppressor . . . God knows that my heart
must be with the oppressed and always against the
oppressor." A man whose words for thirty years
had been half-battles hardly needed to justify himself by this wary plea. There can be little doubt
that Miss Holley entered readily into his conception
of the situation.[1] All the great events of 1859 and
1860 must have shaken her heart as they went by,
terrible as the kings which Macbeth saw upon the
witches' heath. Doubtless the sense of an approaching crisis nerved her to go on if she was ever
tempted to give over the unequal struggle. Nothing could be simpler than the temper of her mission. She remembered those in bonds as bound
with them. She felt in her own sympathetic flesh
their wounds, in her own side their aches and pains
of separation and contempt.   Finding the way
often wearisome, she had great compensations for
its defects and miseries : her lines often fell to her
in pleasant places, and few women have ever been
more rich in friends or been more deserving of their
love.

[1] On the day following John Brown's raid, she thanked God in
the prayer before her lecture at Ellsworth, Maine, for John Brown's
heroic deed.

"WOONSOCKET, R. I., Feb. 28, 1859.

"This morning I give an hour to you, dear Mrs. Porter, who are oftener in my thoughts than you may imagine. This month we have spent with (when I was not
in surrounding villages lecturing) a very dear circle of
friends in Worcester, who have taken us to rare lectures,
entertainments of music, pictures, libraries, skating parties, etc. For instance, the evening we reached Worcester,
an omnibus had been chartered to take a party of admir-
ers to hear Mr. Emerson's grand lecture on 'Fate' in
Grafton, eight miles away, and we were made warmly
welcome to go. Returning we had the wise presence and
talk of Mr. Emerson himself, who was added to the
company.

"But the *skates!* What do you say to nineteen cars
being loaded with twelve hundred men, women, boys,
and girls, all bound for the ice, equipped with skates,
hand-sleds, and the like?

"We went about three miles to a beautiful sheet of
ice covering 'Long Pond.' The ladies in their bright
dresses of scarlet, crimson, blue, green, and high-col-
oured plaids made the scene a gay and animated one.
Some of the skaters were as graceful as swallows in
their gliding, curving movements. The colours in the
scene reminded me of the beautiful description we
heard Bayard Taylor give of the strange, fantastic colours
of Moscow, 'the wonderful city,' as he called it, which he
said must look amid the winter snows of the vast Russian
steppes like a Turk in gay Oriental dress, seated with
his pipe on an iceberg. Mr. Higginson's articles in the *Atlantic*, 'Saints and their Bodies,' 'Physical Training,' and
his lectures and personal efforts seem to have stimulated

everybody, old and young, grave and gay, to participate in this excellent and fascinating exercise. Last winter some rigid-minded people called it 'Higginson's Revival.' This winter he marvels at the excellent skaters among the ladies, and declares they must have learned last summer.

"The last two evenings we had in Worcester, we were at two parlour lectures given by Mr. Henry D. Thoreau, the author of that odd book, *Walden, or Life in the Woods*. The first lecture was upon 'Autumnal Tints,' and was a beautiful and, I doubt not, a faithful report of the colours of leaves in October. Some of you may have read his 'Chesuncook,' in the *Atlantic Monthly ;* if so you can fancy how quaint and observing, and humorous withal, he is as traveller- or excursionist-companion in wild solitudes. Several gentlemen, friends of his, tell us much of their tour with him to the White Mountains last summer, of his grand talk with their guide in 'Tuckerman's Ravine,' where they had their camp. He paid us the compliment of a nice long morning call after we heard him read his 'Autumnal Tints,' and remembered our being once at his mother's to tea, and Miss Putnam's looking over his herbarium with his sister.

"Please tell your good husband that the fine poem, 'All's Well,' in the December *Atlantic*, is by our friend Mr. David A. Wasson, whose sermon we liked so greatly. I regret to say how sad his sickness has made all who know his rare worth and eminent ability, and this poem was written in the beginning of that dreadful affliction which so suddenly suspended his active usefulness,— spinal disease.[1]

[1] Caused by accepting in his youth the challenge of a wrestler much his superior in weight and strength, whom he threw, but at the cost of a life's misery.

" Then poor Theodore Parker has gone off to warm lands [the West Indies] to get health, which many tremblingly fear is a vain endeavour. Others are more hopeful. [The fears were realised, May 10, 1860].

" The anti-slavery festival in Boston was a great success. Whittier was there, Mrs. Stowe and her two daughters. Poor Mrs. Stowe upset a cup of coffee on her superb grey moiré-antique skirt. Are you reading her delightful story in the *Atlantic?* I am charmed with it. [*The Minister's Wooing.*] To-morrow we return to Boston. I had a grand meeting in Mr. Holland's church some six weeks ago. Six hundred people present. Next Saturday we go to New Hampshire for a month or more."

" WORCESTER, May 20, 1859.

" Your very kind and affectionate letter was balm and joy to my heart. Most sincerely do I thank you for it and pray you will not ever again keep the door of mercy shut so long. Heaven grant you are all well and happy as you deserve to be. Dear Maria, I doubt not, is as philanthropic and large-hearted as ever ; Jane as bright and Almira as lovely ; and your good husband in health and prosperity. You must, one and all, accept my warm and unchanging love.

" Miss Putnam and I have just come from passing a month in Rhode Island. We were in the city of Providence during the Rhode Island Anti-Slavery Convention, and I had two lectures there, and we had pleasant walks, rides, and a church-wedding, etc.

" Mr. Phillips made two magnificent speeches ; one against *caste* schools, which now disgrace the three cities of Rhode Island : to us splendid in its philanthropy and awful in its indignation at the spirit of contempt for humanity shown by these separate schools for coloured children.

"The scene of Mrs. Stowe's new story is laid in Newport, and when there we did not neglect to hunt up 'Hopkinsian' reminiscences. I read there a little memoir of Dr. Hopkins, saw the church he preached in (now Unitarian, which Dr. Channing dedicated, after it was remodelled), visited his grave, and the old house where he lived so many years and where he 'used to walk his room with hands clasped in rapturous ecstasy, thinking how the Law had been magnified and made honourable, through the atonement.' The old house was just sold to be entirely renovated, so we were in the very nick of time to see the Doctor's study just as it was, and the enormous kitchen fireplace, where the Doctor's outer man was prepared for, and the time-worn front and back stairs. Afterwards we called upon a brisk, bright-eyed, entertaining maiden over eighty years of age, who was the last occupant of the house and who told us many things of the Doctor. She said he was one of the 'excellent of the earth.'

"Two weeks before, Prof. Stowe and Mrs. Stowe had been to see her and collect *Hopkinsiana*. She had a little, black, round frame, with silhouette of the Doctor, hanging on the wall, which greatly interested the Stowes.

"What a grand chapter that is where Candace takes her freedom! A similar instance is recorded in Dr. H.'s life, where a slave man was given his freedom as suddenly, through the Doctor's persuasion of his master.

He was truly, as Mrs. Stowe says, ' an honest, grand old boulder,' and we blessed his memory in that slave-traffic-accursed town (there being once one hundred and fifty vessels engaged in the trade from Newport), for lifting up his voice in denunciation of the Heaven-daring

wickedness and for purging his church from slave-trad-
ers and slaveholders.

" It is said the summer-visiting slaveholders are rarely
disturbed now in their pews in the Newport churches, as
a terribly conservative, pro-slavery atmosphere abounds
here still. Even the brisk old maiden lady said she
had never read and never wished to read *Uncle Tom's
Cabin.* Mr. Phillips said, ' Mrs. Stowe has the genius to
make the negro character lovable.' [1]

" I wish I had room to write you about a real ' Candace,' an old negress one hundred years of age in Newport, and a beautiful story of Rev. C. H. Malcolm's
taking her into his own pew at church, there where a
negro gallery is, and where the modest Grace Russell
(Emily's sister) was so persecuted for sitting with an
English lady who invited- her, after Grace came back
from London and the patronage of the noble Earl of
Shaftesbury,—but these things will keep till I see you.

" I ought not to forget that Charles Howard Malcolm is
a noble exception to the time-serving clergy there. He
opened his church to my plea for the slave, at the risk of
losing his pulpit. He was driven from Virginia two

---

[1] This was to give Mrs. Stowe credit for God's work. Emerson's
was a better word :

> " He has avenues to God
> Hid from men of Northern brain,
> Far beholding, without cloud,
> What these with slowest steps attain.
> If once the generous chief arrive
> To lead him, willing to be lead,
> For Freedom he will strike and strive
> And drain his heart till he be dead "—

less a prophecy grandly fulfilled under the lead of Col. T. W.
Higginson, Col. Robert G. Shaw, and many another, than a record,
October, 1863, of the accomplished fact.

years ago for persisting in teaching slaves to read. What a great test of Christian courage and fidelity in this country the slave is! How much it costs to be a Christian in this age! I wish you would take the *Anti-Slavery Standard*, and read all the grand speeches at the late New York meeting."

TO THE PORTERS

"BATH, ME., August 30, 1859.

"Mr. May has laid out anti-slavery work for Miss Putnam and myself to keep us in Maine until November. How pleasant a letter from you would be!

"Everything here as dry as dust, from the corn and potatoes to the forest trees, parched with drought. Gratitude was in every heart when, last Thursday, the obdurate heavens yielded and poured out their refreshing showers. I spoke twice in Portland, and beside our anti-slavery work, had several social visits and went to the 'Islands,' a grand resort for the Portland people in summer. The sea air was so healthful and the views were so fine, every minute it was luxury and happiness to be there.

"Rev. Frederic Frothingham [1] gave a beautiful speech in my meeting last Sunday here. In the evening we went to hear Mr. Sheldon, who has changed from a Baptist to a Unitarian, and coming home we witnessed an astonishing display of Northern Lights, lighting up our room as if the moon shone, with sheets of pink and red light that spread over half the sky.

"While in Boston we saw Charles Sumner's picture of *The Miracle of St. Mark*, by Tintoretto. The deliver-

[1] Then a Unitarian preacher in Portland; afterward in Buffalo, N. Y., and Milton, Mass. A man who mixed the scholar, the hero, and the saint in about equal parts.

ance of a white slave who has been bound for torture, by St. Mark suddenly plunging down from above ; the axe and cords are broken in pieces to the astonishment of the excited multitude. It is a very appropriate possession for Mr. Sumner, who has so nobly vindicated liberty. But I felt while standing by Mr. Garrison that a greater than St. Mark was there,—that he was permitted to perform a grander miracle than this picture represents ; for not only has one slave had his shackles broken, but those of four million are being unbound, and at length they shall go forth rejoicing in freedom. This picture once belonged to the poet Rogers in England.

"Is it not more and more amazing that the people of this country can be so apathetic and dead to the enslaved condition of four millions here ? It is one of the great comforts of my life that I am not cursed with such infidel stupidity ; that I have made some effort, some struggle, to stand for the holiest, most precious truths known to the human soul,—Justice, Freedom, Holiness, Eternal Right.

"I hope none of you failed to read Mr. Phillips's faithful and noble temperance letter to Judge Shaw and President Walker of Harvard University [criticising their countenancing the use of wine at the Paul Morphy dinner], which I was glad to see the *New York Tribune* copied from the Boston papers. It has made a great sensation here in New England. Mrs. Stowe dined with the Atlantic Club, on condition no wine appeared on the table, just before she sailed for Europe."

TO MRS. PORTER

" CALAIS, ME., September 30, 1859.

"We are here in sight of British soil, so dear to the heart of the poor, hunted, fugitive slave. It seems a

long way off, and just think of Boston's being spoken of
as at the West! You would rejoice to know how our
way in this country has been gladdened at every step by
the kindest sympathy and warmest interest in our dear
cause, as well as most genial courtesy and hospitality to
ourselves personally.

"I wish you and Mr. Porter could have shared with
us the beautiful view at Eastport. It was the most marvellously lovely interweaving of land and water my eyes
ever enjoyed. We had the happiness to stay with George
Richardson, a young Unitarian minister, and I thought
him the most single-minded, unworldly human being I
ever knew. [To be distinguished from James Richardson, an exceedingly erratic friend of Samuel Longfellow,
Samuel Johnson, and their set.] It seems to me that in
this part of Maine Anti-Slavery walks in silver slippers.

"This afternoon we are asked to take tea with Mrs.
Pike, the authoress of *Ida May*, *Caste*, etc. I am told
she has made a fortune by those books. [Two of the
many that started up in the wake of Uncle Tom's
ploughshare.]

"Afternoon.—Mrs. Pike has just left us, after giving
us two hours' animated conversation. Her husband
gathered a fine audience for me last evening. Mrs.
Cooper, with whom we have a delightful home, and
Mrs. Pike spent a winter in South Carolina a few years
since, when Mrs. Pike learned much which suggested to
her the narrative of *Ida May*. She has given us many
reminiscences of that Southern winter, some shocking
atrocities which *she* could not shut her eyes to. Once
the Mayor of Aiken, South Carolina, waited on these
ladies with a *warrant!* They were addressed, 'Ladies,
you are suspected of being abolitionists.'

"This morning Mrs. Cooper took us in her carriage to

ride across the river St. Croix in New Brunswick, along a pleasant road with fine views all the way ; but the happiest feature to us was, that it was absolutely *free soil :* no slave there ! "

"CHERRYFIELD, ME., Oct. 7, 1859.

"At Dennysville we had the happiness to stay at Theodore Lincoln's. He is grandson of General Benjamin Lincoln of Revolutionary fame. Both himself and Mrs. Lincoln are very hospitable and social. They live in a large old mansion, full of open fireplaces, with handsome fires blazing. Some twenty-five years ago, Audubon passed some time with them, pursuing his bird studies, and he named a bird after Mr. Thomas Lincoln, ' Fringilla Lincolni.' Miss Putnam was in ecstasies. Her enthusiasm knew no bounds. She has formed acquaintance with some sea birds that have added not a little to her rapture. The sandpipers she especially admires. We saw one large grey gull that she mistook for an eagle."

"WORCESTER, March 29, 1860.

". . . You must have enjoyed the rarely mild and sunny weather we have had this winter. Its quality never was finer, it seems to me. Such lovely dawns I never knew before. No wonder the old Greeks had such pretty fancies about Aurora ! Do you remember what Dr. Channing said ?—' I welcome every day with new gratitude ; I almost wonder at myself when I think of the pleasure the dawn gives me, after having witnessed it so many years ; and the blessed light of heaven, how dear it is ! and this earth I have trodden so long, with what affection I look upon it ! ' "

"CAPE COD, Sept. 20, 1860.

" . . . As Charles Lamb wrote his friend Manning in China, removed from him by the whole breadth of the continent, 'You remember France?' so I may, blunting the point of the humour, ask if you have any recollection of the Cape Cod of school-books? I dare say you thought of it distinctly as having villages, farms, gardens, salt-works, fish-flakes, homes, and every kind of human interest that other places have. Fishing, salt manufacture, and cranberry culture are the most obvious distinctions of the Cape from any part of the world I know. We are hospitably entertained in a handsome house, the last one on the Cape. There is a charming grove of oaks on the grounds, and there are pines bristling all over with their bushy, squirrel-taily boughs, the true Cape Cod forest. All the trees have a dwarfed appearance. Here too are beach *plums*, beach peas, beach grass, and much else that has only existed, to me, in name before. It is wonderful how these Yankees thrive on sand, rock, or ice ; nothing daunted by any forbidding aspect of nature. Every third man you meet is ' Captain ' somebody, and larger, liberal views seem the result of the wide activities and foreign association.

"Last month when we were in Boston I looked over Franky Garrison's book of autographs. This was what Lydia Maria Child had written for him[1] :

"' How a very small mouse helped to gnaw open a net that held a great lion :

"' I believe it was in the winter of 1834 that my beloved friend Ellis Gray Loring said to me, " Maria, a very talented and agreeable young man called on us last evening. He said he had been reading your *Appeal*, and that it made a strong impression on him. When he

---

[1] Francis Jackson Garrison, youngest son and child of William Lloyd Garrison, born 1848 ; named for the father's loyal friend ; the principal collaborator with Wendell Phillips Garrison (born 1840) in writing the *Story* of Garrison's life.

bade us good evening, he said, with a charming smile,
that he did n't know but he should be obliged to come
out an abolitionist ! " I inquired his name and they told
me it was *Wendell Phillips!* I had never heard of him
and did not then think much of the circumstance ; but
now it makes me proud and happy to remember it.

"'[Signed] L. MARIA CHILD.'"

TO MISS PUTNAM

" Dec. 30, 1860.

"   .   .   . What fools people can make of themselves,
having their minds stored with a knowledge of *mean, bad*
things concerning their acquaintances ! It seems to me
always a proof of a lean soul and a commonplace character and an ill-tempered heart. Such characters are
to be avoided as far as possible. They make nobody
happy, and never win respect."

TO THE PORTERS

" BOSTON, Jan. 31, 1861.

" Friday afternoon Miss Putnam and I had a very interesting call on Mrs. Theodore Parker. While she was
showing us the library she took from a very small, old-
fashioned bureau the *first book* Mr. Parker ever owned—
the Latin dictionary he bought with money earned by
picking huckleberries. It used to be on the shelves
with the other books, but when so many people were
anxious to see and handle this nucleus of the fine library,
and hear its story, Mr. Parker found the binding was
being torn and put it carefully away in the little bureau.
The bureau is one that Theodore kept his clothes in
when a boy. Such was his attachment for it, that he
obtained it a few years ago although it had gone out of

the family. On the fly-leaf of the old dictionary was written 'Theodore Parker, 1822.' He was then about eleven years old. I could not but look with reverence on this token of the boy's eager thirst for knowledge, and thought of the hopes that stimulated his hands to pick the huckleberries that he might buy a treasure which would never perish. All the books (except this one)[1] are to be removed to the public library in the spring, being given to the city by Mr. Parker's will and with Mrs. Parker's consent. 'This,' she said, 'was Theodore's darling wish.'

"These dreadful times of mobs are thought to be the last struggle of the slave-power in the North, and it remains for time to prove whether such a precious life as that of Wendell Phillips is to be given up to satisfy the minions of slavery. God grant that such a costly sacrifice may be spared. I wish you could have been with us on that sublime occasion when the hosts of abolitionists sat looking danger and violence in the face as serenely as if the light of Eternity's morning had dawned on their souls. I think it was worth living a great many years to be present at the meeting in Tremont Temple last Thursday morning. I may never live to witness another day so great as that was in courage, devotion, and fidelity to principle.

"The platform was crowded with the faithful and true—many a tried soldier in Freedom's long battle: Francis Jackson to preside, Edmund Quincy to aid; Mr. Phillips, like a conquering angel, with wit and wisdom on his tongue, and beauty and honour on his head; James Freeman Clarke, glorious in speech and action; Ralph Waldo Emerson, serene as the sphinx of six thousand years ago; Samuel J. May, reading the Ninety-fourth

[1] The dictionary ultimately followed.

Psalm, that seemed to come from the prophet's pen of
to-day ; Mrs. Lydia Maria Child, as full of enthusiasm as
she could express by flashing eye, glowing cheek, and
waving handkerchief, as she sat by the organ on the
highest seat of the platform, making everybody glad by
her presence ; Mrs. Maria Chapman, sitting with the
calm dignity of a queen, her sister and daughter beside
her ; T. W. Higginson, ready with brilliant eloquence of
tongue or with the revolver's bullet—so it was said—to
do battle for free speech that day ; William I. Bowditch,
with his venerable and dignified mien, looked quite distinguished among them all. Once when he took his
place at the front of the platform, the mob called out,
' There comes the old bald eagle ! ' and well may the little
insignificant mice and weasels look out when such a
glance is abroad."

With such a sound of trumpets does Sallie Holley
herald a new blood-red dawn, the substitution of
bullets for ballots, the exchange of pro-slavery and
anti-slavery ideas at the cannon's mouth. Phillips's
speech, which she admired so much, was of disunion
all compact. He cried, " All hail, then, Disunion !
Beautiful upon the mountains are the feet of her
that cometh ! " He said of South Carolina's seceding from the Union, " Build a bridge of gold and pay
her toll over it ! " But a little later he was speaking
" Under the Flag," applauding the awakened spirit
of the North, " the uprising of a great people," and
Sallie Holley was not slow to catch the step of the
new Union and Emancipation March.

CHAPTER XII

IN WAR TIME

" Not as we hoped ; but what are we ?
   Above our broken dreams and plans,
   God lays, with wiser hands than man's,
   The corner-stones of liberty."

MR. GARRISON'S non-resistant principles were of such a consistent and yet elastic kind that they easily expanded to the breadth of the new situation in which the country found itself in the spring of 1861. His attitude towards the John Brown affair was perfectly explicit and made it unnecessary for him to violently readjust himself to a state of war.

" I thank God," he had said, " when men who believe in the right and duty of wielding carnal weapons, are so far advanced that they will take those weapons out of the scale of despotism and throw them into the scale of freedom. It is an indication of freedom and a positive moral growth ; it is one way to get up to the sublime platform of non-resistance ; and it is God's method of dealing retribution on the head of the tyrant. Rather than see men wearing their chains in a cowardly and servile spirit, I would, as an advocate of peace, much rather see them breaking the head of the tyrant with their chains. Give me, as a non-resistant, Bunker Hill, and Lexington, and Concord, rather than the cowardice and servility of a Southern slave-plantation."

When the war had actually begun no people in the North waited upon its awful chances with more breathless hearts than the abolitionists. Many of their dearest friends had sent their sons, as Garrison his own,[1] to the embattled field, and their hearts ached for them with anxiety and sympathised with them tenderly when such sorrows came as those that fell to the share of the Winthrops, the Lowells, and the Shaws. Henceforth their non-resistance was that of the Quaker on shipboard, who having done his best to prevent the captain from running down a hostile craft said finally, " If thee is bound to do it, thee hadst better port thy helm a very little."

The abolitionists did not find their occupation gone. It was quite otherwise than so, and they were never more efficient than in the years which brought the Emancipation Proclamation every day more near.

[1] George Thompson Garrison, born 1836 ; named for the great English "carpet-bagger" (so called by Dr. E. E. Hale), for whom Garrison had a just admiration bordering upon reverence. The son was a second lieutenant in the 55th Massachusetts, the coloured regiment formed immediately after Colonel Shaw's 54th. One of the most dramatic moments of Garrison's life is thus described by his biographers : " As they [the 54th] marched down State Street, sing-ing the John Brown song, Mr. Garrison stood, by chance, on the corner of Wilson's Lane, the spot over which he had been dragged by the mob of 1835, and there, with emotion too deep for words, he watched the solid ranks go by, the fair-haired officer at their head who was never to return."

The war was rapidly making their doctrine of immediate emancipation a more practicable doctrine than
it had ever been, and their business was to hasten as
much as possible "the wonderful day of the Lord";
to applaud every forward step and to denounce
every one that was backward or too slow for their
impatient hearts.   In all the movement, anticipation,
and triumphant realisation of the war time no one
was involved with keener interest than Sallie Holley.
The war did not make her work as an agent for the
Liberator any easier.

> "Most could raise the flowers now,
>   For all had got the seed ;
> And so again the people
>   Called it but a weed."

The paper lost its special character in the wide
diffusion of its most characteristic sentiments.   As
dying, yet behold it lived, and she was wise to understand the meaning of the hour.

TO MISS PUTNAM

"ELMIRA, Sept. 7, 1861.

"It is four weeks since I came here, and it seems
hardly one, so happily has the time passed.   You see by
Mr. May's letter and Mrs. Garrison's and the *Liberator*
and *Standard*, the 'old guard' think this is no time for
abolitionists to stop working.

"Personally, I should not object to remaining in one
spot all winter, rather than have again the dreadful cold
and fatigue and hard work of another lecturing campaign ; but I confess my conscience and heart would

not be satisfied with doing nothing for the noble cause, and now of all times, to give up seems to me weak and wrong. I have no doubt we could advance the cause as we have hitherto done, even if we only get a few sub-scribers, and small collections and donations. *I* think we ought to work. What do you think? You know my hope and faith of old. Not many years longer *can* we work. You and I will be too feeble to go on many years more as we have done. Let us work while we can. I believe it would greatly gratify Mr. Garrison and Mr. May to know we kept faithfully working this winter. I expect my 'treatment' here [at the Elmira Water-Cure] will be of immense service to me."

" ELMIRA, Sept. 22, 1861.

" Miss Seaton of Washington is here. She has that indescribable charm of manner and tone that Dr. Johnson used to say can only belong to superior birth. You know of old my almost passionate admiration for that sort of culture, and can readily imagine how much Miss Seaton interests me. Her father is the editor of the *National Intelligencer* of Washington, D. C. Her father is a Union man, but her heart is in the South. Friday evening I had a delightful time walking with her on the verandah and listening to her fascinating convers-ation. She has known Daniel Webster ever since she was six years old. She said, in part : ' No American ever received such attention in England. When he arrived in London the Duke of Portland placed his own carriage at his disposal. When he entered the Court there (equivalent to the Supreme Court here) all arose, and he was at once invited to take a seat among them. The Queen asked him to dinner *before* he was presented at Drawing-room, an honour never before offered an American. In his own home and circle of intimate friends, Mr. Webster was overflowing with good-nature, wit, humour, and childlike gaiety. He died of a broken heart, not because he had wanted so much to be president, but, as he told my father, because he wanted it to go down to history that his countrymen thought him worthy their confidence.' She has seen bank bills stuffed in his inkstand for a stopper. He was 'that careless.' "

" ELMIRA, Sept. 29, 1861.

" Have I ever written what Mrs. Gleason denominated my disease? It is 'torpidity of the liver.' It is such a satisfaction to know.[1] Are n't you glad to have it positively stated? Did you ever hear of the Irishman who, when his physician told him he had torpidity of the liver, understood that he had a torpedo in his liver?

" Miss Seaton tells the story of Fanny Kemble being in Washington, at Willard's hotel, and ringing the bell for the waiter and demanding candles. 'Hain't got none.' 'What do you suppose,—that I will read by gas? Bring me some wax candles instantly.' There was a fight and a scuffle among the waiters as to who should go, every time her bell rang. She frightened all the servants who came near her.

" At breakfast this morning a gentleman from Connecticut told a story of a Yale College student who advertised for board ' where his Christian influence would be received as part pay '! Perhaps you think one reason I am so welcome here is that my influence is considered part pay. Do you remember A——a P——e, at Ober-

[1] One is reminded of Mrs. Bulstrode in *Middlemarch*, who liked to have " names for her diseases suitable to the dignity of her secretions."

lin, who only wanted boarders who ' could take a part'?
There is a comical side to life, is n't there? I don't
know, but I am inclined to think that when a person is
so happy as I am here it should be received as an indication from Providence to remain. It is certainly a rare
chance in my life."

" ELMIRA, Oct. 1, 1861.

".   .   . Miss Seaton went to Mount Vernon with the
Prince of Wales and his company. She it was who
asked him to plant the horse-chestnut tree at the grave
of Washington.

" October 4th.—I have been sewing a good deal for
Mrs. Gleason ever since I came, and right glad have I
been to do it.

" In various little ways, such as showing the establishment to strangers, aiding them about the grounds and
Glen, reading an hour a day to Mrs. Gleason while she
rests on the lounge, taking the reading and the prayer in
the parlour when Dr. Gleason is away, reading stories to
the children, lecturing in the parlour evenings, and reading aloud to patients there, I try to show my grateful
acknowledgment of the generous and open-hearted
hospitality given me by Dr. and Mrs. Gleason. But I
cannot accept it all without returning some money or
gifts. You know I never stayed anywhere without making compensation.

" October 6th.—Mrs. Sargent, a patient here, who is
dangerously ill, bears her illness very patiently and
sweetly. Every day for weeks I have read to her.
Sometimes in the Bible, also praying with her. She is
kind enough to say I am a great comfort to her.

" October 24th.—This evening, by special request, I
was at the college to give recitations and readings to the

young ladies. What a pretty sight all those young ladies make !

" Are you not about tired of my water-cure chronicles ? Do you feel as Lord Jeffrey did about the Micawbers when he wrote Dickens that he 'should be well content to have heard the last of 'em ' ?

" You may judge I 'm like poor Pilgrim sleeping on enchanted ground, to stay here so long, and, I confess, every 'cowerin', sleekit, tim'rous beastie ' in my character begs and pleads for exemption this winter—every nerve in my body protests against going. How can I again face audiences, meet so many strange faces, endure the cold and fatigue, go through the nervous excitement, mount up in courage and daring, encounter the battle and the breeze, work in thought and feeling equal to the requisite exertion of public speaking—as in the past ten years ? But let me give you a grand passage from Carlyle :

" ' The nobleness that inspires a human soul to struggle heavenward cannot be taught by the most exquisite catechisms or the most industrious preaching and drilling. No ; alas ! no. Only by far other methods. Chiefly by silent, continuous example,—silently waiting for the favourable mood and moment and aided then by a kind of miracle, well enough named " the grace of God,"—can that sacred contagion pass from soul to soul. How much beyond whole libraries of orthodox theology is sometimes the mute action, the unconscious look of a father, of a mother, who had in them devoutness,— pious nobleness ! In whom the young soul, not unobservant, though not consciously observing, came at length to recognise it, to read it in this irrefragable manner, a seed planted thenceforth in the centre of his holiest affections forevermore ! '

"You know that I have a feeling that my dear father is the inspirer of my work in the anti-slavery cause, and more and more do I bless his holy memory.

"October 29th.—When Jenny Lind visited Mount Vernon, Miss Seaton was with her. John A. Washington gave Jenny a history of Sweden, in French, with marginal notes and comments in George Washington's own hand. Jenny was much affected. Miss Seaton said, 'You are not an American, yet you reverence Washington so much?' 'Whoever loves *mankint*, must love the name of Washington,' replied Jenny.

"The house of Miss Seaton's father was the last in this country that Lafayette was in. Her mother gave him a Ball, and at the close he took boat down the river and went directly on board the *Brandywine*.

"Yesterday morning, by special invitation, I breakfasted at Mr. Beecher's.[1] *He* got the meal. We had 'pop-overs'—a delicate kind of muffin—hot coffee, and clams ; cold roast beef, bread and butter, and a pleasant time. When I read him your question about Paul's singing in prison, he said that he never heard that Paul sang 'Old Hundred,' but, if he did, that was why the angel let 'em out,—to stop the singing.

"November 12th.—I have been in my room nearly all day writing anti-slavery letters, and hope I have done my duty. At least I think I should not feel so happy as I do, if I had not."

"ELMIRA, Nov. 18, 1861.

"Oh, my heart yearns toward you this morning, and the heaviest disappointment of my life would fall if *you* should die. Again and again I thank you for all your

---

[1] Rev. Thomas K. Beecher (younger brother of Henry Ward), long settled in Elmira.

love to me.[1] I wish I were more deserving of it.
Please God I may be some day. How I should love to
put my arms around your neck and kiss you !

"Nov. 23d.—Coloured Sarah has just left my room
after my hearing her lessons. What a cruel thing it is
that every being should not be taught to read while yet a
child ! Sarah tries hard, but makes what seems to me
slow headway.

"Nov. 27th.—Do not forget to give me the names of
some abolitionists to whom I can write for aid. I am
determined to be faithful and fulfil my promise to Mrs.
Garrison in this point ; and may God in mercy grant
that I be more faithful to meet all the obligations of
coming life !

"Your letter, noble, true-hearted, and full of dear-to-
me love, is here. I am inadequate to express my appreciation of your goodness and kindness ; and, as the best and
most comprehensive of all thanks and grateful affection
possible to offer, pray *God bless you.* ' Be still and know
that I am God,' has a deeper, fuller significance than
ever before.

"Nov. 29th.—In reading Hase's *Life of Jesus,* I am
surprised he should all along tell what *it is not,* of any
passage or scene, before affirmatively declaring his own
understanding of the part. You know my old liking for
positive affirmative statements, rather than for negative
assertions. What an ever fresh and living interest the
life and character of Jesus has ! I bless my dear sainted
father that very early in childhood my love was awakened
for this beautiful soul. More and more human it becomes
to me as I live and grow myself.

---

[1] Which was to go on growing all the time for the next thirty years
and more, and to prove itself stronger than death. And it was well
deserved.

"Dec. 10th, 1861.—Poor Mrs. Sargent is worse. When I come to a knowledge of what most other people bear and have borne, I exclaim afresh, How singularly light and happy my life has been! I would n't turn my hand over to change any outward event of my life.

"Dec. 24th, 1861.—I have now thirty-six dollars to send Mrs. Garrison, and wish I could make it fifty. Can you beg or send me a dollar?"

"ELMIRA, Jan. 16, 1862.

"   .   .   .   Who ever wrote hymns like Watts? This verse occurs in the one we sang this morning :

> "'Satan may vent his sharpest spite
>   And all his legions roar ;
> Almighty mercy guards my life
>   And bounds his raging power.'

"Who has not experienced the reality of the great opposing Force—Tremendous Adversary—in his own conflict? Call it Satan, evil, devil, or what you please, there is the awful and solemn fact. Sometimes I believe there are two Sallie Holleys. One fair, good, faithful, generous, and the other bad, worldly, mean, selfish ; and am anxious which shall gain the victory in all this mortal strife.

"Jan. 18th.—Was not Mr. Garrison's reply to the *Journal of Commerce* capital?—'When I said I would not sustain the Constitution because it was a covenant with death and an agreement with hell, I had no idea that death and hell would secede.'

"Jan. 26th.—It is incalculable how many letters I have written to get even the sum of forty dollars for the festival. If every abolitionist has worked as constantly as I have for this end, a large sum will be realised."

TO MISS SEATON

" ELMIRA, Feb. 4, 1862.

" . . . What you say about the 'influx of snobs and free negroes into Washington, in lieu of the grand old society,' has, I take it, a significance of great moment. Not so *pleasant*, to be sure, as a social element. As one imagines the illuminated missals and libraries to have been unwillingly exchanged, by those accustomed to artistic luxury, for the simple printing of the diviner art, which was for the multitude ; yes, if you will, the 'great unwashed,' but which was to make a 'new heaven and a new earth' for the million ; so this democratic idea of freedom and justice for all will in no way abridge the elegancies and privileges of private culture." [1]

TO THE PORTERS

" FARMERSVILLE, Jan. 22, 1863.

" . . . For the last six weeks I have been begging warm, woollen clothing for the 'contrabands' from these farmers, and have had the satisfaction of sending a large box to those destitute ones of God's poor."

Here, and so soon after the Emancipation Proclamation, is the first intimation of a new order of activity which was to engross entirely her last twenty-three years—work for the emancipated slaves.

" FARMERSVILLE, March 12, 1863.

" You can't think how unceasingly active dear Miss Putnam and I have been in this little corner of the world. The Sunday School, the Bible Class, and Temperance meetings about use up all our Sundays.

[1] The argument here would seem to be a *non sequitur*, but the spirit of it is sufficiently clear.

"On the principle 'Do the duty nearest you,' Miss Putnam thought she ought to remain here and wishes me to aid and labour with her, feeling that no work we could do elsewhere would be more important. Anti-slavery-wise I have not been entirely idle. I have sent $100.00 to the dear old Anti-Slavery Society from friends who know I am always agent for the cause. In the subscription list are more than one hundred names of individual abolitionists, scattered from Maine to Michigan, upon whose kindness and hospitality we have been from time to time 'quartered.'

"You will be pleased to know that my 'contraband' box arrived in Washington and gave great satisfaction. I have another nearly ready to send.

"What a great variety of scenes has human life ! As Edmund Quincy said, 'This is a very entertaining world.' The only party I have attended this winter was a 'donation party' at the Baptist minister's, where the chief amusement was the game of 'snap and catch.' I tended a woman's baby while she played."

"FARMERSVILLE, Sept. 12, 1863.

"Every fibre of my heart is aching to hear from you. Are you playing 'hide and seek' with me ? And won't you 'coop' loud enough, pretty soon, for us to hear you here in Cattaraugus ?

"I have just despatched to Oberlin, for four years, study, a fair-haired, rosy-cheeked girl, a German of nineteen, out of Wurtemburg six years. She wanted to study, had the 'spirit of improvement,' which Miss Putnam thinks is the greatest blessing in life.

"Have just received a nice letter from Miss Putnam's sister. She says, 'It was a beautiful sight—four hundred young ladies dressed in white, for Commencement.'

"She wore my white book-muslin, that I graduated in twelve years ago ! Was n't that a talent wrapped up in a napkin for a good use at last ?

"She seems to be enjoying her opportunities at Oberlin more and more, and we are unutterably glad to have her there. It seems to me like 'setting the captive free.' To emancipate one such soul from ignorance, is well worth all the conflicts, hard toil, and antagonisms I have gone through in 1863, the hardest year of my life."

For 1864 the letters are but few. Apparently she and Miss Putnam were still "wandering on from home to home." In October I find her applauding the temper of Miss Elizabeth Porter, who had refused a visit of condolence made on her by a "Copperhead" ex-governor. She held him responsible for the death of her brother, Col. Peter B. Porter. The sternness of Miss Holley's political temper for the remainder of her life was foreshadowed by this approval of her friend. Henceforth she was one of the most zealous of Republicans. The party which, under God, had been the immediate instrument by which slavery was abolished became "a thing ensky'd and sainted" in her eyes, while the Democratic party was to her simply and only the party that had supported slavery. She could not but distrust it, with whatever protestations it might come before the people ; while to the shortcomings of the Republicans she was, judging by her letters, habitually blind. All this was very natural and quite inevitable.

Lincoln's Emancipation Proclamation had only emancipated the slaves in the seceding States. It remained for the Thirteenth Amendment, passed in

February, 1865, to make a clean sweep, abolishing slavery everywhere in the United States, only thirty-four years from Garrison's public declaration of his plans and purposes. He had been heard at last, and it was granted him to " see what he foresaw." If Sallie Holley had ever doubted the logic of his position, she was reassured by the passage of the Thirteenth Amendment. " So it seems," she wrote, "the Constitution *was* a covenant with death and an agreement with hell."

CHAPTER XIII

NEW OCCASIONS AND NEW DUTIES

THE abolition of slavery did not prove an un-
mixed happiness to the abolitionists, for the
reason that differences arose among them as to the
line of action that should be taken with reference
to the several organs and instrumentalities of the
anti-slavery propaganda. These differences were
the more painful because for a time they brought
Garrison and Phillips into conflicting attitudes;
Garrison, with more of formal consistency and
dramatic appreciation, advising that the anti-slavery
societies be dissolved and the *Liberator* and *Anti-
Slavery Standard* be discontinued; Phillips advising
that "old Marley's sign" be still kept up. There
were differences more strongly marked; for example,
those between Phillips and Edmund Quincy, on
which Colonel Higginson has commented [1]:

"Nothing could be more curious than the difference
between his later days and those of Phillips. When
slavery fell, Phillips simply shifted the harness for service
in other reforms; while Quincy, like a tired steed, merely

[1] *Outlook*, Sept. 3, 1898, "Anti-Slavery Days."

shook himself and dropped the reformer's equipment altogether; utterly denied that there was anything left to fight for, and pronounced woman suffrage, for instance, a case in which there was ' no grievance.' He simply became a reformer *emeritus*, in the university phrase; was for the rest of his life a brilliant and delightful flâneur; went to the theatre with the constancy of a Parisian; became secretary of the learned societies which had rejected him in earlier days; resumed, in short, that life of the cultivated Bostonian which Howells has so well painted in his *A Modern Instance* and elsewhere."

By a vote of 118 to 48, Garrison's resolution to close the operations and existence of the American Anti-Slavery Society was rejected, and, though he was immediately elected president, he could not, of course, accept the office and it devolved on Wendell Phillips. This was at New York in May, 1865, and in the following December the *Liberator* was brought simultaneously to the end of its 35th volume and the conclusion of its great career. Very beautiful and affecting is Gibbon's story of the inception of his famous history and its conclusion, when he took a quiet turn in his garden at Lausanne and felt as if he had parted forever with a beloved friend. Even more beautiful and affecting to me the story of Garrison's inception of the *Liberator* and its end, when he set the final paragraph with his own hands and inserted it in its proper place.[1] Well might the hearts of those who stood about swell with tenderest emo-

[1] I have seen the " stone " on which this was done—" the stone of stumbling," Garrison called it; and few relics have I found more eloquent.

tion. Garrison turned away to go immediately to a
meeting of the New England Freedman's Aid Society. Slavery was dead, but what of its spirit still
survived he was as alert as ever to seek out and de-
stroy, while he knew better than most how much
remained to do for the emancipated slave, and dedicated his remaining strength to the new work.

At the parting of the ways in 1865 Sallie Holley
went with Phillips and his party, contending for the
perpetuity of the old societies and other instrumentalities. There was no *Liberator* for which to solicit
subscriptions, but she remained an agent for the *Anti-
Slavery Standard*, from the editorship of which Oliver
Johnson, who was in perfect sympathy with Garrison,
had retired, Mr. Aaron M. Powell succeeding. Yet
she bated not one jot of admiration for Garrison at
any time, so far as I am able to discover. She could
say as Phillips said, after the day of separation, " I
have never uttered an anti-slavery word which I did
not owe to his inspiration ; I have never done an
anti-slavery act of which the primary merit was not
his." And, happily, there came a time when not
only the differences springing from the victorious
event, but those which arose from time to time in
the course of the great struggle,

" melted
From the smallness of a gnat to air,"

in comparison with the dignity and grandeur of the
common work, and hope, and joy.

From the conclusion of the war there are certain
scrap-books made by Sallie Holley which supplement
the letters collected by Miss Putnam. They fill up

various gaps; they afford Miss Holley's comment, or
her friend's, on various situations in which they were
interested or engaged, many of the scraps being letters written by one or the other of them to the *Standard* or some other paper. Thus, at the outset we
find Miss Putnam describing a visit which they made
together to "A Leicester Home," that of Samuel May,
and the inference is clear that though he had stood
fast by Garrison there had been no breach in the
friendship which was then fifteen years old and had
nearly thirty more to grow. If he was no longer the
director of her work, he was her faithful counsellor.
Those of us who know the Leicester home will appreciate the force of her description,—"a grand prospect of sky and land, vast enough to give the feeling
of a sea-view"; "no white caps, but an immense
sweep of woodland," in the October weather "gorgeous with the orange, scarlet, or crimson of many a
burning bush"; and then, the fireside talk and
kindly cheer.

Miss Holley and Miss Putnam had come from
Rhode Island, where "the real ocean had roared
gently for them, rolling up its surf and spreading it
out in exquisite lace-like borders along the hard
sandy beach." Both were as keenly alive to any
natural beauty as to the work in hand, the obtaining of subscriptions for the *Standard* and the pleading of the Freedmen's new-born necessities and
rights. A week had been spent with Theodore D.
Weld in Milton, Massachusetts, looking with reverence on his beautiful head, taking long walks with
his wife.

Frederick Douglass

"She and her sister, Sarah Grimké, give the impression of radiant youth, they are kept so fresh and bright with the life of thought and principle. After Miss Holley's lecture, Mrs. Weld declared that she felt like going out herself again in this great crisis to plead for the black man's right of suffrage."

They went to hear Frederick Douglass speak in Music Hall. "He looked very well, in no way an unfit companion for the Beethoven[1] statue behind him and the bust of Sebastian Bach on the organ." We find them together at the funeral of Thankful Southwick in April, 1867. She it was who called the Chardon Street Convention. The next month they were at the thirty-sixth annual meeting of the New England Anti-Slavery Society, enjoying its "baptismal flood of light and power." The same letter that reports this meeting criticises Charles Sumner for omitting in his address on Russian America any mention of the humming-bird that haunts as far north as Sitka.

Later in the year there is a letter from Miss Holley to the *Standard*, giving an account of her meeting Harriet Tubman, a coloured woman of remarkable character and of great ability, especially in the way of giving slaves their liberty and putting them out of danger.[2] "Forty thousand dollars was not too great reward for the Maryland slaveholders to offer for

[1] Bearing a certain resemblance to a well-known lithograph of him. In 1887, eight years before his death, I came upon Douglass suddenly in London on the Strand, and I met no manlier-looking man upon the London streets that day.

[2] See article by Mrs. Lillie Chace Wyman in *New England Magazine*, March, 1896, and Siebert's *Underground Railroad*, for accounts of this heroic woman, who is, I think, still living.

her." Undated among the letters and other memorials of these years I find an article by Miss Holley on James G. Birney, which shows how warm was her appreciation of the man whom Myron Holley chose to be the standard-bearer of political anti-slavery. All of Miss Holley's anti-slavery work had been done under different auspices; but her sympathies were wide, and her father's memory bound her to a generous view of the Liberty party, especially in its original form and spirit. Moreover, she always did her thinking quite as much with her heart as with her head. All her thought was touched with emotion, and sometimes the logical distinctions were consumed as by the breath of fire.

TO THE PORTERS

" OBERLIN, Aug. 30, 1865.

". . . Here we are, hourly expecting the arrival of a young coloured girl from Washington, to go through a four years' course here. I have obtained a scholarship for her and a boarding-place where she can work for half her board, which is $2.75, including wood and room. She is to be educated as a teacher. Miss Putnam's sister recommences her studies this term. You can't think how heartily I enter into all the little details of these girl-students' lives, their 'work hours,' 'study hours,' economical devices, educational desires, etc.

" 'Emily,' whom I told you of, from Elmira, is doing nobly. She has been here a year ; earned all her board, and her teachers tell me she recited 'admirably' in all her classes. She taught this summer in the Union School here, part of the day, and is going out West with another young lady to teach next winter. After she graduates she will study medicine in Philadelphia. So you see Oberlin turns out doctors, lecturers, and preachers among its women-students.

"Our Class-Tea at Prof. Ellis's was a unique affair— the Class of '51. They all told what they had been doing these fourteen years since graduation. I was surprised and delighted to find myself belonging to such a distinguished Class. One had passed years in Washington as private secretary to Senator Chase. General Cox [1] very modestly told of his march through Georgia with Sherman. Mr. Cooper and Charles Finney had been three years in the army. [To which Oberlin gave 166 undergraduates and 87 alumni, 100 of those enlisting losing their lives in the service.] Of the ladies present, two were teaching and one was a farmer's wife. They insisted on my relating what I had been about. I said I was afraid they would n't care to hear how I had been holding anti-slavery meetings all these years and still 'spoke in public.' Mr. Cooper asked what I lectured upon now. 'Oh!' I said, 'Black folks must vote all through the country.' Helen Finney, who was present with her husband, General Cox, said she thought I wanted women to vote. 'Oh, yes!' I said, 'that's inevitable,' whereupon there was 'immense sensation,' as the newspapers say."

"McLean, Tompkins Co., N. Y., Nov. 7, 1865.

". . . While at Elmira Water-Cure during those golden October days, our friends, the Tylers,[2] made a tea

---

[1] J. Dolson Cox, soon after Governor of Ohio, and latterly a publicist and critic of very great ability.

[2] Friends of long standing, lasting to the end, and as faithful now to Sallie Holley's memory as to her person and her work when she was living.

party for us. During the evening Mr. Lewis told us
this interesting incident about Florence Nightingale.
When Lucretia Mott was in England in 1840, Florence
was a young girl and heard Mrs. Mott talk about the
importance of young ladies having some other ambition
than that of being married, and how much happier they
would be in some career of useful benevolence ; and
Florence said she would like to live to do good. Shortly
after, she was visiting some hospital with an aunt ; and
as they went through the wards, Florence would say,
Such and such an improvement ought to be made ;
when her aunt said, ' Florence, you are the very one to
make it ; this is the work for you to do; you have been
wanting something to engage your higher and better
energies and here it is.' So, from the idea and spirit of
our own noble Lucretia Mott, sprung the inspiration
to Florence Nightingale's beautiful and philanthropic
work."

" NEW YORK, May 8, 1866.

" We came from Elmira with Mrs. Stowe. I like her
face. She looks like a victorious saint, full of goodness
and kindness. There is human sympathy and noble
power in her expression. Sunday morning we heard
Mr. O. B. Frothingham. I enjoyed the sermon exceedingly. I am perfectly satisfied that I belong to the
Radicals, and eye hath not seen, ear hath not heard, my
joy and thankfulness for the privilege."

" PROVIDENCE, R. I., July 21, 1866.

" . . . I am still lecturing and getting subscribers
for our noble *Standard*. In the last two months I have
obtained $100.00 for subscriptions."

" BOSTON, Nov. 9, 1866.

"   .   .   .   My friend, Mrs. Anna Shaw Greene (aunt
to the lamented Colonel Shaw, who fell at Fort Wagner),
called to see me and said that Mrs. Putnam, mother of
young Lieut. Lowell Putnam, wished very much to see
me.   Miss Putnam and I had a lovely visit with her at
her country house in Jamaica Plain.   After receiving us
in the parlour she soon invited us to Lowell's room, where
she talked out of her mother's heart, telling a great deal
of his life.   The family lived in Europe with their children while they were at school.   Their son Alfred died
in Italy.   Her daughter is now the only one left.

" When they were in Dresden, Lowell was then, as he
had been before in Paris, painfully impressed with the
privations of the poor, and the inequalities of human
condition.   It could not be, he said to her one day, that
God loved *him* better than he did so many others, in
giving him so much more.   If he thought so he could
not love God so well as he did.   No, he had only be-
stowed on him such large favours, that he might do for
others with his abundance.   This was his idea, though
only a boy of twelve.   After they came home from their
long residence abroad, he wanted to see his own country,
and visited the West, and among other points, the Mam-
moth Cave in Kentucky.   He studied it so well that he
could act as a guide through it.   It was the fall of
Abraham Lincoln's election, and every day, as the
parties were going in, they voted at the mouth of the
cave for their several candidates for President.   He
voted for Lincoln, day after day, *alone*, not one other
vote.   The ladies gave their voice for Bell and Everett,
mainly, and the gentlemen declared for Breckinridge.
Mrs. Putnam said it not only showed the principles of
her son, but also that it was safe to pronounce in Ken-

tucky in favour of Lincoln at that time. Did this handsome, gracious boy disarm prejudice and violence ?

"His idea was to be a traveller and study the histories of countries from their memorable places. How soon he became an historic personage, great and heroic in character, up to the level of his opportunities, in a battlefield of his own country!—that sad, terrible one of Ball's Bluff."

TO MISS PUTNAM

"ELMIRA, Aug. 1, 1867.

"To-day was spent at Watkins. In the morning we visited the Glen, so wildly beautiful, and in the afternoon we heard Frederick Douglass in a grand speech before three thousand people, a third coloured, at an open-air meeting. Amelia Tyler says, 'Douglass is no negro ; I would n't mind being his complexion.'

"When Douglass was demanding for the negro equality before the law—that Government should know no black, no white—a man cried out, 'That 's a damnable sentiment.' Douglass said, 'The Copperheads are saying I am no negro ! Then, as a white man, I declare I have no objection to negro equality before the law. I do not believe it will lessen my chances for the Presidency ! The negro would not refuse to vote for me on that account.'

"He introduced his newly arrived brother Perry, from whom he had been separated forty years. He had often tried to find him,—sent agents down South again and again,—but could get no trace of him. Slavery had whelmed him in its bitter flood. He spoke of his unspeakable joy in being restored to him. It was a tender and beautiful sight. Those two brothers, standing there side by side, moved the audience to tears of glad sympathy. Perry's honest face won, at first sight, confidence and interest, which his words of good sense and religious trust deepened.   It was the first time he had ever heard his brother speak in public."

"SHERWOOD, Oct. 6, 1867.

" . . . R. Howland sent me here October 1st (the day after the funeral of Mrs. Howland) : Mr. Howland and Emily were very glad to have me come.   Emily has been home since August, nursing her mother.   She is as heroic and self-denying as ever.   She and her father, in a few weeks, will make a journey to Northumberland County, Virginia, to look after her people.   She has four hundred acres of land there and ' every prospect pleases.'

" Emily wants you to work and teach among her people in Virginia.   She thinks you would be an admirable person to go.   If ever you will go, you have only to write her to secure a place."

Here is the first suggestion of what proved to be " The Holley School," and might have been " The Putnam School " but for the fact that Miss Putnam *would have her way* in doing loving honour to her friend.   Emily Howland, from whom the suggestion came (inspired by Sallie Holley !), was ever counted by our two evangelists as one of their most precious friends.   She was born in Sherwood, New York, November 20, 1827, and that town has always been her home except when exchanged for some field of active service.   Her father was an abolitionist and her principal reading as a child was that of abolition books and papers.   She writes me, October 24, 1898 : " I think I could not have done much but feel until

feeling became agony, and in 1857 much against the
wishes of the most of my relatives I went to Washington and taught a school for free coloured girls
which had been started some years before by Miss
Myrtilla Minor." In this work she continued for
two years. In 1863 she returned to Washington to
work in the great camp of Freedmen there, called
Contraband Camp, and kept at this until 1866. In
1867 her father bought a tract of land near Heaths-
ville at the mouth of the Potomac, and Miss Howland took there several of her "first families" of
Virginia blacks and started a school in a log cabin.
Her object was to sell the land to the Freedmen for
homes, and this object was accomplished. Hence
the importance of her suggestion that Miss Putnam
should go down to Virginia and follow her example.
It was a suggestion that determined the future of
Miss Putnam and Miss Holley to a remarkable degree, as we shall see a little farther on.

TO MISS PUTNAM

" Oct. 15, 1867. On board the *Aurora*, en route for Elmira.

"This morning I left the dear and sacred home of
Emily Howland. I found that the soldiers, and the people
whose sons, brothers, and husbands starved in Southern
prisons, all hated Horace Greeley's going bail for Jeff
Davis. They said if his son had perished there he
would n't have done it."

" PETERBORO, Oct. 28, 1867 .

" . . . Mr. Gerrit Smith is surprised at the bold and
aggressive side of my character, and never having seen

Emily Howland

it before, declares I am 'changed.' He says I am 'a regular old Puritan ; quote the Bible as they used to.' I well remember when Mr. Alcott first heard me lecture sixteen years ago, in Abington, he said to me, 'I am glad to see the Puritans are not all dead yet.' "

" PETERBORO, Nov. 4, 1867.

"I am in the home of Gerrit Smith. His unceasing benevolence and great, sweet heart are a wonder and delight. As Lowell wrote of Lydia Maria Child, ' His heart at high flood swamps his brain now and then.' He is extremely kind and obliging to me now as always ; writing letters to his friends to appoint my meetings and then sending me in his carriage to the meetings.

"Harriet Tubman came Saturday. She wants Mr. Smith to help her get her claim allowed against the Government. She has a letter from William H. Seward to Maj.-Gen. Hunter, dated 1865, in which Mr. Seward says, ' I have known her long, and a nobler, higher spirit, or truer, seldom dwells in human form.'

"Mr. Bridge is doing good work here preaching and teaching. Yesterday afternoon in this little church,¹ this small band of disciples celebrated the Lord's Supper ; all sitting around the table as in the beautiful picture of Leonardo da Vinci. I joined them, and it was a very tender and touching scene. The poor woman, a hunchback black man, beautiful, fair-complexioned Mrs. Bridge, the grand and noble head of Gerrit Smith, sincere and devout Rev. Mr. Bridge, and others."

¹ Built by Gerrit Smith for the uses of an independent, unsectarian congregation. Originally a Presbyterian, he had by this time reached a position so radical that he was a vice-president of the Free Religious Association.

"CAYUGA BRIDGE, Nov. 18, 1867.

"I an stopping at a small hotel and have laughed till I am tired, over the landlady here.   She said I had kept the servants trotting ever since I came, because I asked for a clean bed, and a fire, and water to drink."

"TRUMANSBURG, Nov. 25, 1867.

"Well, the deed is done ! I have spoken in Trumansburg, to a large audience in the Baptist meeting-house. Some people went out, evidently because they did n't like my sentiments.   There are many Copperheads in the Baptist Church, but I got all the good Republican farmer members in this vicinity to call on the minister and insist upon opening the door.   There was quite an excitement about it. This year (1867) I have sent the *Standard* nearly five hundred dollars for subscriptions."

"FARMER VILLAGE, Dec. 16, '67.

"Last night the Baptist church was full and I spoke for an hour or more. The Presbyterian minister adjourned his Sunday evening meeting and, with all his people, came to mine ! After the lecture he took my hand and said, ' I congratulate you on your large audience.'   The feeling that can assume such a thought on my part always offends me.

"Yesterday Farmer Covert and I drove sixteen miles for a subscriber, and I got him.   Mrs. Covert's grandmother was first cousin to the great painter, Hogarth."

A letter of Miss Putnam's in the scrap-book reports the Anti-Slavery Festival of January 22, 1868, which she and Miss Holley must have enjoyed exceedingly. Phillips was there, with younger men—O. B. Frothingham, D. A. Wasson, and Col. Higginson.   Apparently Mr. Wasson had not yet developed his intense antagonism to negro-suffrage. Frothingham praised Dr. Furness's devotion to "the greatest moral question of the age," and found here the reason why he had been "the profoundest interpreter of the life and spirit of Jesus of all the two hundred writers who had attempted to interpret them in the last thirty years." February 11th, Miss Putnam[1] writes from Salisbury, Connecticut, where Myron Holley was born, and gives a charming account of his daughter's visit there—the first one that she made. Her father's nephew, Ex-Governor Holley, greeted them with cordial hospitality. Sunday evening the old church was crowded, galleries and all, with a sympathetic audience, including many relatives. Spots that had dear associations were visited, no doubt with throbbing hearts. The iron mines suggested one of Miss Holley's first lessons in protection, of which later she became an ardent scholar and teacher, making this exception to liberty-loving principles, which but for this were wellnigh universal. March 4th, we have a letter from Miss Holley to "Dear Mrs. —— " in answer to the question, "What is the sense of keeping up an Anti-Slavery Society when there is not a slave in all the land?" It may be confidently surmised that we have here the burden of her prophecy in those distressful reconstruction times. The tone is very earnest and impassioned: The Anti-Slavery Society

[1] Miss Putnam finds in the practical efficiency of Myron Holley and his grand-nephew, Alexander L., the Bessemer steel inventor, a very happy correspondence with the work of Sallie Hollie for "improvements" more profoundly "internal" than theirs—the emancipation of the coloured people of the United States from slavery and ignorance.

was the only society demanding unfalteringly a guaranteed equal liberty, equal justice, for the black race. Harriet Tubman had just then been brutally thrust out from the street-cars in Washington. Was there no need of anti-slavery teaching there? In the following June her mother died at the age of eighty-two suddenly ending a life of splendid health and practical efficiency. The daughter, summoned from New England for the funeral, was soon back again on the long trail.

TO MISS PUTNAM

" West Gouldsboro, Me., Aug. 17, 1868.

" Mrs. McKaye, from Newport, who is here, told me that, when Governor Andrew brought the remains of Lieut. Lowell Putnam home, the mother was sick in bed, but the sister met him at the door, smiling, but tears falling thick and fast, and said, ' Governor Andrew, we thanked you when we got Willie's commission and we thank you now.' The Governor completely broke down under his emotion."

" Orland, Me., Oct. 9, 1868.

" Sunday was passed at Deer Isle. An agent of the American Bible Society preached there. He said that Bibles should be sent to the poor ignorant freed people. I could n't help thinking of the time when our American Anti-Slavery Society offered $500 to the American Bible Society if that Society would make the attempt to give Bibles to the slaves. But, so cowardly was it, it declined even making the attempt."

" Great Falls, Oct. 26, 1868.

" As I got out of the cars here Saturday evening, you could have knocked me down with a feather when I

heard my name called out in thundering tones ! They
had got the Town Crier to advertise my meeting ! It
was awful."

TO THE PORTERS

" BUFFALO, Nov. 23, 1869.

" Dear Miss Putnam is ' roughing it in the bush ' in
Virginia. Has been there a year. I have beautiful
letters from her every week. I spent five months at
two different times with her there. I have just come
off from a lecturing tour in old Cattaraugus County.
You will be glad to know that Miss Putnam's young sister, whom we educated in Oberlin for three years, is now
Lady Principal of the Olean Academy. So you see the
' bread cast upon the waters ' promise is fulfilled, as
always.

" As for myself I am as ever engaged in the Great
Cause. The negro is not yet where I wish to place
him."

" PETERBORO, N. Y., Dec. 16, 1869.

" . . . I preached here yesterday all day. Sunday
accompanied Gerrit Smith and Rev. Mr. Bridge to Mor-
risville to a Temperance Convention where Mr. Smith
made a beautiful speech. Some years ago Mr. Smith
was making a speech, when an Irishman called out,
' A great man ye are ! May ivery hair on your head be
a tallow candle to light ye to glory.' "

TO MISS PUTNAM

BOSTON, Feb. 17, 1870.

" It seems to me a sad mistake to discontinue the organisation of the Anti-Slavery Society or the *Standard*.
The mere fact that the coloured race has such friends
and guardians is a strong defence and high tower of de-

14

liverance from more wrongs and insults. The American Nation is not good enough to be trusted with the care of the black race. The blacks still need their long-tried and faithful friends of the American Anti-Slavery Society, which is a very different individual from the Nation. To discontinue our earnest defence and guard will be the signal for a volley of abuse and scorn let loose upon their defenceless heads, which Mr. Phillips should still cover with his strong and loving wing.

"Does not the simple fact of the existence of such a Society in the nation's midst, such a watchful, wise friend, save the poor black race from much neglect, contumely, and wrong? Does not such a fact guarantee a respect and aid they cannot afford to relinquish?"

"BOSTON, Feb. 21, 1870.

"It has been a thoughtful, not to say a sad day to me. Never more to have any New England Conventions! Perhaps I shall never come to Boston again. Anti-Slavery meetings all over with! It seems too soon to give them up. I am to stay in and around New York until after the meeting to commemorate the admission of coloured people to equal political rights—our Fifteenth Amendment rejoicing. Probably it will be the last public meeting of our Anti-slavery Society. The meeting[1] will be held next Saturday, after the Secretary of State announces that the Fifteenth Amendment has became the law of the nation."

[1] The scrap-book gives a full contemporary account of it. It was a great occasion, adorned by one of Phillips's most eloquent addresses. But the last meeting of the American Anti-Slavery Society was somewhat later, April 9, 1870.

CHAPTER XIV

COMING TO HER OWN

HER own were the black people of the South and they received her heartily ; but not so the white people. Miss Putnam, as we have seen, was her forerunner in the work, but in the two years of her priority Miss Holley made her two visits and nothing could have been more natural or inevitable than their entering into partnership. They had been too inseparable for twenty years to think of living separate lives. But there were reasons far less personal for Miss Holley's going to Virginia and spending the last twenty years of her life in teaching negro children and making herself a good providence to their people round about. Her action here was the natural continuation of her anti-slavery work. This had always been intensely personal and human. Never did the zeal of the reformer less burn up the human heart. She had remembered those in bonds as bound with them. The slaves were human beings to her, not so many mere units in an abstract "cause." She had kept the field so long as the Anti-Slavery Societies maintained their organisation and the *Standard* floated to the breeze. With the dissolution of the one and the suspension of the other she was foot-free for pastures new. She found them at Lottsburgh, Virginia, Northumberland County, at the mouth of the Potomac, about ten miles from the school established by Miss Howland in the "faw'est." A good account of the enterprise is found in a printed letter of Miss Holley's dated August 3, 1875 :

"It is nearly seven years since we established this Freedmen's school in Virginia. We came from our great love and pity for the poor coloured people. We are not the agents of any society, we have no salary, but give purely volunteer service. Nothing could be more bare, and blank, and hopeless than our material surroundings were to begin with. But upon a two-acre strip of this desolate land, exhausted a hundred years ago with miserable tobacco raising, we have succeeded in building a cheerful Teacher's Home, and a spacious, airy, pleasant new schoolhouse. We have made flower-borders, strawberry-beds, melon-patches, grape-arbours, and fruit trees to blossom and flourish, to the admiration of all around us. There are seven hundred coloured people in this town. Our school keeps from Christmas to Christmas, without vacation, the year round. The tides of its blessings reach every soul. The all-absorbing business of the country is corn-raising. Most of our scholars are intermittents, for they have to work nearly all summer in these immense cornfields. But by keeping the doors of our school ever open, hundreds have learned to read and write. When we first came, they did not know a letter of the alphabet, or the names of the days of the week ; could not count on ten fingers,

or name the State they lived in. And the ignorance
of these white Virginians, too, is appalling—a striking
illustration of the truth of what the great Wilberforce
said : 'No man can put a chain around his brother's
neck and God not put the other end of the chain about
his own.'—These slaveholders, in shutting out the light
of knowledge from the blacks, also shrouded themselves
in the gloom of wretched ignorance.

. . . .

" As we have no salary ourselves, we can offer others
none. So their aid must ever be a labour of love. One
great compensation for living in Virginia is the climate,
the most delightful I ever knew. The winters are short
and mild. In summer we have a refreshing breeze from
off Chesapeake Bay and Potomac River. We never
know a hot night. "The Evening Wind" is to us all
that Bryant sings it. After having been out to play upon
the wild, blue waves, it comes to cool the twilight of our
summer day.

" We have no white society except when our Northern
friends visit us. The poor coloured people come to our
door every day and almost every hour. Every want in life
is theirs. We are glad to help clothe them from the boxes
and barrels sent down from the North. In return they
weed our gardens—cut our firewood, 'tote' water from
the spring, etc. Sometimes their joy at seeing us is highly
amusing. One day an old coloured lady came to see me.
She seemed greatly satisfied with the interview; when she
rose to take leave she seemed to think she ought to
apologise for such exuberance of spirits, and she dropped
a very low courtesy, saying, 'Please 'scuse me ma'am,
Ise so proud when I gets 'long side of de Norf population ! I knowed you was Norf population as quick as
I seen you.'"

Help came to them in many ways.

> "He that doth the ravens feed,
> Yea, providently caters to the sparrow,"

has many "great allies" and some of these knew
of the Holley School from the beginning and others
found it out in course of time, some of them going
to see the work with their own eyes and reporting
on it in public and private letters to the public
and their friends. The scrap-book is enriched with
many of the printed sort. They describe the situation; they indicate the character of the work; they
tell of the delightful celebrations with which Misses
Holley and Putnam marked the anniversaries of
great days of patriotism and freedom and religion.
Some of the brightest of these letters were written
by that Mrs. Elizabeth Oakes Smith whose elaborate
toilet had so scandalised the sober-minded women
of the Woman's Rights Convention in 1855.

In a sketch of Miss Holley's life written for the
Silver Cross, July, 1893, there is a good account of
one of the most interesting features of her work:

"It was a great day for her people when word came
from Lodge Landing, on the Potomac, that 'The *Sue*
had brought a box for Miss Holley from de Norf,' and
when the two-wheeled ox-cart, which she would send for
it, arrived, a crowd of both blacks and whites would
gather around, and with great expectancy await its opening. Then, they would offer in exchange, chickens,
eggs, and services, for the commodities so generously
sent. Miss Holley never encouraged pauperism, but
taught her people that it was honourable to *earn*, or buy

their comforts, not to *beg* them. So one young darkey would say, 'Gim me dat coat, and Ise build a heap o' dat fence.' 'Gim me dem collars and cuffs and neckties, and I done pull de weeds outer dat ar strawberry bed o' yourn,' and so on, till all had been distributed, except the articles she retained to be presented to them upon special occasions, and as rewards of merit. There were certain days in the year which she singled out to be celebrated with appropriate ceremonies ; among these the anniversaries of the Emancipation Proclamation, the Opening of the School ; and at Christmas and other holidays, also, at the close it was her unfailing custom to give a present to everyone, young or old, black or white, who attended the services. This was a great source of pleasure to them, and the gift helped to impress the lessons of the day upon their minds.

"In various ways she endeavoured to give her people a practical knowledge of the good results of labour. She, herself, had a garden planted with vegetables, fruit, and flowers, to show them what they might have and enjoy, if they would only work for it. In many instances the object lesson proved a success, while some pronounced the good things to eat, very nice, 'but oh ! a heap of trouble.' 'Very well,' she would reply, 'you can go without.' 'He that will not work, shall not eat.'"

One of the best of many accounts of the School is from a correspondent of the *Lyons Republican* writing from Lottsburgh in 1877.

"This is the centre around which everything else revolves ; and whatever else may fail, *this* goes on uninterruptedly from year's end to year's end, an ever active centre of influence constantly operating upon this community in the diffusion of intellectual light, and the awakening into life of a higher order of ideas than commonly prevails here. In this school Miss Holley gives personal instruction or procures the necessary teachers, labours for it directly or indirectly, and has at all times a supervision over its welfare. The results of this work are certainly encouraging. Much of the former darkness of mind, ignorance, and consequent wretchedness, that prevailed so long throughout the entire community, have been dispelled ; those of the pupils whose attendance is at all regular have a bright, wide-awake aspect, possess a creditable fund of information concerning the times in which they are living and some of the causes that underlie the effects that are visible all around them, show an ability for, and give evidence of, mental discipline, and an awakened capacity for improvement, which promises well for their future."

The letter from which this paragraph is taken yields a concluding one of a more general character.

" In brief, Miss Holley's enterprise means two things. To her, it means incessant toil, privation, and care ; a continual strain on all her physical and mental energies ; constant vexations and interruptions ; and the total absence of all congenial society, with the added penalty of unfriendly demonstrations from those of her neighbours who would not be sorry to see her labours perish with her. To her many beneficiaries, on the other hand, it means the daily stimulant of precept and example ; the means of intellectual and moral culture and growth ; and the opportunity of obtaining in return for such small services as they can offer—and which here find a market and a price they could find nowhere else—necessities, conveniencies, and comforts otherwise wholly unattainable. And no disinterested observer can look upon the results that have been and are being accomplished here, without expressing the wish that these ladies may be prospered in their philanthropic and self-denying labours to the fullest extent of their desires."

So many friends, with equal sympathy if not with equal ability to help, came to the aid of the Holley School in various ways, that it seems invidious to name particular helpers. Yet it would be ungracious not to name such loyal friends as the Porters of Rochester; the Tylers of Elmira; Mr. James S. Rogers of Chicago[1]; Gerrit Smith and his daughter, Mrs. Elizabeth Smith Miller; Emily Howland; the Otis Shepards of Brookline, Massachusetts; Mrs. Francis George Shaw, the mother of Col. Shaw; his aunt, Mrs. Anna Shaw Greene; Mrs. Putnam, the mother of Lieut. Lowell Putnam; and Dr. and Mrs. Frank Fuller of New York.[2] The Doctor,

---

[1] Ever one of the most devoted friends of the Holley School and the two friends who had it in their charge, he crowned his service by selecting from Miss Holley's letters those which seemed to him most fit for publication. He did this to satisfy Miss Putnam's loyal soul. He confessed that his admiration for Miss Holley made a coldly critical attitude difficult for him. His work upon the letters has made mine much easier than it would otherwise have been. He anticipated that much of his choosing would be finally omitted; but I, in my turn, have erred, perhaps, on the side of a too liberal inclusion. Mrs. Rogers, one of the Worcester (connected with the Leicester) Earles, was to Miss Putnam what Kadijah was to Mohammed—her first convert; *i. e.*, to her faith that Sallie Holley's story must be written for her friends if not for a wider public.

[2] To which names must certainly be added, says Miss Putnam, "as faithful and long-devoted helpers of the Holley School," those of Photius Fisk, Sarah H. Southwick, Mr. and Mrs. Russell Marston, Col. C. W. Folsom, Louisa M. Alcott and her mother, Miss Ellen Emerson, Senator George F. Hoar of Massachusetts, Miss Ellen

we are told, was "never without a box or barrel in
his office in process of packing for Miss Holley, and
she often used to tell with peculiar satisfaction of
her 'Fuller Fence' built entirely by means of the
contents of the ' Fuller barrels.' "

Another helper of most enviable fame was Mr.
Thomas N. Rooker, named in a former chapter as
one of her youthful playmates. A chance remark
of Oliver Johnson's in the *Tribune* office brought
her to his mind after many years of separation and,
perhaps, mutual forgetfulness. He wrote and invited her to his home in Brooklyn to renew the old
acquaintance. She came with Miss Putnam one
snowy, icy Saturday evening in February, 1868, just
after the visit to Myron Holley's birthplace in Connecticut. Ezra Cornell had just left, full of plans for
his new university. "Would women be admitted?"
asked Miss Holley, always on the alert where her
characteristic principles were involved. Mr. Rooker
thought " of course"; his sister doubted and was
right ; but before long there was a happy change.

Miss Putnam on her way to Virginia with Miss
Howland in 1868 met Mr. Cornell and "withstood
him to the face," not because he, but because the
trustees, "ought to be blamed." Miss Howland had
girl friends whom she wished to have admitted and

Collins of New York, Mrs. Elizabeth Preston of New Hamsphire,
Col. and Mrs. J. S. Lockwood of Boston. Some of these names have
for me no personal associations, but all of them seem to have that
place in Miss Putnam's heart that Calais had in Mary Tudor's and
Italy in Robert Browning's :

" Open my heart and you will see,
Graved inside of it, ' Italy.' "

Thomas N. Rooker.

Mr. Cornell advised her to send them on sufferance as he did his own daughter, but her claim on the consideration of the faculty was not so evident as his. When she next met Mr. Rooker, in 1871, he was glorying in Mr. Henry W. Sage's gift of $200,-000 to Cornell to make it a bi-sexual university. Meantime Mr. Rooker had given the Holley School $100 towards its present schoolhouse and he was unabating in his sympathy and help until his death, in 1898, and his support meant that of the *Tribune* also, with many a timely word.

It was perhaps, but I think not,¹ during Miss Holley's visit to Mr. Rooker in Brooklyn that I made her acquaintance and had the pleasure of welcoming her in the evening to my pulpit. My recollection of her appearance is very clear. I can see, as if they were now before me, the eyes so softly bright, the fresh complexion as if the roses that she loved so much had given their colour to her cheeks, the beautiful hair lying smoothly on the forehead, which was broad and full. The face had little formal beauty; could have had little, I should think, at any time, despite the ardent protestations of her friends; but that expression which is "feature in the making" overflowed her lineaments and the general impression was singularly interesting and engaging. When she came to speak there were, as the saying goes, "tears in her voice"—a very sweet and penetrating note which went far to explain the sympathy which

¹ That she attended my church in the morning at that time, Miss Putnam is confident, and Miss Putnam saw her first English sparrows on the way.

she had commonly excited in her hearers' minds. I
recall, too, a certain tremulous sensibility which
made it wonderful to me that she could bear the
strain of so much public speaking under conditions
sometimes fearfully adverse. But that sensibility
was one of the purest sources of her persuasive
eloquence.

Turning again to Miss Putnam's file of her friend's
letters, we find her established in the work which
was to be the sacred passion of her remaining years,
subordinating to itself all the other joys and sorrows
of her life.

TO THE PORTERS

" LOTTSBURGH, Aug. 28, 1870.

"I have been here all summer and incessantly busy.
Indeed our work here seems to me like the twelve labours
of Hercules. These coloured people are awfully poor
and destitute. Every want of life is theirs, from a
lump of sugar for the sick baby to an acre of land for
a homestead. I think it was dreadfully mean and disgraceful in the United States Government not to give
some land to these poor negroes who had worked all
their life-time without wages. 'Oppress not the poor.'"

TO MRS. PORTER

" LOTTSBURGH, July 20, 1872.

"How I wish it were possible for you to visit me
here ! We are very quiet in the depths of the country and
were it not for my constant labours of various kinds and
degrees I might feel keenly this exile life. It is a perpetual wonder how people possessing so few of the com-

forts of life can be so cheerful and uncomplaining as
these poor black folks are.

"I have just read Gerrit Smith's speech and rejoice
that he is for Grant and Wilson. If by a frown from
Providence, Greeley is elected, we shall have awful doings here. All the old rebels are earnestly trying to get
our coloured men to vote for Greeley. I hold regular
monthly Republican meetings in our schoolhouse, and
don't mean a single man shall vote for Horace Greeley."

"LOTTSBURGH, Sept. 1, 1872.

"Oh, how I wish you were here to spend this lovely
Sunday with me ! I am alone, but our schoolhouse is
only a few rods off, and I hear the coloured people in
their morning meeting singing

"'I want to rise with the heavenly choir
When the old Archangel rings the bell.'

"You can scarcely imagine how remote from all I
used to know, this kind of life is. I have too much to
do to feel at all lonely, but a visit from Northern friends
would be wonderfully sweet to me.

"Sept. 23d.—This climate is lovely for me. All summer long I have known no distressing heat. We have a
delicious breeze from off the river and bay daily and
mild, charming weather up to Christmas.

"You must not envy these poor people their 'faith.'
It is very small, not enough to save them even in this
world. Their language is often striking and poetical.
Yesterday, in their meeting, one man prayed, 'Oh, Jesus,
this day may hell be balked of her large expectations.'
And the minister, good William Downing, exclaimed in
his sermon, 'Jesus is the everlasting flagstaff of eternal

victory.' But many of them never dream that religion has anything to do with honesty or truth.

"Dec. 26th.—Yesterday we held our Christmas festival in our schoolhouse, and had a green cedar tree loaded with all sorts of good things for our dark scholars, big and little. Twelve of our children recited one of *your* Christmas poems, and did very nicely. I wished you could hear them. Indeed all the pieces were said so correctly and admirably, and, afterwards, their fathers made such sensible remarks, and tender and eloquent speeches, that our New York lady visitor declared, 'though it was cold and snowing without, within it seemed that " December 's as pleasant as May." ' She, with Miss Putnam and our assistant teacher, Miss Sterling, has gone to-day to attend the wedding of Mary Ann Diggs. They all drove off in an ox-cart and I am left at home with only one young coloured maid, Harriet Porter, who is now pursuing her literary avocations before the parlour fire, while I am reporting to you. I made a loaf of cake for the wedding. The raisins, currants, and citron were given me in New York, and I don't suppose such a nice fruit-cake was ever seen here before."

TO THE PORTERS

" LOTTSBURGH, Oct. 13, 1874.

" We have two acres of land about us, but it was such poor, worn-out soil that it 'aggravates my life near out of me,' to get it all fertilised to grow my fruits and flowers. What I especially plead with you to be sure to put into Maria's barrel, is some root or vine from your garden that I can plant here. I should like a young grape-vine and a rose-bush to keep the memory of dear old times fresh and green even in this far-off country.

"Miss Putnam and I have tugged and toiled, and striven and struggled on through this summer, and though our new schoolhouse is not entirely completed at this date, yet I rejoice to write, the second coat of plaster is this day successfully going on, and by November 1st our school will enter triumphantly.   These Virginia rebels are fairly confounded to see our schoolhouse spring up so magically, and our fortunes revive so elastic from their hostile tread.   Like the camomile bed, the more it is trod upon, the more fragrant and lively it becomes.   Our coloured friends are cheered to the very marrow of their bones.   Their faces shine, as day after day they call on us to exult and crow.   Still we know the enemy ever sits with lance in rest to take advantage as often as he can make a deadly thrust.   These Virginia rebels are no more reconstructed than those in Louisiana or Alabama.

"It was so cool when I rose at 4.30 this morning that I put on those nice, warm, grey stockings that Mrs. Porter knit with her own fingers and sent down.   As we are our own servants and cooks, for ourselves and our workmen, we are compelled to rise very early in order to run our daily race of duties.   What a never ending burden these household cares, especially when one expects *ravens* to bring the supplies."

TO MRS. E. S. MILLER

"LOTTSBURGH, Jan. 5, 1875.

"Yesterday's mail brought me the painful intelligence of your noble father's death.   I and thousands of human hearts are to-day mourning that we shall see his beautiful face no more on earth.   I think of you and your angelic mother and pray God to bind up your bruised

and wounded hearts. And for your blessed father—
what a great awakening it must be for him, upon that
life unmeasured by the flight of time ! And all that life
is Love. All those tender and noble affections, his love
of justice, his heavenly aspirations, his thirst for more
and more knowledge and wisdom—how unspeakably
precious and imperishable they must ever be !

"I cannot doubt he was met by loving and kindred
souls who welcome, cherish, and appreciate him. What
a great blessing he was to us all ! How much I owe to
him ! Those delightful visits to Peterboro' where he
always made me so glad and happy ! I have the very
first letter he ever wrote me, and it is marvellously graceful, elegant, and beautiful.

"How he stands out in clear relief from the rest of
the world in all his benevolence and pure, unselfish
sympathy for the poor and needy ! How rich and
privileged I feel that I knew and loved him ! How
singularly free he was from pride and vain-glory ! I feel
so deeply moved by his death, and such a crowd of
thoughts, emotions, and tears come, that I must write
you in sympathy and grief. I praise God for all your
father was and did on earth."

"LOTTSBURGH, Jan. 28, 1875.

"'The loveliest of the lovely and kindest of the kind,'
was the very instant feeling of my heart and speech of
my lips, about you, as I read your beautiful letter, with
irrepressible tears of admiration and affection over all
your noble generosity to us and our school. How good
and unselfish to spare your time and effort to us at such
an hour, when, I know, your own grief and loss press
you sorely. I thank you for communicating to me so

many particulars of your father's last earthly days. Every one of them is of tenderest interest to me. How I wish I could have seen him at the last! But no power can make me doubt that I shall again see him and know him. Yes, as Bryant sings,

" ' In the resplendence of that glorious sphere
    And larger movements of the unfettered mind.'

It has been the habit of my whole life,—as it was my father's before me,—to cherish an unfaltering faith in immortality. In the highest and most real experiences of my spirit, I always see it the clearest and most distinctly. In the deepest griefs and most trying trouble, the assurance comes to me—like a voice from heaven. In the human soul I see proofs. How can death have power over the great affections,—the noble mind, the rich character, the high hopes, the long, patient, self-denying efforts after growth and improvement, the sublime trust in hours of test? Why should we ever have this exalted faith and purifying hope unless it be eternally vital? Why should we be subject to such great and joyful attraction unless our destiny is proportioned?'

" Oh, my dear friend, I believe with all my might and mind in immortality. I think of your dear father with all his beautiful disposition, as a disencumbered spirit, intensely interested and supremely glad in all the heavenly life opening largely before him. Not one of his hopes will be disappointed. In unutterable reverence and changeless devotion, I bow in grateful humility before the Great Father, to thank Him for the gift of Everlasting Life."

---

[1] A clear reflection of the celebrated doctrine of Fourier: " The attractions are proportioned to the destinies."

"LOTTSBURGH, March 26, 18—.

"Your 'only a line,' has reached us to-day. I sympathise most deeply in your loss of your beloved mother.
Yes, we did love and prize her pure, beautiful spirit very
greatly. I remember how very lovely she looked while
singing at the grave of my father when the monument
was erected at Mount Hope, in Rochester, more than
thirty years ago. I always admired the delicate taste of
your sainted mother in wearing white. It was so peculiarly
appropriate to her character. What an exquisite appreciation she had of flowers! We can never forget her
pleasure in the rhodora I sent her from Worcester. She
had read Mr. Emerson's poem, but had never seen the
flower.

"Miss Putnam wrote you last Saturday, telling of our
grateful joy and loving thanks for your large barrel of
nice comforts to us and our people here. And now you
mention another barrel! Every garment ever worn by
your dear father seems sacred. It is impossible to tell
you how dearly we thank you for sending them to us.
You cannot fully know how much your good gifts have
done to make our life in Virginia easier, brighter, and
more happy and useful."

TO THE PORTERS

"LOTTSBURGH, March 27, 1875.

"We are congratulating ourselves on the agreeable
fact that two of our young coloured women are now educated far enough to be able and willing to conduct our
Sunday-school! This morning they made their début,
and I am happy to say, with very good results.

"In week-day school Miss Putnam keeps forty-eight
little slates and pencils, and two hundred and forty right-
hand fingers busy in humble imitation of what she saw

in your own beautiful school in Rochester. So, dear Mrs. Porter, you, in a manner, are teacher still. Classes have the luxury of books alike, thanks to the Rochester box.

"For the past week our Boston crocusses have been in bloom. My tomatoes are up, in my little hot-bed. The ninth of March I planted a square of Irish potatoes and in June I expect to eat them. Vice-President Wilson sent us 'Champion of England peas,' that we will plant to-morrow. The weeping willow I planted three years ago is now ten feet high, with long, lithe branches sweeping the ground, and putting forth its young, tender green leaves.

"Our new schoolhouse, we can't be too thankful for. It is a constant comfort and satisfaction and is almost entirely paid for."

TO MRS. E. S. MILLER

" LOTTSBURGH, Jan. 15, 1876.

"Your two beautiful lamps with their high, delicate chimneys and elegant, soft shades give us the most delightful parlour illumination we have ever had in Virginia. They, with our open pine-wood fire, lighten and glorify our little parlour in a way splendid to behold! The lamps seem like a piece of Peterboro' come down to Virginia. I remember them as they stood in your father's library and in the drawing-room—a part of the sweet peace and distinguished charm of that dear home. How much happiness we do owe to you!"

" LOTTSBURGH, Feb. 13, 1877.

"Next week our school celebrates Washington's birthday, and all are eager and interested. A class of eight recites Buchanan Read's patriotic poem, 'The Eagle and the Vulture ' ¹ with immense spirit. Another class recites Schiller's ' Diver ' very well. I really take pleasure and delight in hearing their clear young voices declaim what was the favourite poem of my childhood. The scholars never were so interested in their studies as now. The greatest punishment is to be sent home from school. The large, cheerful room, with walls covered with beautiful pictures—the warmth of our big stove—the big windows at the south—all form such an attractive contrast to their poor, little, dark, smoky cabins. No wonder they cry and feel great distress if told they must leave school !

" The dire ignorance of all this community, both white and black, is astonishing. Even the old Bible stories, they never heard till we came ! An old coloured oysterman was so immensely taken with the story of ' Joseph and his Brethren ' when I told it in Sunday-school, that since then he never can hear it often enough, but is always asking and begging to hear it over again. And ' Ruth ' made his tears come ! "

In May, 1878, she went to England, and returned early in October. For a time the chills and fever she had contracted in her wonderful Virginia climate clung to her, but eventually the summer proved "a season of refreshing" both for her body and her mind. She heard Moncure D. Conway preach with delight born in good measure from the fact that his father was a Virginia slaveholder, while the son was a champion of Freedom in whatever guise she came. Spurgeon she found repulsive in voice and matter. She did an immense amount of sight-seeing, and

¹ The *Kearsarge* and the *Alabama.*—C. F. P.

wrote long, bright, pleasant letters about it to the
Lyons Republican. Westminster Abbey overwhelmed her with emotion, wonder, and awe; with
gratitude and joy. Apparently she did not ask
Charles Lamb's question, " Where are the bad people buried?" nor remember Carlyle's reflection on
the Abbey, " What a jail-delivery there would be!"
—at the general resurrection. But she was ever prone
to find the good in life, and pass by the evil on the
other side unless it threatened injury to her chosen
people.

TO MRS. MILLER

" LOTTSBURGH, Dec. 30, 1878.

"I wish you a happy New Year! We celebrated
Christmas in our schoolhouse and shall also New Year's
Day. These poor white as well as coloured people
flock to our doors to get a present holiday times. Last
Wednesday more than three hundred souls came, and to
each one I had the pleasure of giving something off our
gay Christmas tree. It is pitiful to see these poor whites
with their blank, lean faces. Too silly or proud to attend, or to allow their little children to attend our *coloured* school! And to grow up without knowing the
alphabet!

"The religion of these coloured people is very demoralising. It has no connection with moral principle.
They have just had a ' three days' meeting ' in the old
stolen schoolhouse, and made night hideous with their
horrible singing and prayers, and dancing in a wild, sav-
age way. The noise and shuffling and scraping can be
heard in every direction, and our house, though not very
near, seems almost shaken by their dancing. It is like

the tread of an army in weight and sound. One of our young lady teachers says it reminds her of a heavy sea beating against a rocky beach ! They get drunk on tobacco [another of Miss Holley's deadly enemies], and then in their high excitement go to meeting and keep up till almost morning, in their fearful, exhausting action !

"I am glad to say that my new, tight oak fence, that I have been struggling years to build, is at last completed. Our next summer garden fruits will be safe, I think."

" LOTTSBURGH, March 25, 1879.

"The little pamphlet in one of your barrels, entitled *Benefaction of William Evans to the Town of Smithfield*, interested me greatly. Especially the speech of your father where he so modestly attributes most merit to Mr. Evans. 'He toiled for his wealth, I inherited mine. His was acquired in the sweat of his brow ; mine cost me nothing. Great praise is due to him while little praise belongs to me,' etc. I think your father had great humility of soul. Wonderful in a man of so much worldly possession ! "

" LOTTSBURGH, June 10, 1879.

"I thank you very much for the beautiful verbenas. They are now growing in our garden. I love to find myself in the country near green trees, and with flowers growing about me. I took great delight in walking in Kensington Gardens and under those grand old trees in Hyde Park. Just now the glory of the garden here is 154 tall white Annunciation Lilies ! "

TO THE PORTERS

" LOTTSBURGH, July 8, 1879.

"   .   .   .   Give a great deal of love to Maria, and thank her for her kind *wish* to send me the needed money.

I seldom get a sight of any money. In this country it is all barter and exchange of eggs for soap or starch, corn for sugar, etc. A friend of mine who deals in hats, sends me every summer a big box of them, which I exchange here for various necessaries at the small variety store, and also get firewood, pine lumber, nails, etc., with —hats.

"You write you would like to see some of the results of our 'labours of love.' You would have to travel about considerably to do so, for our older pupils almost all go away, to Baltimore, Washington, New York, New England, etc., to get higher wages. One of our girls has lived in Senator Blaine's family the last three or four years. One is learning dressmaking in New York City. Two go to Saratoga every summer and receive excellent wages. One has travelled all over Europe as lady's maid. One thinks there is no place like Connecticut; she has been there six years. These idle, shiftless ways of Virginia can never redeem the State. Northern people must volunteer to come down and show what civilisation means, if this country is ever to be lifted out of rude barbarism."

TO MRS. MILLER

"LOTTSBURGH, Aug. 5, 1879.

"This is the hottest summer I ever have known in all my life, anywhere. Sometimes I can't help wishing I was where I was last July and August—in *cool* England. For months here scarcely a drop of rain fell. All over England there have been prayers offered for fair weather.

"I thank you for every letter you are so kind to write. In this very secluded and confined life of ours, letters are the overflowing fountain of pleasure. Never, before I came to reside in Virginia, did I fully appreciate those lines of Pope,

> " ' Heaven first sent letters to some wretch's aid,
> Some banished lover or some captive maid.'

How many things we read in early life whose meaning does not unfold until our own personal experience translates it. Don't you find it so ? "

TO MRS. PORTER

" LOTTSBURGH, Aug. 26, 1879.

" This whole summer long I have had nobody to talk with but Miss Putnam and these poor coloured folks ! These white women who hold themselves high, are sick with bilious fever or rheumatism a great part of the time. Their habits of living are horrible. Fat bacon, poor black coffee, and bread made with saleratus and eaten hot from the fire. It is awfully rainy and the coloured people are holding their 'protracted meeting.' I expect nothing less than that all will be down sick with chills, after it is over. They use immense quantities of tobacco,—men and women both smoke,—then hold all-night meetings and shuffle and scuffle and sing and scream in the greatest excitement and call it being ' happy in the Lord.'

" Steptoe Ball, as he was hoeing my garden the other day, near the morning-glories, remarked : ' In old rebel times the horn blowed at break o' day : time then to get up, cook, an' eat. Then at sunrise, horn blow agin an' we had to go to work, whether we eat or not. No time then to look at mornin' glories, or *night* glories. Mebbe dey might been here. Never heerd the name of 'em befo' you ladies come. Awful times then ! nobody knowed *a* from *b ;* but sence you ladies come, so much

THE HOLLEY SCHOOL

light has sprung up all roun' that now there's nobody hardly that don't know *a* from *b*.'   I thought it valuable testimony."

TO MARIA PORTER

"LOTTSBURGH, Dec. 2, 1879.

"This is 'Old John Brown's Day,' and what better time could there be to acknowledge the gifts sent to these poor, long-enslaved people, whom the glorious old man died to make free? The well-filled barrel and box were deposited at our door last evening. I thought of our departed Almira [one of the Porter sisters] as each garment was taken out. They had a double and more tender welcome as coming from her generous hand, and as the last labour of love for us and our school. Please give Mary Anthony and her mother my love, and say how tenderly touched I was on reading the few lines attached to her dear father's last coat :—that it was to comfort some poor, black man here in Virginia. I shall give it to Solomon Porter, an honest, well-intentioned man, who suffers awfully from rheumatism,—and is not considered as cunning and bright, intellectually, as some of his race are. But Captain Dawson says, 'Anybody who takes Solomon Porter for a fool will lose his money.' Solomon knows enough to be honest and to keep his word, which can't be said of everybody, either black or white, in my circle of acquaintance ! His wife loves her ease and is disgracefully lazy, and poor Solomon toils on to get corn, sweet potatoes, and meat to keep off starvation.

"Our scholars, big and little, still look to us for wraps to keep off cold Winter's bites, and to make them decently presentable in the garb of modern civilisation. With the help of barrels like yours they appear quite stylish.

My cup of joy runneth over with gratitude for your kindness."

TO MRS. MILLER

" LOTTSBURGH, July 13, 1880.

" Yesterday morning a nice cooking-stove was landed at my door. I want to thank somebody for this very welcome comfort so rarely to be found in this poor Virginia wilderness. 'There is no guessing its kith and kin,' as was the case with the Pied Piper ; nevertheless I venture to write you whose open, generous hand has so often supplied our needs here—to say how very glad I am to have the stove, and how truly and sincerely I thank the good giver.

" Have you read Tourgee's *A Fool's Errand?* I think from all I hear of the book, it must be my own story of my life here in Virginia. How hopeless it seems ever to educate the Southerner up to Northern civilisation ! "

TO MISS TYLER

" LOTTSBURGH, Aug. 22, 1881.

" Your pleasant letter of the 15th was very welcome, especially in my solitude. The letters I receive from my dear friends do 'cheat absence of its sting.' What did people do before the post was established ?

" Your classing me with Lady Hester Stanhope is amusing. I dare say I am alone as much as she was. My days fly quickly by. Every hour has its task. My house, garden, and schoolhouse are situated on a gentle hill, and very cheerful and cool, with the ever-enlivening sea breeze. Paper-weights are always in requisition whenever a letter is to be written ; otherwise the wind blows everything off.

"You request to know what 'papers I see *regularly.*' *The Boston Commonwealth, The Woman's Journal, The Lyons Republican, The Jonesville Independent, New York Semi-Weekly Tribune,* and a great many others *irregularly.*"

TO MRS. MILLER

" Lottsburgh, Aug. 26, 1881.

"Miss Putnam has been in New England since early in April, but will return here next month. I am entirely alone with school, Post-office,[1] and house and garden. My health sweetens all life for me. The sea breezes always come and the heat is not oppressive. Did you know that Elizur Wright is writing the life of my father? He thinks his manuscript will be complete about the middle of September. It is most generous in him to take so much thought and toil and travel to accomplish this work. Those old abolitionists were a noble circle of men."

The gap at this point between letters of 1881 and 1883 represents, among other things, a winter with her nieces in Germany (1882), which she enjoyed exceedingly and wrote about to the *Lyons Republican* with her habitual enthusiasm in the enjoyment of all beautiful and novel things.

" July 12, 1883.

" I was very much gratified to hear you felt an interest in distributing my father's Biography. I took of Mr. Wright one hundred dollars' worth of the books to sell and return

[1] Whereby hangs a tale. Miss Putnam was made post-master at Lottsburgh in 1869 and still holds the fort in spite of manifold opposition stirred up against her at various times. Her predecessor in the office could not read or write his name.

him the money. My object is to express my grateful sense of Elizur Wright's faithful labour in writing the Biography. He published the book at his own expense. I wish to reimburse him some of the money he expended." [1]

" LOTTSBURGH, Sept. 29, 1883.

" . . . We are now reading *Letters and Memorials of Jane Welsh Carlyle.* She was a much-suffering, much-complaining woman. She struggled hard with her housework and tells very much the same story any earnest housekeeper could, if she chose to picture the shady side in her letters. She had the common experience with her builders, carpenters, and painters that every house-builder and repairer I ever knew, including myself, could relate. Wherever she was,—in Scotland or England or Wales,—East, West, North, or South, there was

" 'One little hut among the bushes,
One that she loved,'—*5 Cheyne Row.*

" She was true to one at least of the 'kindred points ' of Wordsworth's 'Skylark'—Home. No wonder Carlyle mourned the inconsolable loss of such a true and tried ' better half,' and published her staunch faithfulness through thick and thin of their forty years' tossings and growlings and ' earthquakes,' and all the terrible pains and travail of soul in which he produced his fiery-hearted books ! A much-suffering, almost tragical existence, mixed with rare joys of knowing bright and gifted people, who, almost every one, took their turn under her clever quizzing-glasses."

[1] The scrap-book blossoms thick with notices and reviews of the Myron Holley book. The best one is from the hand of Oliver Johnson, though, as we should expect, it antagonises some of Mr. Wright's criticisms upon Garrison.

"NEW YORK, Feb., 1884.

"I am so inexpressibly thankful to taste once more the luxury and ease of this hotel life,—so unlike the place from whence I came! The labour and hardship of Virginia life could not be serenely lived out were it not for the celestial consolations my work there, among the poorest of the poor and the saddest of the sad, yields me. Is it not some drop of comfort even to be the least in 'the noble army of martyrs' who have helped to elevate and redeem the human race?

"Did I write you about the long fight, the earnest battle we had to keep our Lottsburgh Post-office in my schoolhouse? The Democrats were very miserable over their defeat. For months they tugged and toiled to effect a removal of the Post-office, but all in vain. No new appointment was made, though every Republican postmaster for miles and miles about, was turned out. Our one hundred and three coloured Lottsburgh voters were all right, and the Democratic candidate for State Legislature lost his election. He said, 'Oh, Lord! those Lottsburgh niggers are all drilled.'"

TO MARIA PORTER

"LOTTSBURGH, May 22, 1884.

"Miss Putnam left a week ago to spend the summer in New England, and I am entirely alone on my plantation of three acres. The garden is full of singing birds, and they sing as if they thought 'life worth living.' To-day our thermometer registers ninety, yet the air is charmingly cool and fresh. I am cased in flannel from head to foot: should not feel comfortable in any less heavy drapery.

"I have a great deal to do. The Post-office affairs

absorb many hours of my day. Registering letters is a real study : such infinite precaution against the possibility of their being stolen. Wickedness is always awfully expensive.

"Snakes like this warm, sunny weather, and nearly every day, when poor, old Steptoe Ball comes to work in my garden, he kills two or three big ones—hideous creatures ! And yet, all life is to me so wonderful, and so very mysterious, I shrink from extinguishing the lowliest."

TO MISS TYLER

" LOTTSBURGH, Aug. 15, 1884.

". . . You say ' religious life is at a low ebb in Elmira.' Not so here. The white folks' campmeeting has just ended. Over thirty conversions ! The coloured ' protracted meeting ' is this week in full blast, making night hideous with terrible noises. All this kind of religion seems to me *worthless*. It does n't save from lies and stealing. Nobody's character is elevated or ennobled. Vanity and self-conceit are fostered. People pray and shout and say the Holy Ghost is moving their souls ! It is awful.

" I have a delightful visitor, Mrs. Elizabeth Oakes Smith. She writes descriptions of this place and people to Northern newspapers. She is amazed at all my fruit. Says she never had so much to eat in all her life. ' Quite Arcadian living.' She has seen seventy-eight years, but she is the *youngest* human being I ever knew. Such freshness, vivacity, sweet cheer,—always abounding in lively talk,—full of life and action. Personally she is very handsome. Age does not wither her beautiful eyes and features and lovely mouth.

" Last Sunday we had a drive. The people were a novel sight. More than a thousand assembled in an oak-

YEOCOMICO CHURCH, COPLE PARISH, VA.

(Built in 1706)

grove, eight miles from my door.   This campmeeting is very popular.   Everybody in these four counties seems to make haste to attend.   It is the Grand Annual Feast of the year.

"I must tell you of our visit to the old Episcopal church.[1] This old church is about the only lion we have in this region.   There is no tower or steeple, and the quaint, steep, pitched roof does not need either.   Its pure, artistic outline is not disfigured by chimney or any other excrescence.   It is a beautiful architectural monument, and, aside from religious feeling, deserves to be carefully cherished.

"On the wall inside the church are still inserted the canvas imitations of black marble, on which is inscribed in faded gilt letters the ancient scripture, 'Thou shalt have no other Gods before me.'   Yet in defiance of this plain commandment, slavery was, as all the world knows, exalted above all that is called God.   The canvas is sadly torn, and as I picked up a fragment to restore it to its place I wished for needle and thread to sew it in. The quaint, long, old-fashioned s's made it difficult at first to read the text, but I soon made out, 'Thou shalt not steal,' and could not help thinking how nothing but stealing went on all those two hundred years, by Christ Church communicants, priests and people,—for all were slaveholders,—continually trampling on the eternal laws of Justice and Honour.   No wonder their sacred places are now a desolation and a waste, their tombs desecrated, and their haughty pride humbled almost in the dust of oblivion.

[1] Christ Church, Lancaster County, which Miss Holley described much more elaborately than here for the *Lyons Republican*, for which she wrote at one time a lengthy series of reminiscences : " Lyons in the Olden Times."

"As we took our parting look at the old church standing in such deep and awful solitude, we piously closed the great door we found open ; the bright sun was setting behind the western pines, and what a picture of the past that old church was, with its very bricks brought over from England ! As we drove away the full moon was radiant, and the whole jaunt was one of uncommon pleasure."

The name of Mary Ball, the mother of Washington, is often associated with this church. She is *said* to have been married there, but the family church of the Balls was White Chapel, across the river in the same parish.

Another favourite excursion was to the old Yeocomico Church in Westmoreland County, where Washington was not baptised as fabled, but at Pope's Creek. In the War of 1812 the communion table of the Yeocomico Church was used for a butcher's block by the American soldiers, and the font " as a vessel in which to prepare the excitements of ungodly mirth." There was no greater satisfaction for Miss Holley or Miss Putnam than to arrange and carry out an excursion for Northern friends who came to visit them. It was thirty-five miles to Christ Church, many less to Yeocomico, and the way was beguiled not only with the novel scenery and situation, but by Miss Holley's bringing out of her treasure things new and old,—the poems which had delighted her imagination and sustained her heart on many a weary quest.

CHAPTER XV

FAINT BUT PURSUING

WHETHER we read one account or another of Miss Holley's school or see one photograph or another of the days and feasts which she observed, as regardless of St. Paul's injunctions in this respect as in the matter of women's public speech, we find the method of the school to be that of teaching by picture and poem to a remarkable degree. This method jumped with her own nature as well as with the simple intelligence and childlike heart of those she fain would educate into some fuller life. If both she and Miss Putnam had not taken kindly to these ways, it would have been very difficult for them to prosper in them as they did. But so instinctive was their inclination to them that their scholars, big and little, named or renamed for their Northern friends and for the heralds and champions of freedom the world over, were simply sharers of their joy. Indeed it may be doubted whether, when Decoration Day or the Glorious Fourth, or West India or United States Emancipation was celebrated, any of the scholars viewed the cheerful

16

spectacle with so much delight as warmed the teachers' hearts. Lydia Maria Child made many picture-scrap-books, and it would have been just like our Lottsburgh friends to do so, whether they did or not.

Over the new schoolhouse floated the American flag, " not a stripe erased, not a star obscured," and hence the more hateful to an unreconstructed neighbourhood; and there were many threats of shooting the teachers and burning their " nigger schoolhouse " over their heads. Plucky as Barbara Frietchie or May Quantrell,[1] she stood fearlessly in the doorway of the hated building, and answering their threats to shoot her, cried: " Shoot, if you want to, but let me tell you that, if you do, the North will send down a dozen to take my place. Burn the schoolhouse if you like, but the Northern people will build twenty others! " As time went on much of the early prejudice wore off, and Miss Holley's kindly influence was extended to many white families in her vicinity. In 1885 Mrs. Elizabeth Oakes Smith spoke on Sunday to a large company of white people, enjoying a privilege won for her by Miss Holley's persistent interest in them and her perfect fearlessness.

In a letter to Mrs. Anna Shaw Greene Miss Holley gives an account of one day's occupations, a fair sample of many hundreds and thousands that she suffered and enjoyed from 1870 to 1893. She was up at five o'clock in the morning preparing for herself the simple breakfast she had learned to like in

[1] See Whittier's note to " Barbara Frietchie " in *Collected Works*.

England. Next she baked five loaves of good flour
bread, and then put her house in order upstairs and
down, laying the fire for the evening, bringing in
more wood, etc. At nine o'clock she goes down to
the schoolhouse and calls the roll, and then returns
to the house and sends off Sylvester Fauntleroy to
exchange sixty eggs for eighteen candles; while he
is gone making a small spiced cake for him, to reward his service. Next, letter-writing, and then
" dressing up " for lunch; after that to the school-
room again to hear the Natural Philosophy and
History classes recite their lessons, and certain
poems and psalms by way of preparation for the
celebration of Washington's Birthday.

Martha Parker, Mary Lizzie Burgess, and little
Willie Eskridge recite their several psalms; another
scholar, Schiller's " Diver," an old favourite with
Miss Holley; Wendell Phillips a rhymed paper,
" The Fox and the Cat "; Willie Whitlow, Byron's
sonnet to " The Prisoner of Chillon "; Judson Eskridge, Addison's " Spacious Firmament," which
always stirred the heart of Thackeray to secret
tears; Gerrit Smith all the time remaining so still
and attentive that he was praised as a model scholar
before all the rest. At two o'clock Miss Putnam
takes the helm and puts her fourteen boys through
" The Pied Piper of Hamelin " before the arrival of
the mail. Meantime Miss Holley is cutting out a
winter dress for poor old Winnie Beale and at 4 P.M.
lugging in more wood for the evening fire and the
kitchen supply for the next morning and her own
chamber wood-box. Next, back to the school again

to release Miss Putnam and exhort Laura Porter, *nominis umbra*, to " sweep the room as to God's law " and so make that and her stockings fine, the stockings being a reward of faithfulness. Governing the seventy " young barbarians " is the hardest labour of the day. Nothing is said about dinner, but I trust it was not forgotten. Soon after six the household were gathered snugly round the evening lamp, Miss Putnam reading Green's *History of the English People*, while the others were busy with their sewing or knitting. Early to bed was the rule, with its proverbial concomitant. Have I not a letter from Miss Putnam written at 12.30 A.M. !—her " beauty-sleep " enjoyed already and her conversation with the stars.

To fully appreciate what a long succession of days like this one meant for Miss Holley, we must remember that she was not by any means indifferent to the soft and pleasant side of life. She liked nice things as well as anybody. There is a recurrent note in her letters which is proof of this. Naturally she shrank from things sordid and disagreeable. She uses the word " elegant " so frequently that we may be certain that it expressed one of her most attractive ideals. And yet she went right on as if she loved her mean surroundings and her lowly tasks. She loved the ends to which such things were the predestined means. After twenty years of missionary work she had saved enough from her modest wages to settle down somewhere and be comfortable for the remainder of her life. She chose instead to invest her savings in the Virginia " plant " known as " The Holley School," which yielded for usurious interest the satisfaction of " remembering those whom God seemed to have forgotten " and helping them to the enjoyment of a more intellectual and moral life.

TO MISS TYLER

"LOTTSBURGH, Nov. 29, 1884.

". . . I design to arrive in New York Dec. 19. I wanted to be there sooner but imperative labour will detain me. No Peri ever more longed to enter the gate of Paradise than I to escape all this grinding toil and incessant work,—and enter New York City, and taste of its ease and happiness. The other day a lady wrote me that she thought I must be very 'lonely' down in this wilderness. Why ! I don't know the meaning of the word. If she had used the word 'fatigued,' I could earnestly respond to it.

"The result of the election is appalling to us, it is such a victory for our enemies and their hostility to our school is now greater than ever; their whole manner to us uncivil and unkind."

TO MRS. MILLER

" LOTTSBURGH, Dec. 14, 1884.

"Yesterday your large, generous trunk was brought down from Lodge Landing.'

" Last night, by lamplight, Miss Putnam and I unpacked it in our front hall. We were again, as so often in times past, impressed with your ever overflowing love. The old trunk itself is a curiosity—eloquent to us of your travels : its lid all lined with records of hotels in the capitals of Europe. We especially prize the splendid picture, all framed, of your distinguished father ; also the smaller cards of him and of your sainted mother.

" We have just been reading Carlyle's story of Voltaire and Frederick in Berlin, Potsdam, etc. With all his marvellous genius, what a nervous, fidgetty, hot water–y creature, the little Frenchman was ! In Westminster Abbey I heard Dean Stanley preach on the Voltaire anniversary, when he bravely testified that Voltaire had greatly enlarged and liberalised human thought, and that the world was indebted to this extraordinary man. I thought it remarkable fidelity in a Church of England dignitary, and was exceedingly gratified myself.

" Carlyle's *Life in London,* Froude's last volumes, have given us many evenings of stirring entertainment. How Carlyle did sit in judgment over his fellow mortals ! With what contempt he mentions Gladstone, Stuart Mill, Harriet Martineau, and many others. He said Cardinal Newman ' had not the intellect of a moderate sized rabbit ! ' "

" LOTTSBURGH, April 7, 1885.

" . . . The delightful books you sent are very refreshing. Ramona gives us pictures of those Southern Missions extremely interesting. What a beautiful, un-predjudiced, catholic spirit of humanity the author pos-sesses ! It is an honour to Secretary Teller that he gave her an official errand of mercy to ask after the rights of Indians there."

" LOTTSBURGH, Sept. 2, 1885.

" The little vine you sent from Rochester in the spring grows and flourishes in living green and is climbing up my summer-house in the middle of the garden. The Ivy I brought from Warwick Castle is now a great vine cover-ing a dead cedar tree. My Wistaria vine is so immense

as to form a long arbour, and suggests Queen Anne's walk
at Hampton Court. A garden is like a child, requiring
constant care and diligent cultivation to grow a success.
But what a resource and indulgence! and not without
good effect on all these Virginia people."

"LOTTSBURGH, Oct. 12, 1885.

"Miss Putnam is still in office. But oh, what an
excitement we have had! The coloured people have
been intensely excited. They gathered night after night
in the Democrat's little store to express their feelings
against any removal of this post office. These Virginia
Democrats are very unhappy and bitterly disappointed.
The more liberal Democrats say they don't want the office
removed. How much we are indebted to yourself and
Col. Miller for all your large hearted interest in Miss
Putnam's keeping the office! Without you we should
have lost it."

"NEW YORK, Jan. 11, 1886.

"A day or two before Christmas, I came North for rest
and refreshment. I feel thankful every hour for the
enjoyment.

"No express nearer Lottsburgh than Baltimore, and
business so feeble in our part of Virginia that the 'Sue'
discontinues her trips in the winter season. So I cannot return before March. The only communication is
by mail, which is carried by a coloured boy in a sulky."

"LOTTSBURGH, Sept. 23, 1886.

"It seems very long since I have heard from you. I
should love to know how you have enjoyed the summer abroad. It has been heavenly weather here. The
shortest summer of my life,

"We have had a very interesting earthquake. The rocking of my bed seemed droll and quaint enough. Some of our neighbours were alarmed,—got up,—lighted lamps and sat up till morning! Southern people, white and black, are far more timid than Northerners. Thunder and lightning always seem to strike them dumb. Hell and the Devil are ever present in their minds. It would be pitiable were it not so ridiculous.

"I hope you welcome these glorious fall days as ardently as I do. George Eliot said she should be content to look forward to a heaven of long autumn afternoon walks! How she delighted in outward nature!"

TO MISS TYLER

" LOTTSBURGH, Oct. 7, 1886.

"I think this October the most radiant and golden I ever knew. The forests are green yet. We have the bluest of skies and gorgeous sunshine shedding a glory over all the earth. It is a pleasure to be alive. We have the red maple which in early spring is bright with red flowers, but no sugar maple."

TO MRS. MILLER

" LOTTSBURGH, Oct. 18, 1886.

"As the little boy said, 'God knows better than I how to make all the best words out of the letters, and they will tell my love to Him.' So no words of mine can express to you how grateful I am for all your kindness to us. The charcoal dyspepsia biscuit are a decided curiosity to me. I have some neighbours both white and black who suffer from dyspepsia, and I will give the biscuits to them. I never know indigestion, for I live an intensely active out-door life and my food is

almost as simple as that of the 'Infidel Saracen' who
figures in Walter Scott's 'Talisman.' When after the
fight with the 'Christian Knight' on the hot sands of the
Red Sea desert they both sat down to refreshments, the
Englishman lunched off dried hog's flesh and wine, while
the Saracen took a few dried dates, a piece of coarse
barley-bread, and a drink of water.

"I am writing in haste, for I have to cook dinner for
three men who are here working on a new room we are
making for a lady teacher who comes from the North in
a few weeks to teach in our winter school.

> " ' I pray for light and strength to bear
> My portion of the weight and care
> That crushed into dumb despair
> One half the human race.' "

TO MISS PORTER

"LOTTSBURGH, Oct. 21, 1886.

"Miss Putnam has just returned from a summer in
Boston and vicinity, which she declares 'paradise' in
contrast to desolate Virginia. We have had no rain for
many weeks, but I have wonderfully enjoyed it and admired all the glorious autumn days. I wish most earnestly you would spread all sails and get a barrel of old
clothes sent down here. We have had a tough time to
keep all this work going on here these eighteen years,
with no salary and no income except as kind Northern
friends send us barrels, boxes, and donations.

"We are now building a new room for our lady
teacher who comes in December. I have four men to
tear down the dilapidated room and build anew. Every
man, woman, and child moves slow in the south. I lay

their inertia to the amazing amount of tobacco they smoke and chew. We will not allow smoking on the grounds or in the Post Office. At first the men demur, but we are resolute and conquer. Life with all its stings and contumelies I find very delightful,—a very great pleasure, and

> ' joyfully onward I go.' "

" LOTTSBURGH, June 12, 1887.

" This beautiful Sunday is enough to make us all rejoice with great joy. Virginia never had a more charming June than now. My three hundred Annunciation lilies are a vision of white loveliness. How I should love to show you around my garden to-day! With my own fingers I have picked, by actual measurement, four bushels of strawberries during the last thirty days.

"We have recently read the very interesting memoirs of General Grant, and have learned to admire him anew. With what a loyal grip he took Vicksburg and crushed the Rebellion! He grandly earned all the honours paid him."

TO MRS. MILLER

" LOTTSBURGH, July 12, 1887.

" My very dear Lady Bountiful :—For such you are to me ever and always. Late Saturday night ' what to my wondering eyes should appear ' but a coloured man driving two horses before a big waggon holding your two generous boxes all coming straight to my door! I was delighted to see your beautiful bureau, and nice, convenient stand with bowl and pitcher, soap-dish, etc. Not a crack or nick or injury to anything, all so securely packed for the long journey by railroad and steamboat. For nineteen years, here, I 've had only a very rough pine board stand, that I improvised a day or two after I first

Elizabeth Smith Miller

MRS. MILLER AND DAUGHTER

arrived. Now your washstand is a very welcome substitute. The pretty bureau I have put in Miss Putnam's room. When she returns from her visit to Massachusetts she will rejoice to see what she has long wanted to possess. Every item you send is gratefully received. The boards, nails, etc., of the boxes are just what our washerwoman, Flora Blackwell, has been sighing for all summer to make her a little room to cook in through the hot weather. Nothing could be more timely for her. I assure you it is pleasant to meet this want of hers. She will take all to her cabin to-morrow."

"Lottsburgh, Aug. 9, 1887.

"Your letter, breathing love and kindness, came in yesterday morning's mail. . . . It was delightful for you to wish I could feast my eyes on your lovely lake that perfect night. I found exquisite enjoyment in those glorious moonlight nights here last week. Day and night I feel intensely the beauty of the sky here. I care most to look at all the clear, blue loveliness overhead and the green forest around me.

"During those tremendously hot days I lay under my thirty-feet long Wistaria arbour[1] two hours daily, and lost myself and all the loneliness, care, and responsibility of my Virginia life in the pages of a charming book,— *Rambles in Palestine and Syria.* As Emerson said, ' The great law of compensation holds everywhere.' "

TO MISS PORTER

"Lottsburgh, Sept. 30, 1887.

"You were kind enough to write that you intended to send a barrel to me this fall. If you can send it in Oc-

[1] Here, too, were read the two thick volumes of Darwin's life, a gift from Mrs. Miller.

tober it will be an untold comfort to us here. During hot summer time rags and patches do for these pensioners, but when the time of outside chills and inside fires arrives, they suffer. This coloured race is improvident and lacks management. It will take generations to make them like Northerners, in industry, economy, and thrift.

"It is nigh twenty years [reckoning the visits to Miss Putnam in 1868 and 1869] since I first began this struggle down here trying to educate and elevate these poor, ignorant, low-lived ex-slaves. I can see good results. I have not laboured in vain. But the work is not yet done, though I shall, before many years, be compelled by old age to retire from this field of conflict. It is wonderful to me that I have persisted and persevered in the face of almost every conceivable obstacle all these nineteen years, to keep this school open. This life in its awful isolation has been exile and martyrdom to me."

"LOTTSBURGH, Oct. 30, 1887.

"Yesterday our factotum, John Newton, brought from Lodge Landing your generous barrel and trunk. Never was anything landed at my door more truly welcome. Who *did* donate all those excellent coats and garments of all kinds? Somebody has been 'lending to the Lord,' as I could plainly see, when taking out article after article.

"The long rain has been a great pleasure to me, on account of the rest these poor mules and horses have enjoyed. Oh, how pained I have felt to witness the abuse and neglect of them. I have been tempted to comb and wash and curry and feed one pair of grey mules especially, who are prematurely old and worn and weak in consequence of cruel treatment. Solomon's merciful man does n't reside in Lottsburgh. The owner of these grey mules has just 'embraced religion,' as these people say, and if Southern religion were good for anything, these mules should know the bliss of kind usage henceforth.

"The chief excitement before your barrel came, was watching large flocks of wild white swans, flying south-ward over my garden. The rustle of their great wings and the encouraging call of the leaders could be plainly heard. How far they had come or how far going, we could not conjecture, but in a few minutes they would be out of sight, hurrying on as if storm-sent : and then another flock would appear."

"LOTTSBURGH, Nov. 1, 1887.

"No apologies are needed for not sending better things. They are to me a ' whole loaf,' and a very good one too. It seems wonderful you are eighty-two years old, my dear Maria. You are still one of the youngest people I know. Don't you think what are called ' young people ' are amazingly old and dreary ? Youth is not the happi-est time of life, according to my experience and observa-tion. There 's George Bancroft, who celebrated his eighty-seventh birthday in Newport last summer. I have a neighbour who was born in 1799. He came to Virginia thirty years ago, from Pennsylvania,—the great-est regret of his life. He is dreadfully disappointed in this naked, poor, miserable country. The ignorance, indolence, and poverty are indescribable."

TO MRS. MILLER

"NEW YORK, Feb. 24, 1888.

" .   .   .   I thank you for your little letter of the 21st. I am not well and strong this winter. I took cold soon after my arrival and had a touch of pleurisy.   But after days of lying in bed and taking Turkish and electric baths, I am now up and about enjoying the heavenly weather of these last February days.

"I must return to my post of labour some time in April, not doubting my out-door life and luxurious supply of fresh air and space will tone up my physical powers.

"I have listened to a course of parlour talks, by Mrs. H. M. Poole, on mental science.   They impressed me deeply.   You know I incline with all my being, to the spiritual and immortal side of life.   The lectures were, to me, of irresistible power and beauty."

" NEW YORK, Feb. 27, 1888.

"I thank you sincerely for the invitation to go to Washington, but it does not seem wise and best for me to accept.   My old elasticity and vigour of body are declining.   I am seventy years old.   I look forward with intense joy to an interminable existence, independent of flesh and blood."

" March 23, 1888.

"I thank you for your generous thought about me.   I have no ache, no pain ; only 'nervous prostration,' as they call it.   I weigh only one hundred pounds.   I have no depression of spirits.   To-day I am ordered to keep in bed.   People advise me to take some 'tonic,' but I think only out-door air will restore me.

"March 28th.—Last Thursday afternoon I did not resist my great desire to attend the woman's suffrage convention here in Masonic Temple.   The result was I became so deeply interested and deeply moved by the eloquent speakers that I was taken with a chill and had

to leave before the meeting closed. Mrs. Dr. Miller
and all the ladies in the house are very kind. Will you
smile if I tell you something ? Some time ago, one of
the ladies, seeing that my appetite was rather dainty,
went across the way to St. James Hotel, and brought
me a cooked bird on toast and some French peas.
Nothing ever tasted more delicious to me. But I dare
not expatiate on the treat, for the lady is a working
woman and a widow, and ought not to spend a cent
on me. She is educating her only child,—a young lady,
—and needs all she earns to do it."

TO MISS TYLER

"LOTTSBURGH, July 24, 1888.

"Yesterday a coloured woman and myself cleaned the
immense school-room. We swept, dusted, and washed
it with water. After the crowded school, Sunday morning, thorough work was decidedly called for.

"We celebrated Fort Wagner and the brave Colonel
Robert G. Shaw, who fell there fighting for Right and
Freedom. It was a touching scene,—all these coloured
people repeating the name of the

"'Fair-haired Northern hero, with his guard of dusky
     hue.'

"I gave out hundreds of presents on the occasion and
so gladdened many little hearts.

"Steptoe Ball feels he is an old man. He sings,

"'In the shadow of the rock I shall be resting soon.'

"Soon after our storm the other day, he called and remarked : 'When the thunder was rending the sky and
lightning was flashing white, I searched myself and re-
paired back to my mind and did n't find anything was

wrong, and I was n't afraid because I don't want to do nothing against God's will. And it looked like it give me comfort.

> "' Sweet prospects, sweet birds, and sweet flowers
> Mid summer's sunshine's but dim,
> But when I 'm happy with Him
> December 's as pleasant as May.' "

TO MISS PORTER

" LOTTSBURGH, Nov. 1, 1888.

" Your affectionate letter came in this morning's mail. I was not aware of your sister Libbie's death. She has been such an invalid, her release from pain must be considered a blessing. She was so still and quiet, and bore her pain so bravely, we should be grateful for her heroism and fortitude. Her peaceful ending was like her quiet life.

" It will not be very many years before you and I will be laid beside her in beautiful Mount Hope. If you, dear Maria, should die before I do, may I ask that Mary Farley and her brother attend to my burial[1] beside my blessed father ? I shall leave money enough to meet all expenses. I have always thought you would outlive me, and so, made you promise, years ago, to see to my burial. I expect to die in New York, and have already engaged kind friends to superintend the necessary details, and left money in their hands.

" I fully believe in a life independent of flesh and blood, a spiritual life of unending growth, of love, truth, and holy obedience to Right. At the centre of our grand universe is the beneficient Power who holds us all in the ' hollow of His hand.' "

---

[1] A request granted in due time, and her expectation that she should die in New York was *accidentally* fulfilled.

A HOLLEY SCHOOL FESTIVAL. ANNIVERSARY OF THE WEST INDIA EMANCIPATION

TO ROBERT MORVILLE

"Lottsburgh, Nov. 19, 1888.

"Twenty years ago this very month, out of pity, commiseration, and sorrow for the poverty and ignorance of these people, I came down to Virginia to lighten their burdens and kindle their souls to a better life. To-day I cannot but believe this school and its influences have accomplished a solid and enduring blessing, good for time and good for eternity. We have taught hundreds and hundreds to read and write and cipher, besides some knowledge of geography, history—especially that of the United States—the story of our own Government, the eloquent biography of its reformers and martyrs, saints, and apostles.

"As ours is a free school,—no tuition exacted,—and we have no salary, it is only by such interested and large-hearted people as yourself, who donate the means to keep up our work, that we can continue this mission year after year.

"Some of our old pupils are now teaching public coloured schools in this part of the state, earning, every month, twenty-five dollars. Many of our boys and girls are in service in Baltimore and New York. A few of the older scholars have married here and are now in homes of their own.

"Not one of our coloured men failed to vote the Republican ticket on the sixth of November last.

"This month our school counts seventy scholars and the Sunday school adds a score or two more. Our mild November days favour many little young beginners coming, who for the first time have a slate and pencil to work out the profound mystery of writing their own names.

"We now have two young ladies from Massachusetts,
17

who are mobilising this little army of students after the pattern of Boston. It is touching to see these little dark faces light up with new thought as expressively as the pale-complexioned Saxon children's ever do. Again and again I thank you for your generous donation."

TO MISS TYLER

"LOTTSBURGH, Dec. 6, 1888.

"The great charm of Robert Elsmere is his earnest conscience. It is so hard for anyone to make life express his real thought. The reason ' why the evangelical clergy don't meet the book on its own ground,' that is, fight *Robert Elsmere* with another novel, is because *they cannot do it.* No more could slaveholders meet *Uncle Tom's Cabin* by another book representing the truth and power of slavery. Mrs. Ward reveals the thoughts of too many earnest, greatly consecrated souls and intensely devoted minds,—honest, clear-seeing intellects,—for any earthly genius to answer her book so as to annihilate its wonderful significance.

" ' Life is real, life is earnest,' and people cannot accept the popular creeds as they did in ages past. What a noble, quickening influence *Robert Elsmere* has! The moral and spiritual grandeur of the book makes me grateful to the author to the inmost core of my soul. I have just read Mr. Gladstone's criticism on the book. It is unsatisfactory, a disappointment. I am surprised at its weakness.

"Popular theology puts greater emphasis on a *bodily* resurrection than it does on a *spiritual* resurrection. It exalts the physical above the spiritual. Is more anxious to establish the personal rank of Jesus than his character. How *materialistic* it is! I have no doubt that love of popularity keeps many people from avowing their honest convictions."

"LOTTSBURGH, Aug. 5, 1890.

"Complaint seems to me really disgraceful. We had all better face the battle of life with brave courage and unselfish resolve. Each has a fearful conflict, but let us all march on victorious. I am ashamed to bewail and moan over the hardships of life, and I guess I have as many as most people.

"I have been trying to dry a platter of figs, but so many contestants appeared against me, I had to give it up. I put my figs on a clean platter out in this hot Virginia sun. When in an hour or two afterward I went out to see how the drying process came on, lo and behold, several butterflies, a party of yellow-jackets, a swarm of bees, a company of big flies, black ants, green beetles, etc., etc., had taken greedy possession of every fig with astonishing enjoyment and with no possible prospect of one fig being left for me. So I concluded that ' discretion was the better part of valour,'—' owned myself beat ' and abandoned the effort."

"LOTTSBURGH, Oct. 23, 1890.

"We have a continual struggle to keep up the school and this mission in Virginia. We have to pinch and scrimp all the time. But this work is more and more of a success every year, and I want to persevere a few years longer. Then I shall be worn out in body and shall have to give it up,—though I think old age is the loveliest part of human life, infinitely beyond any youth I ever saw or knew."

" I agree that America is for Americans, in the present age of the world.[1]   All admit that this country is a paradise for poor people.   I believe in good wages for faithful labour.   It is better to pay more and get higher prices for the work.   A Democrat here said to me that in England he could buy a sewing-machine for eighteen dollars, while in this country he would have to pay twenty-five dollars.   ' Oh, yes,' said I, ' but you can earn that twenty-five dollars here in half the time it would take you to earn eighteen dollars there.'   He admitted the truth of what I said.

" I have been hard at work in making an old house look as good as new.   We expect another lady teacher here next week, from South Dakota, and I have done my best to get her a comfortable, cheerful room with a southern exposure.   Success has crowned my efforts. All beholders praise the clean, sweet, pleasant room. My life down here is intense, incessant, hard bodily labour."

TO MRS. MILLER

" LOTTSBURGH, May 25, 1891.

"We have just finished reading Fred May Holland's *Life of Douglass*,[2] and think it a valuable book.   His revival of the dear old Liberty Party story was especially refreshing and delectable.   It seems most apropos when the other side of the shield has been so glaringly thrust forth by Garrison's sons in their *Story* of their father's

[1] Is this a concession to anti-Chinese legislation ?   I trust not, and Miss Putnam is sure it ought not to be so construed.   But in these years she was a very genial critic of the Republican party whatever line it took.

[2] Died February 20, 1895.

life and times. It is droll to read their assertion that the
Liberty Party had nothing whatever to do with the abolishing of slavery. Just as droll as it is in Eli Thayer so
persistently, in the New York newspapers, to proclaim
that Garrison and Phillips only retarded emancipation !
He claims it all for the Kansas Emigration Society !
No more romantic story has ever been written than that
of Frederick Douglass. It seems like a miracle. How
can we account for genius ? In a Douglass, a Dante, a
Shakspere, heredity does not seem to solve the riddle."

TO MISS TYLER

" LOTTSBURGH, July 29, 1891.

"While I sit here in our post-office this morning,
waiting for the coming of the mail-carrier with the
Lottsburgh mail, I take pleasure in acknowledging the
receipt of your interesting letter of the 23d. These
Southern people seem to have no appreciation of regular-
ity, promptness, punctuality, or method. Our mail-carrier comes at any hour, at all hours, and at no hour. He
often exasperates people dreadfully.

"Elemental fires burn in these human hearts as in
others all the world over. What a serious affair human
life is ! What suffering, struggle, tears, and despair con-
tend with us while going over the ' burning marl ' !

"One of our nicest coloured men, who has been
thought the strongest and healthiest, was taken poorly
last Christmas, and ever since has been gradually declining. His wife does washing, cooking—anything to
earn food for her three little children and dying husband.
The neighbours are more generous to this stricken family
than I ever knew them to be before. Yet it is a sad
case. I make bread for them every week, and share my
tea, rice, sugar, pickles, hominy, etc., with them. But

my resources are too small to do a great deal. Poverty and sickness together make a very bitter cup ; though a dinner of herbs with love is better than roast ox with hatred. It is touching to witness the affection that unites the hearts of this poor family. I am thankful that I am able to lighten their burden."

"LOTTSBURGH, Oct. 14, 1891.

". . . Don't you think newspapers unreliable? They seem to exaggerate greatly. What astonishing praise went the rounds of the Northern newspapers last year about me and this Virginia school! I did not know where to hang my head, but I could do nothing about it. Any explanation from me would only create greater notoriety. I was compelled to preserve total silence, yet I felt keenly the misrepresentation.

" Poor Charles Stewart Parnell must have gone through agonies the last years of his tempestuous life. I cannot explain the awful suffering of human beings. Dante did not exaggerate the facts. *Personal righteousness* is the only thing that makes it worth while for the sun and moon and stars to roll on so grandly.

" In reply to your question as to what I think of Unitarians having a liturgy : it seems to me an affectation. I should not enjoy it. I think it deadening to spiritual vitality. I used to laugh over what Henry Ward Beecher said in a public meeting to discuss the question,—'Why, I should as soon think of going a-courting with my father's old love-letters as praying to God out of a book.' "

TO MRS. MILLER

"NEW YORK, Jan. 26, 1892.

" I am here in this city of grand opportunities praising and thanking every day for these happy dispensations.

Next week I join a class in *The Soul's Progress in God*, a book written by one of the saints of the middle ages— Professor Davidson's lectures in Dr. Newton's All Souls' Chantry. I wish it were possible for you to join me every Saturday in this rare feast of thought. Every Sunday morning I am a joyful partaker of Felix Adler's spiritual banquets at Chickering Hall."

" NEW YORK, May 3, 1892.

" As a letter has come to me from Miss Putnam announcing the sad intelligence that her half-sister (the only sister she has) is dying in Dakota, and that Miss Putnam will be obliged to leave Virginia as soon as I reach there, I shall leave here next Thursday, *viâ* Baltimore, for Coan Landing, Virginia, reaching there Saturday at sunrise.

" I enclose you a programme of the delightful summer school in the Adirondacks. I can think of no earthly bliss that would compare to passing the summer with those cultured, scholarly, elevated people. But my duty compels me to work at the old post in Virginia. With Miss Putnam away, I shall be like Persephone in Hades :

" ' Among the dead she breathes alone.'

For can an inhabitant of that dark region be any more *dead* than these poor, benighted, uneducated Virginians ? "

" LOTTSBURGH, May 19, 1892.

" Your affectionate letter of May 8th came several days ago. But I and my seventy-five years have been so overwhelmed with things to do—house-cleaning, tending post-office, waiting on poor people, and repairing generally—that this morning affords the first disengaged hour. If the sun shone and the ways were dry, I could not write even now ; so many people are after me with their legion of wants. I feel as though my hard-working days must come to an end before many more years fly by. My advanced age, my impaired physical powers, and nervous, high-strung, weakening organisation, all assure me that not always can I keep on working so incessantly."

CHAPTER XVI

THE LONG DAY'S END

" The long day wanes ; the slow moon climbs ; the deep
Moans round with many voices. Come, my friends,
'T is not too late to seek a newer world."

THE consciousness of failing strength touches
many of the letters written before 1892 with a
pathetic intimation of the approaching end, but it
alternated with brave hopes and plans for future
work for others and the improvement of her own
mind.   Like Michel Angelo she " carried her satchel
still " ; was interested in every new development of
thought ; in New York heard Heber Newton and
Felix Adler with delight, and the lectures of Prof.
Thomas Davidson, especially those on Dante, with
immeasurable gratefulness and satisfaction.   Yet
there was no slackening of the lifelong loyalties,
reverences, and affections.   We find her writing to
Miss Tyler a letter about Unitarians in literature,
claiming almost everything good for them :

" How striking it is to see that American literature is
Unitarian literature : the most distinguished Poets—

Bryant, Longfellow, Lowell, Holmes . . . ; the Historians, too—Prescott, Bancroft, Motley ; the Philan-
thropists—Miss Dix, Peter Cooper, Gerrit Smith, and
hosts of others." [1]

Her views of revelation and inspiration were of
the most radical description, but they cost her—as,
indeed, why should they ?—no particle of admiration
for the old Hebrew and early Christian Scriptures.
She had always had something akin to Garrison's
biblical mind and happy gift for apt quotation from
the words of the Old Testament and New. She
writes of Mrs. Colonel Greene (Anna Shaw Greene):

" I regard her as the fairest among ten thousand, and
one altogether lovely. She was kept when young upon
Isaiah and Jeremiah, which accounts for her wonderful
moral height of character. Those blessed old Hebrews
had the yea and nay of the gospel. What an ever-abid-
ing comfort and joy they are ! "

Much given to mental hospitality, she was less
afraid of harbouring some spiritual tramp than of
failing to entertain some angel unawares, and so it
happened that " Mental Science " and " Christian
Science " found in her a sympathetic auditor,
mainly, perhaps, because of elements of thought
and phrase to which Emerson and other Transcendentalists had given currency, and on which the

---

[1] Emerson's name should stand where she put Whittier's, among
the poets, and Parkman's with the historians. Coming to statesmen
there were Sumner and Andrew and Lincoln, in spirit if not formally,
but also (alas for Miss Holley's boasting !) Webster and—Calhoun !

Caroline F. Putnam

patent had so long since run out that they were anybody's who cared to take them up.

In the way of personal friendship no one ever permitted himself " the delights of admiration " more freely than did she. It was not that her geese were swans, but that she " knew the gift of God " when it was vouchsafed her, and that she was singularly fortunate in the friends she made and kept; most fortunate in that friend who was to her

> " a nearer one
> Still, and a dearer one
> Yet than all others,"

from whom she enjoyed an affection and devotion fully equal to her own. Indeed, I tend to the persuasion that, of all the beautiful things in any way associated with Miss Holley's life, the most beautiful and tender was the love which she inspired and kept alive for more than forty years in Miss Putnam's generous and noble heart. I have read in books of many beautiful friendships, but of none more beautiful than this.

Intellectually and spiritually, Sallie Holley was never more alive than when the last good years were swiftly passing by. Martineau has said that frequently the mind, as life draws to its close, rouses itself, like a traveller who has drowsed a little on the way but pulls himself together as he approaches his journey's end.

Sallie Holley was always so alert that there was little need for her to rouse herself, but certainly there was no falling off from the high standard of her habitual life. And so far as the outward aspect of the world was concerned it was as if she feared that the new life could never be so beautiful as this. At any rate she dared not hope that it would be the same, and, therefore, she would make the most of this; " let no flower of the spring pass by her, " or any other lovely natural thing. Oftener than ever she reverts to the amplitude and beauty of the Virginian skies, a compensation for the lack of mountain scenery and much beside. She writes to Miss Tyler: " This morning I rose just as Aurora was getting ready for her chariot, and now it is ten o'clock and she is in the golden splendour of her drive with all the lovely and graceful hours dancing attendance." Such early rising was no uncommon joy. Of one summer she writes that she had hardly missed a sunrise, and wonders how she could get along without the daily spectacle. Once at least she tried to put her morning gladness into verse. She set out bravely to write a sonnet, but she had never, like Wordsworth, felt " the weight of too much liberty," and the resulting verses have no other characteristic of a sonnet than the required number of lines. The arrangement of the rhymes obeys no sonnet-law, and some of them are very imperfect. But, if the verses lack the form of poetry, they have its soul.

SUMMER DAWN IN VIRGINIA

" O summer dawn ! Fresh and fair thy beauty lies
O'er all the scene of amber eastern skies :

New, young, glad presence pure ! like Paradise !
Kindling my inmost soul with the sweet trance
Of peace and joy and heavenly influence.
Such fine enchantment is thy power o'er ill,
To silence thou hast hushed the whip-poor-will :
No right has selfish misery to moan,
And mar the harmony of holy morn.[1]
The mocking-bird tunes up her matins many ;
The soft brown wren sings, Cheerily ! Cheerily !
I fain would bear celestial love, so born,
A charm, through all the cares and toils that throng,
To plume the day with tender grace, O summer dawn ! "

Her active disposition is reflected in a letter of
the later years to which there is no date.

"The young teacher we have now is as sweet and
willing as she can be, but rather too orthodox for my
conscience. Before I was aware of it, she had taught
the children to sing a hymn about

> " ' How sweet to rest forever
> On my Saviour's breast.'

The coloured people are already a great deal too much
for ' rest.' They are disinclined to effort, and the prospect
of an eternity in heaven where all is ' rest,' is amazingly
alluring. It is only by immense and long-continued effort
that I can rouse them to a very moderate degree of
labour, and it seems to me a positive injury to minister
to their laziness by teaching such hymns. I greatly pre-

---

[1] Miss Holley's appreciation of the whip-poor-will seems to have
been a variable quantity. In an early letter she speaks of him as a
favourite bird ; later of learning to like him. Here he seems out of
favour, perhaps because she was growing more cheerful in her tastes
as she grew older.

fer those that inculcate the *truth*, that life here and
always must be a battle, a warfare, a march on to higher
and higher work, under 'the great taskmaster,' as Milton expressed it. 'Life is real, life is earnest,' as Longfellow sings.

> " ' Be not like dumb, driven cattle,
>   Be a hero in the strife.'

Such are the sentiments I aim to impress upon my
pupils. 'Taskmaster' may be a word of unpleasant
association,—what Theodore Parker used to call 'damaged phraseology,'—but I believe it contains a great
fact. I know I am under sacred 'tasks,' which I believe
I am constrained to perform faithfully ; and nobody
can be more alert and active than you, my dear friend,
always have been.

"Don't you find consolation in *work ?* "

Another letter without date, but which certain
earmarks assign to 1888, is good, as a report of any
of the closing years. It is to Mrs. Miller.

"I am entirely alone on my three-acre farm. With
the dawn of day I

> " ' Awake my soul, and with the sun
>   My daily course of duties run.'

To draw water from our well, fifty feet deep, light my
fire, boil potatoes, make tea, pick peaches from the garden, breakfast, wash up the dishes, make my bed, sweep,
etc., consumes the time until half-past eight, when I put
on dry clothes and take myself down to the schoolhouse
to tend the mail, which, thanks to your faithful efforts,
is still in our keeping. Although the Virginia Demo-

crats all the time write letters to Washington and predict
we shall not have the post-office another year, they
acknowledge it has the reputation of being the best kept
post-office in the 'Northern Neck.'

"The Sunday school goes on regularly. I have a nice
class, each one of which recites a psalm. Gerrit Smith
Payne reads very well. His psalm is the thirty-third,
beginning 'Rejoice in the Lord.' How well I remember
your blessed father's fine recitations from the Bible, on
my Peterboro' visits. What a beautiful accomplishment
it was! Once when I told the children they could
select the closing hymn for the Sunday school, little
Carroll innocently began 'Way down upon the S'wanee
River.' It made us all smile, but it was sung very
prettily.

"There has been so much sickness among the people,
both white and black, I have tried to aid and comfort
them with tea and sugar and 'loaf-bread,' until I have
fairly wished a bread tree grew in my garden.

"Yesterday we had a long, splendid autumn afternoon.
It was a treat to be out in the air and sunshine. I worked
two hours weeding in my garden. The sky looked grand
and spacious, and it was happiness to see the blue
heavens stretched out like a tent above me and to feel
the everlasting arms about me. Like Count Tolstoi, I
like to work with these poor people. It helps to educate
them as well as myself. In fact, it seems to me as solid
and valuable a work has been accomplished here among
these people by my garden and housekeeping, mending
and other economies, as by the school studies."

WITHOUT DATE OR ADDRESS

"My roses still bloom in the garden. This climate is
charming. I was alone all summer, night and day, but

not afraid. No railroads within a hundred miles of us, consequently no tramps. I could sleep with all my upper windows and blinds wide open, and see the beautiful stars as I lay in bed. No sultry nights, but cool evening winds, always. Do let me hear from you soon in exchange for this 'airy nothing' of mine. I am human and love all my friends as much as ever."

TO MISS TYLER

"LOTTSBURGH, Aug. 22, 1892.

"The fierce heat of this summer has proved fatal to very many people. People do not obey the laws of life and health, and God never suspends law to accommodate a sinner. I live so simply that heat does not overcome me. These Virginians eat so much pork they cannot know what good health is. The Baptist camp-meeting goes on all this week, and fresh pork is the popular dish there. Of course afterwards, malarial fever will kill many, but an *inscrutable providence* will be cited as the cause.

I count it a misfortune never to see the sun rise. I see it rise nearly every morning all summer long, and I hope to see it rise next summer from the top of Mount Hurricane, in the Adirondacks. I find intense and constant companionship in all out-door nature, and the stars at night look significant and friendly to me."

"LOTTSBURGH, Sept. 16, 1892.

"I mourn to have G. W. Curtis [1] and John G. Whittier die. But they leave a glorious memory. Well done

[1] This kindly judgment upon Curtis is very different from one expressed in 1884 after the election of Cleveland, to which Curtis had contributed so much. He had proved a friend in need to Miss Holley and Miss Putnam in their post-office straits.

good and faithful servants ! Shall we ever be sufficiently grateful for the noble band of thinkers. Paul's 'cloud of witnesses' has grand additions from our day and generation."

TO MRS. MILLER

" LOTTSBURGH, Sept. 21, 1892.

" Your great, loving, tender heart came to my door last evening in shape of a box full of the nicest and best things. How did you ever learn to be so full of kindness and human sympathy ? There does n't seem to be a single chord of ordinary selfishness about you and all your make-up. It is delightful to me to receive your generous gifts and still more precious to have your love and interest. Every item in the box will make some human heart beat with gladness. You never forget to do a liberal and unselfish act. Sometimes I wonder how you ever got to be so unselfish and thoughtful for other people's happiness. Was it the result of conflict, or did it come to you by the grace of God at birth ? You seem to me a miracle of self-command and I believe that ' He that ruleth his own spirit is greater than he that taketh a city.' I am very grateful to you for all your unending kindness to me."

" LOTTSBURGH, Sept. 29, 1892.

" Another of the expressions of your heavenly love in the shape of a beautiful letter and check for freight charges. I thank you from the bottom of my heart.

" I congratulate you on all your pleasant guests. Such people are among the sweetest joys of life. I rejoice I know so many, though I don't see so much of them as I would like.

" I hope next winter I may be so fortunate as to meet you in New York and take you to the Dante class. You would have enjoyed the Tennyson class, for Professor Davidson interpreted *In Memoriam* with rare power and beauty. I mail you to-day his little book, and beg you will write me exactly how well you like it. Tennyson believed in a personal God and our own personal immortality.

"This clear, cool September air and golden sunshine are delightful.

"I have just read Mrs. Oliphant's *Life of St. Francis of Assisi*, a tender and touching story. [What a pity that it was not Paul Sabatier's!] It is wonderful what power the soul has over the body! How it can make darkness light and people solitude with lovely spirits."

[No date.[1]]

"I must confess to the surprise and pain your sentiments about the book gave me. I value highly frank and fearless expression of honest opinion and conviction. In no other way can truth become manifest to us. I thank you, though I have great sorrow in our wide difference of views. To me Prof. Davidson's rendering of the poem is beautiful. It brings out so clearly and with such eloquent distinctions all the religious fervour and the passion of immortality which breathes through *In Memoriam*. I feel endlessly enriched.

"No, I have never seen Miss Brackett's *Technique of Rest*, though last summer, in an old magazine, I read a charming article of hers upon 'Lycidas.' She must be a woman of rare culture and scholarship. The great burden and grief of my life is that I have not studied more."

[1] But evidently answering a letter from Mrs. Miller which objected to Prof. Davidson's book.

MISS PUTNAM STARTING FOR EUROPE

" LOTTSBURGH, Oct. 12, 1892.

"The poem of Whittier's is very beautiful,—in the same spirit with so many others of his poems. I love his beautiful religious faith. The last stanza is lovely.

" ' There from the music round me stealing
    I fain would learn the new and holy song.
And find at last, beneath Thy tree of healing,
    The life for which I long.'

"You kindly ask me what are my pleasures. I can count up a good many here on my little hill, surrounded with forest trees. I look up to the sky with never ceasing pleasure. I am up nearly every morning of the summer before Aurora mounts the chariot for her daily drive, and the summer dawn is exquisitely lovely. The broad, blue sky with its exalting influences is a very great pleasure to me, and the summer night is perpetually soothing and comforting. My garden, all summer, has abounded in fire-flies, ' piloting through airy seas frail barks of light.' My grounds are like cities of refuge to the birds of this country. The little wrens build nests in the school-house and rear their young. Bluebirds, mocking-birds, robins, cat-birds, brown thrashers—all like my garden and build their nests every summer in it.

" My flowers now in bloom are nasturtiums, dahlias, roses, princess feathers, asters, and the lavender with its little greyish blue flowers and nice perfume.

" My Sunday-school has been a great pleasure to me, but, also a great fatigue. I have the entire care of it three hours, from nine until twelve. The two oldest boys chose the story of David for our summer study. The eloquent and famous lament of David over the deaths of Saul and Jonathan, each girl and boy has committed to memory. I have a higher appreciation of the character of David than ever before. He was a most extraordinary man. The children and I have had a very interesting time. They can tell the whole story. Few men of any age or country have ever been equal to David. Perhaps no king that ever ruled has manifested as high virtues, as much tenderness of heart towards man, as much piety towards God. The sore self-reproach and the floods of tears produced by a consciousness of his sins, seem to me the most extraordinary example of humble and deep repentance in a man so powerful and so respected that royalty has ever offered to human consideration.

" It does not seem strange to me that in the strongly hyperbolic language of the Hebrews, David should be called a man ' after God's own heart.'

" Another of my ' pleasures ' is the affectionate letters of my friends. Aristotle said ' Without friends no one could choose to live, although he possessed all other blessings.' You, my dear friend, are a great ' pleasure ' to me. I value your regard, your approval, your attentions, above all price, and forever and forever I thank you and your disinterested soul.

" Books are an ever-flowing fountain of pleasure to me. This summer I have had hours of pleasure in reading the history of Greece. I have learned by heart two poems : Shelley's ' Arethusa,' and Jean Ingelow's ' Persephone.'

" Last month a friend wrote me asking if it would not be a pleasure to study and analyse one of Shakspeare's

¹ Look upon this picture and upon that in Renan's *History of the People of Irsael*. They differ much, and I fear that Renan's crafty, cruel, and treacherous bandit is more like the real David than Miss Holley's " happy views."

plays. So we are to take *Hamlet* as one of the 'pleasures' of autumn."

TO MISS TYLER

" LOTTSBURGH, Oct. 16, 1892.

" My garden just now is very attractive with the rich, crimson colours of the crape myrtle trees. The dogwoods, too, are very handsome. Miss Putnam has just returned and is busy with her various writings. She has engaged a Chicago young lady to teach here this winter. The lady writes she will be here November first.

" You are right in supposing I am one of those who think it not solitude to be alone. One of the best things Byron ever sung was,

" ' There is society where none intrudes,
By the deep sea, and music in its roar.'

And such a radiant, heavenly day as this, even Lottsburgh is charming. Though scarcely a bird is heard, general Nature's deep delight is felt in every fibre of my being."

TO MRS MILLER

" LOTTSBURGH, Nov. 27, 1892.

" . . . Your letter to Miss Putnam was a great relief and comfort, as, since the election our Lottsburgh ex-slave-holders boast they will get the post-office in March. One of the most bitter told a white woman that ' The old Yankee,' meaning me, ' has ruined these Lottsburgh niggers, making them think they are as good as anybody.' An ex-slave-holding lady said to me, ' I am as great a rebel as I ever was.' I do not for a moment believe any Virginian has met with a change of heart.[1] I am profoundly disappointed at the victory of the Southerners. They could not have won with a fair and honest count. Nobody of intelligence denies this fact. Grady [the Atlanta editor, since dead] admitted it in his banquet-speech in Boston, and insolently and impudently asked, ' Do you blame us ? Wouldn't you do the same in our case ? What are you going to do about it ?' And he got applause and honours from *Boston* for it ! He made the bold declaration that the South would effectually defy and resist the rule of the majority, and his reason was because he was ' opposed to nigger domination.' But George Bancroft wrote, ' We are indebted to the black race for the continuance of the Republic.' "

TO MISS PORTER

" LOTTSBURGH, Dec. 5, 1892.

" It is a great pleasure to acknowledge the receipt of your big barrel. How kindly and carefully you packed it, full of things we need down here all the time. Every item will meet a pressing want of poor coloured people. They have never known Yankee economy and care.

" This December weather is beautiful. Not quite so warm as October, but still very pleasant and enjoyable. I am the busiest of the busy, preparing to leave the day before Christmas.

" A Wellesley College young lady is coming here on next Saturday's boat. She will teach through the winter and be company for Miss Putnam. She was anxious to

[1] The situation has not bettered much with time. That slavery was an economic failure is now generally conceded by the more intelligent, but artifices nullifying the Fifteenth Amendment have been legalised in Mississippi, Louisiana, South Carolina, and North Carolina, and the lynching of coloured people upon suspicion of crime has become frightfully common.

come. I only hope this solitude and privation will not
be too much for her. This life is self-denial to any
Northern lady. Fortitude is absolutely necessary to endure this exile with equanimity."

The plan which this letter forecasts was duly carried out, and there is one other, her last to Miss
Tyler, in which the winter's anticipated pleasures
shine with alluring light. It was written December
7th, and gives the particulars of her successful search
for Indian arrow-heads for a Rhode Island friend's
town-museum. For more than a month she had
been collecting—walking over the fields, driving to
others farther off, soliciting help from every man,
boy, woman, or girl, that she might send off her
box of trophies by the *Sue* on her next trip. A
collection of seventy arrow-heads rewarded her exer-
tions, and one stone axe, and she writes:

" All this thought and handling has seemed to bring
the poor, old, wild Virginia children of the forest very
near to me. The night winds, as they moaned about the
house might be, for all I knew, the spirits of Indians
wandering about their old haunts. Where are they if
not here ?

" It is a lesson in history to me. Is it not interesting
to find these arrow-heads all over these fields ?—where
stones have always been scarce. The very spot on which
I live was once tenanted by a strangely different kind of
woman, whose joys and sorrows, whose toils and pleasures
were as sacred and precious as mine; and these arrow-
heads are the only traces left of that ' untutored mind '
who saw God in the winds, storms, sun, moon, stars—
all animated nature.

" This December day has been delightfully sunny and

warm. Birds are singing; black crows fly over in large parties, very noisy, too. [Here, as if their stridulence suggested what was harshest in her own experience, we have a passionate lament over Cleveland's second election, similar in terms to the letter sent to Mrs. Miller ten days before.]

" I expect to arrive in New York the day before Christmas. O happy day! after nine months of this Virginia labour, 'joyfully onward and upward I go.' If my winter is as happy as the last two winters have proved, I will bow in gratitude to the great giver of every good and perfect gift. I have learned to love New York passionately. My friends there are inexpressibly dear to me. Your next letter must be addressed to me at Miller's Hotel, 39 W. 36th St., where I shall not have to draw water every day from a well fifty feet deep, nor lug in heavy oak-wood to keep fire in the house, nor be the servant of servants."

The letter did not end upon this note, but with the savour of a barrel of the best Baldwin apples she ever saw, " from Gerrit Smith's daughter, whose heart seems as big as the world." Perhaps it was these apples as well as the quail-shooting in her vicinity that almost persuaded her to be a vegetarian. In about a fortnight she was on her way to New York, little imagining that she had seen the last of the Virginia life, with all its pleasures and its pains. In many large and many humble ways it had ministered to her mind and heart: " We have no mountains, no ocean, but we have what is grander than either, the beautiful blue sky. I enjoy it by day, and by night the stars amaze and awe me." " A perpetual comfort " she says elsewhere of the sky. And the home and school were dearer to her for every sacrifice she had made for them, and for all the love they signified from the friends who had never forgotten her in her loneliness and had done what they could to enrich her meagre life. There were scores of things that called up some beloved face and voice. If, after the manner of De Maistre, she had made " a voyage round her room," what freight would she have found of precious memories and generous cheer! There, too, she had enjoyed a friendship such as few women in this world have ever had. And she had had her work, her patient service of a race to which she had dedicated her life in its fair prime, nor failed to keep her vow. Even when many let the burden slip from their shoulders into the grave where slavery was buried, she had shifted hers a little and again taken the long road. It had been hard work always and frequently disheartening, but in the main she never doubted its reality, and it brought her many moments of great thankfulness and peace.

With what genial hopes and plans she found herself once more in New York we can easily imagine from a letter written soon after her arrival the previous year, January 12, 1892, exactly one year before her death.

"I am overjoyed," she wrote, "to be here amidst 'society, friendship, and love.' It is an amazing contrast to my exile in Virginia. No going hungry here; no army of ragged, dirty, low-lived poor whites and freed negroes to wait upon in this dear old familiar Miller Hotel. Here I can have time to read books and recreate my mind and sleep the sleep of a happy, unwearied woman.   No need to rise till 6.30 in the morning!   Find breakfast all ready when I go downstairs!   Hallelujah! ''

There were to be more such things as the Dante class the year before,—an inexpressible delight,— and Felix Adler's preaching ; and when another summer came she was going to the Adirondacks to climb Mount Hurricane, and loftier heights, to which Professor Davidson would lead.   But, alas!

" The best laid schemes o' mice and men
Gang aft a-gley."

Sallie Holley was not destined to enjoy the doings she had planned.   Her frequent recurrence latterly to the anxieties and burdens of her school had much of humour in it but more of physical exhaustion. Saturday, January 7th, she went over to Brooklyn to visit Mrs. Austin Dall, a valued relative and friend.   The day was bitter cold and she came back to New York thoroughly chilled; woke shivering in the night or early morning to call Mrs. Miller and find herself very sick with pneumonia, which four days later set a period to her long and useful life. She had lived nearly seventy-five years; from February 17, 1818 to January 12, 1893.

On Monday, January 13th, there was honourable mention of her in the New York papers,—'' A Friend of the Negro Gone,'' and other articles; the same issue reporting the death of Fanny Kemble, who had served God in quite another way and had a harder lot.   The same day there was a quiet service

at the Miller House, Dr. Adler and Professor Davidson speaking words of warm appreciation. Then,
as she wished, her body was taken to Rochester, that
it might be buried at Mount Hope with that of her
father. To William C. Gannett, minister of the
Unitarian Church, which had its deepest roots in
Myron Holley's heart, it fell to speak the last words
of farewell. That *he* spoke them is sufficient proof
that they were just and fit. " The impressive thing
about it all," he writes me, " was the occasion itself,
—she, after that strange life, brought home to lie by
her father's side; the still, simple service; those
gathered to greet her, some of them old-time abolitionists, Mrs. Miller, Gerrit Smith's daughter, coming up from Geneva, and—most of all—her own
Dante-like face as she lay in the casket." Maria
Porter had outlived her, but to Mary Farley and her
brother Porter fell the simple tasks required for such
a simple burial.

Here was a life that makes no figure on the historian's page. You will look for the name of Sallie
Holley in the biographical dictionaries and not find
it there. Brief is the mention of it in the *Story*
of Garrison's life, which is our best history of the
anti-slavery struggle. But how much it meant to
her and to her friends ! How much especially to one
of these, the best and faithfullest of all ! How much
to those whose sympathies she quickened with her
apt and fervid speech ! How much to the people to
whom her life was consecrated for more than forty
years ! And how much to those whom for twenty-
three years she made her special charge in her Vir-

ginia school! She lived to see many of them doing useful work in various quarters of the world. Such were her joy and crown. What most she teaches us is, that there are many lives, but little known, that are a gracious benediction on the world. " Some there be that have no memorial." I have tried to raise a very simple one to Sallie Holley, who in many humble ways did loyal service to her fellow-men, and lived in all respects as if she actually believed in God and was resolved to shape her own after the pattern of his righteous will.

INDEX